Office 365®

for
dummies®
A Wiley Brand

Office 365®

3rd Edition

by Rosemarie Withee, Ken Withee, and Jennifer Reed

Office 365® For Dummies®

Published by: **John Wiley & Sons, Inc.**, 111 River Street, Hoboken, NJ 07030-5774, www.wiley.com

Copyright © 2019 by John Wiley & Sons, Inc., Hoboken, New Jersey

Published simultaneously in Canada

For general information on our other products and services, please contact our Customer Care Department within the U.S. at 877-762-2974, outside the U.S. at 317-572-3993, or fax 317-572-4002. For technical support, please visit https://hub.wiley.com/community/support/dummies.

Wiley publishes in a variety of print and electronic formats and by print-on-demand. Some material included with standard print versions of this book may not be included in e-books or in print-on-demand. If this book refers to media such as a CD or DVD that is not included in the version you purchased, you may download this material at http://booksupport.wiley.com. For more information about Wiley products, visit www.wiley.com.

Library of Congress Control Number: 2018956414

ISBN 978-1-119-51335-3 (pbk); ISBN 978-1-119-51337-7 (ebk); ISBN 978-1-119-51336-0 (ebk)

Manufactured in the United States of America

V10004909_100218

Contents at a Glance

Table of Contents

Introduction

O ver the last few years, a massive shift has occurred at Microsoft. Microsoft has transitioned from selling software that large customers install locally to a company that sells cloud-based services. Office 365 is just such a service. Microsoft is not the only company that has done this. Just about every traditional software company now offers its product over the Internet as a service.

As a user in this new service-based software world, you have all the power. You can start using advanced software in a matter of minutes that only a decade ago was reserved for the largest corporate entities with dedicated teams and huge budgets. You can decide to start using software one day and decide to stop using it — and stop paying for it — a week later. You can add more user licenses to your subscription or remove them when you don't need them. In short, it is a great time to be a consumer of software.

About This Book

This book is about understanding Microsoft Office 365 at a fairly high level. It includes some of the administrative tasks of setting up and managing the software along with using some of the most well-known applications. The Office 365 product consists of many applications, and the book walks you through some of the major ones.

Microsoft is constantly adding new features and products to Office 365 so this book should be used as a base to get started. You can then explore further on your own. In fact, in most cases there are books dedicated to each app in particular. For example, if you want to learn more about Excel, you can pick up a book about Excel. The same goes for other apps like Outlook and Word, as well as apps that need extensive administration and management like SharePoint, Exchange, Teams, and others. We try to balance our coverage to provide a high-level view that can be used to get you started. Think of this book as the entry door to the whole enchilada known as Office 365.

If you are considering moving to Office 365 or have already moved, then this book is the first book you should read to get up to speed on the concepts and terms as quickly as possible.

In this book we focus on Microsoft's Office 365 software because we are big fans of it and use it regularly. With that said, it is not the only game in town. You will find similar offerings from Google, Dropbox, Facebook, and nearly any other large — and small — software company on the planet. Much of the feedback we have received from previous editions of the book dinged us for being too obsessed with the Microsoft tools and trying to sell for Microsoft. Though we are fans of Office 365, we often recommend other options as well depending on the specific needs of the customers we are working with. We have decades of experience and we tried hard to bring that to this book on Office 365. We hope that you will get value out of all of our hard work through trials, failures, and successes, and we hope you enjoy the book.

How to Use This Book

This book is designed to be read as you want to find out about specific components of Office 365. You do not need to read the chapters of the book in any order; however, we recommend you read the first part first to gain foundational knowledge of service-based software and in particular Office 365. Then feel free to jump around as you see fit.

The familiar *For Dummies* icons offer visual clues about the material contained within this book. Look for the following icons throughout the chapters:

Whenever you see a Tip icon take note. We use the tip icon whenever we want you to pay particular attention. Throughout the process of writing the book, we worked closely with Microsoft on any bugs or issues that have come up. When we found something worth a special note, we use this icon for emphasis.

Whenever you see a Remember icon, get out your notebook. The Remember icon is used to point out key concepts that you should remember as you walk through the Office 365 product.

Throughout our careers we've come across many roadblocks. It often takes hours to figure something out the first time and then only minutes the next time you encounter it. Often the root cause of your problems is a bug or some quirky behavior. We have tried to call out whenever you should take note of something and beware of how it will affect your Office 365 environment.

TECHNICAL STUFF

Office 365 is designed to be simple and intuitive; however, nothing is ever as easy as it appears. When we talk about something that is fairly technical in depth, we use the Technical Stuff icon. You definitely don't need to understand every technical detail, but it is there if you decide you want to dig further.

Beyond the Book

The Internet is huge! Search www.dummies.com for additional information about Office 365. Simply enter *Office 365 For Dummies Cheat Sheet* in the Search box to bring up several additional articles about the Office 365 tools.

Let's Get Started!

Office 365 is a service-based offering by Microsoft and bundles software such as SharePoint, Exchange, Teams, along with the traditional Office apps, Word, Excel, PowerPoint, OneNote, Outlook, and countless other new products into a single subscription. The software is accessed over the Internet and paid for on a monthly basis per user.

The traditional Office products are downloadable to many different devices, including iPhones, iPads, Macs, and Android-based phones and tablets, in addition to the familiar Windows-based devices. Microsoft runs the server products in their data centers with their engineers looking after them. You can be assured that they know what they are doing. After all, who better to manage these products than the same people who actually built them in the first place? To ease the mind of the risk averse, Microsoft puts their company name and piles of cash behind Office 365 in a very attractive service-level agreement.

This book is the first step in your Office 365 journey and is designed to get you up to speed as quickly as possible. If you're ready to take your first step, then you can get started!

1
Keeping Up with the Cloud Computing Environment

Start with an overview of how the workplace has changed since the arrival of cloud computing.

Get an understanding of the current threat landscape with the proliferation of hacking as a cottage industry. Learn how bad actors use social engineering to trick you into giving away the keys to your kingdom.

Get your feet wet with a broad understanding of the Microsoft cloud and how Office 365 fits into the mix.

Look into Office 365 and all the products stuffed into the offering, including Exchange Online for email, SharePoint Online for your portal needs, Microsoft Teams for instant and ad-hoc meetings and communication, and Office ProPlus for your desktop productivity needs.

Chapter **1**

Understanding Cloud Computing and the Current Threat Landscape

The way we work today is vastly different from the way we worked in the past. Gone are the days when we worked from 9 a.m. to 5 p.m. in one location using one desktop computer and software that didn't connect to the Internet. Today we get our work done using a desktop, a laptop, a smartphone, or a tablet while on the bus, at the doctor's office, during a run, at a coffee shop, and even when we're on vacation.

Welcome to the new world of work. It is the way most organizations are working, and it is the way the modern and younger workers expect to work.

As more companies embrace the opportunities presented by cloud and mobile computing, they also take on new risks. One of the most significant challenges in today's computing environment is ensuring security, privacy, and compliance. In fact, there is a consensus in the business world that there are only two types of organizations: those that know they've been hacked, and those that don't know they've been hacked. By the end of 2017, more than 28,800 data breaches had occurred globally with over 19 billion — again, that's *billion* — records exposed stemming from over 20,000 types of vulnerabilities.

The security issues we know today are not isolated to Fortune 500 companies. The reality is that small and medium-sized businesses (SMBs) are just as vulnerable to attacks. In fact, SMBs face more serious risks for a variety of reasons, including the scarcity of security talent in the industry; their inability to identify, assess, and mitigate security risks; the lack of familiarity with security best practices and the overall threat landscape; and confusion from the multitude of security solutions from which to choose.

One might conclude that the best defense against cyberattacks is to have a computing environment that's not in the cloud (rather *on-premises*, as technologists call it), and is protected by firewalls using the best encryption technology and running the latest anti-virus software. The problem with this approach is that all it takes to start a breach is one simple human error, such as clicking on a link or opening an attachment in an email. The reality is that as software and platforms are getting better at combatting cyberthreats, attackers are shifting their focus to the human element to hack the users through social engineering.

But what is *social engineering?* Consider the following real-life example:

Cloud611, a Microsoft Cloud Solutions Provider, resells Office 365 licenses to SMBs. Recently, a customer forwarded an email to Cloud611 asking why the company was warning him that his account could be deleted or closed. The exact language of the email read:

> *Your account will be disconnected from sending or receiving mails from other users because you failed to resolve errors on your mail.*
>
> *Confirm your activities* here.
>
> *Regards,*
>
> *The Mail Team*

Under the guise of being a solutions provider, the attacker tried to use a scareware tactic to trick the customer into clicking on the word "here," which is hyperlinked to a site that then downloads and installs malware on his computer. Fortunately, the customer did not completely fall for it, and the attacker failed — this time.

Social engineering comes in many forms: phishing, spear phishing, scareware, and more. These tactics all attempt to psychologically manipulate a user into divulging information or influence an individual to perform a specific action. The end game is usually to gain access to the computing environment to do harm.

The good news in this story is that the customer did not have to invest thousands of dollars to implement an end-to-end security solution nor hire an expensive security expert to protect his small business. For a mere $2 per user per month, the customer added Advanced Threat Protection (ATP) to his Office 365 Business Premium license to secure his mailboxes, files, online storage, and even his Office applications against advanced threats.

This chapter is for those of you who have a keen interest in understanding the basic principles of cloud computing with the intent of utilizing the benefits of the cloud to run your business in a way that increases employee productivity while keeping your environment secure. It covers the various services offered within Office 365, including what they cost and the latest security and privacy features built into the services. With the knowledge you gain from this chapter, you will be better prepared run a more secure, productive organization.

Understanding Cloud Computing

The "cloud" is a metaphor for the "Internet." In simplistic terms, *cloud computing* means that your applications or software, data, and computing needs are accessed, stored, and occur over the Internet "in the cloud."

If you've had a Facebook account, played online games, shared files with Dropbox, or shared a photo of your new haircut on Instagram, you've been computing in the cloud. You're using the services of an entity to store your data, which you can then access and transfer over the Internet. Imagine what life would be like if you wanted to share photos of your lunch with all of your 500 friends and cloud computing didn't exist.

For businesses and other organizations, cloud computing is about outsourcing typical information technology (IT) department tasks to a cloud service provider who has the experience, capability, and scalability to meet business demands at a cost that makes sense.

For example, let's look at a small business such as a boutique accounting firm that services over 200 businesses locally. Email is a critical communication platform for the firm. To be productive, the firm decided to hire an independent IT consult-ant to install an email server in the office. The deal was that the IT consultant would train a couple of people from the firm to do basic server administration. Beyond the basics, the consultant would be available to remotely access the server to troubleshoot or show up in person if something breaks.

Like most horror stories we've heard from people who try to manage their own servers without a highly trained IT staff, the situation turned out to be a nightmare for this firm. The email server went down during tax season when the IT consultant wasn't immediately available. In an industry where highly sensitive data is exchanged and customer trust is paramount, you can imagine the stress the company owner experienced dealing with email that contained sensitive attachments ending up in a black hole, irate customers who didn't get a response to their time-sensitive requests, and lost opportunities beyond quantifying.

Cloud computing for members of this firm meant migrating their email to Office 365. So instead of running their own email server, fixing it, patching it, hounding their IT consultant, and dreading another doomsday, they simply paid a monthly subscription to Microsoft, which is the entity responsible for ensuring the services are always up and running. They also know that email will not be lost, because they don't rely on one piece of equipment getting dusty in a corner of their office break room. Instead, they're taking advantage of Microsoft's huge and sophisticated data centers to replicate and backup data on a regular basis.

The basic premise of cloud computing is that organizations of any size can take advantage of the reduced cost of using computing, networking, and storage resources delivered via the Internet while at the same time minimizing the burden of managing those complicated resources.

Breaking down the cloud deployment models

Not all organizations are created equal. For example, a financial organization has different requirements than a nonprofit organization or a government organization. To address these varied needs, cloud service providers offer different deployment options.

Public cloud

The type of deployment model the boutique accounting firm used in the previous section is referred to as the *public cloud,* where the cloud computing service is owned by a provider (Microsoft) and offers the highest level of efficiency in a shared but secure environment. The firm did not own or maintain any hardware. It accessed and used the email and other services from the public cloud on a subscription model. In cloud computing-speak, this firm is referred to as a *tenant* in a public cloud. There are multiple tenants in a public cloud. Each tenant is isolated from the other with security boundaries so there is no data leakage. As illustrated in Figure 1-1, Enterprises A, B, and C can access the same application services in a public cloud, but their data is isolated from each other.

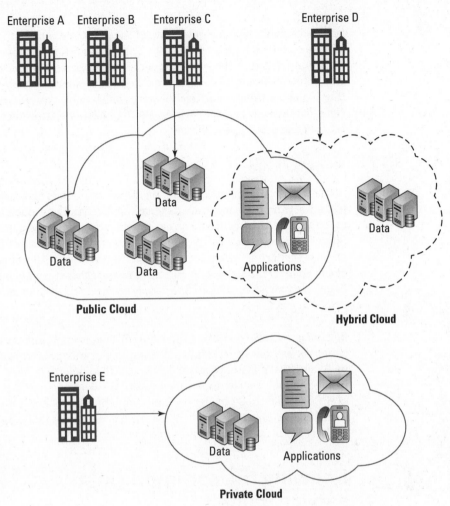

FIGURE 1-1:
Cloud computing
deployment
models.

Using a public cloud is like using electricity. You only pay for what you use. And just like electricity, you don't need to maintain the power plants — the provider does that. You only maintain the devices using the electricity. In this example, you don't need to maintain and patch the servers running your cloud services, but you do need to maintain the computers and laptops accessing or using the cloud services.

Private cloud

A *private cloud* typically is dedicated to one organization on its own highly secure, private network located at a company's on-site data center or at a colocation facility or *colo*. A colo is a data center facility that rents space for servers to other companies.

Unlike the public cloud, a private cloud doesn't share computer, networking, and storage resources with other tenants. This allows for a higher degree of flexibility in customizing the cloud environment, as any configuration done in a private cloud only applies to that environment. Industries with privacy concerns such as financial institutions and healthcare organizations typically opt for a private cloud. The same is true for government organizations, which have more stringent security and privacy requirements.

Hybrid cloud

A *hybrid cloud* is simply a combination of the public and private clouds. For example, an organization may run its email applications in a public cloud, but store customer information in a database in a private cloud to meet business and regulatory requirements. This scenario can be seen as the best of both worlds because an organization can maintain control of the resources it is running on the private cloud, while at the same time take advantage of the scalability of the public cloud to quickly provision additional resources to meet spikes in demand. This is called "cloud bursting."

Regardless of the deployment model used, cloud computing has afforded organizations of any size the flexibility of being able to scale resources up or down based on its needs at a faster pace and lower cost than before. In fact, cloud computing is the greatest equalizer for businesses as it breaks down the barriers for small and even one-man-show businesses from competing in the global market. For a small monthly fee, any business can use the same productivity tools and built-in security features that large enterprises use.

Knowing the common cloud service models

Contrary to general belief, cloud computing isn't a new concept. The idea of an "intergalactic computer network" was first introduced in the 1960s by J. C. R. Licklider, one of the most influential men in the history of computer science. Other people attribute the emergence of cloud computing to John McCarthy, another computer scientist who in the 1960s proposed that computing be delivered as a public utility similar to service bureaus that provided services to businesses for a fee.

Back then, massive computing was conducted with supercomputers and mainframes occupying whole buildings. Thousands of central processing units (CPUs) were connected to divide the computing tasks of supercomputers in order to get results faster. The high cost of creating and maintaining these supercomputers precipitated the discovery of more economical computing means, which brings us to where we are today.

With cloud computing today, not only can businesses use the services of specialized providers for massive computing, they also benefit from the lower cost of these services stemming from the efficiencies of shared infrastructure. Generally, there are three types of cloud computing service models (see Figure 1-2):

>> Software as a Service (SaaS)

>> Platform as a Service (PaaS)

>> Infrastructure as a Service (IaaS)

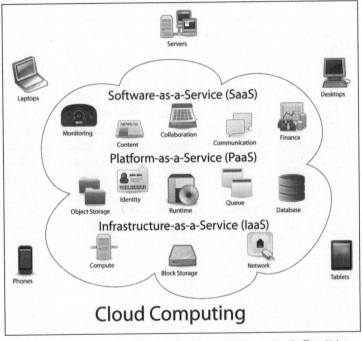

FIGURE 1-2: Cloud computing service models.

Illustration created by Sam Johnston using OmniGroup's OmniGraffle and Inkscape. Computer.svg courtesy Sasa Stefanovic.

Software as a service (SaaS)

A software as a service (SaaS) service model is where a software application is paid for on a subscription basis and installed from the cloud provider's data center. Office 365 is an example of a SaaS model where all your collaboration and productivity applications are bundled together as part of your subscription. You don't have to run your own email servers, for example, nor do you need to maintain and update the servers. For desktop applications like Office 365 Pro Plus, you can install the software from a web-based portal instead of buying the packaged software from a store. After you've installed the software, updates and bug fixes automatically are installed in the background.

Platform as a service (PaaS)

In a platform as a service (PaaS) service model, developers can create online applications ("apps" for short) in platforms provided by the PaaS provider. The developers develop their own code for the apps, store it in the PaaS provider's data center, and then publish the apps. They don't have to worry about planning for capacity, security, or managing the hardware to run the apps — the PaaS provider does that. A PaaS model also cuts the time it takes to develop apps because of the availability of pre-coded application components such as workflows, security features, search, and so on. To some extent, PaaS is similar to creating a macro in Microsoft Excel where you use the built-in components of the software to run a code that automate tasks.

Infrastructure as a service (IaaS)

In an infrastructure as a service (IaaS) service model, organizations have access to computing power, network connectivity, and storage capacity, using a cloud provider's hardware. This model enables organizations to have control over the infrastructure and run applications in the cloud at a reduced cost and at a faster pace. The organization, however, is responsible for managing and updating the operating system running the applications. While capacity planning, security, and hardware management is the responsibility of the IaaS provider (similar to PaaS), it is the organization's job to monitor the performance of its apps and/or add more resources to meet the demand. Amazon Web Services (AWS) offer several IaaS cloud-hosting products that can be purchased by the hour. Rackspace is another player in the IaaS market offering managed and cloud hosting services. Microsoft Azure started out with a PaaS offering, but has since extended its services to include robust IaaS capabilities.

Determining the Right Office 365 Plan for Your Organization

Office 365 is a SaaS solution running in the public cloud offered on a subscription basis by Microsoft. Each subscription is comprised of one or more licenses depending on the organization's needs. Subscriptions can be purchased directly from Microsoft or through a Microsoft Cloud Solutions Provider (CSP). When you purchase your subscription directly from Microsoft, your support comes from Microsoft. If you purchase your subscription from a CSP, support for the services is provided by the CSP.

TIP

It is important to note that Office 365 comes in two versions: Home and Business. As the name implies, the Home version is intended for home use and does not include the productivity solutions such as Exchange Online or SharePoint Online, which are typically used by businesses for productivity and collaboration. This book is focused on the Business version of Office 365, which includes various plans to meet the needs of small business, enterprise, government, education, and nonprofit organizations.

Choosing between Small Business and Enterprise plans

Office 365 comes with four key technologies (or "workloads" as your IT team might call it):

>> **Exchange Online:** A messaging application that powers business-class email.

>> **SharePoint Online:** A web-based collaborative platform that is typically used for online storage, document collaboration, intranets, and more.

>> **Teams:** Formerly called Skype for Business, the technology behind web and audio conferencing, chats, screen sharing, voice communication, and more.

>> **Office Applications:** Productivity tools including Outlook, Word, PowerPoint, Excel, Access, and more that are available in both desktop and online versions.

In additional to the four key technologies listed here, the Office 365 suite also comes with a host of other features, some of which may only be available in the Small Business plan, such as Microsoft Bookings, and others that are available in all plans, such as Planner, StaffHub, Forms, PowerApps, and more. As a SaaS solution, Office 365 will continue to evolve, so don't be surprised to find new features in your subscription that may not be covered in this book.

TIP

You can view what services and features are currently available across the various Office 365 plans from the following link:

```
https://technet.microsoft.com/en-us/library/office-365-platform-
service-description.aspx
```

While it's true that all organizations should have access to productivity and security tools, not all organizations need the same bells and whistles to run their business or pay the same price for the services. It doesn't make sense for a small business, for example, to pay the same fees as a large enterprise that has more advanced needs such as eDiscovery for legal purposes.

To address this need, Microsoft designed a variety of plans and subscriptions from which organizations can choose. There are, however, so many plans, subscriptions, and license combinations that sometimes it can be difficult to know which one is right for your organization. To help narrow down your options, refer to the decision tree shown in Figure 1-3 to quickly determine what's best for you by answering three questions.

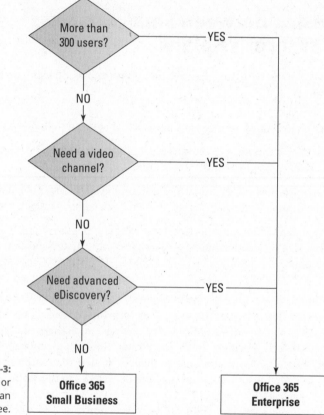

FIGURE 1-3: Small Business or Enterprise plan decision tree.

Office 365 Small Business

The Small Business plans are designed to meet the typical needs of small businesses with 300 or fewer users. There are three key offerings in the Small Business plans:

>> **Office 365 Business:** $8.25 per user per month; ideal for users who only need the Office desktop applications and access to online storage.

- >> **Office 365 Business Essentials:** $5 per user per month; ideal for users who need business-class email and collaboration tools but do not need the Office desktop applications.

- >> **Office 365 Business Premium:** $12.50 per user per month; ideal for users who need business-class email and collaboration tools and the Office desktop applications.

For small and mid-sized nonprofits, Microsoft offers two plans that correspond to the Business Essentials and Business Premium plans but at zero cost and $3 per user per month, respectively.

Office 365 Enterprise

There are four key offerings in the Office 365 Enterprise plans ranging from $8 per user per month to $35 per user per month:

- >> **Office 365 ProPlus:** $12 per user per month; ideal for users who only need the Office desktop applications and access to online storage.

- >> **Office 365 E1:** $8 per user per month; ideal for users who need business-class email and collaboration tools but do not need the Office desktop applications.

- >> **Office 365 E3:** $20 per user per month; ideal for users who need all the features in Office ProPlus and E1 plus security and compliance tools such as legal hold, retention policies, data loss prevention policies, and more.

- >> **Office 365 E5:** $35 per user per month; ideal for users who need all the features in the Office 365 E3 plus advanced security functionalities, analytics, and voice capabilities such as the ability to make and receive phone calls or allow meeting participants to dial-in to a meeting for audio conferencing. Please note that there is an additional fee of $24 per user per month to make domestic and international calls. For domestic calls only, the fee is $12 per user per month.

TIP

You can mix and match a variety of enterprise subscription plans based on the needs of your users, and there is no limit to the number of users on the enterprise plans.

The education, government, and nonprofit sectors have corresponding Enterprise plans. The education plans are called A1, A3, and A5; government plans are called G1, G3, and G5; and nonprofits are called Nonprofit E1, Nonprofit E3, and Nonprofit E5. Take note that prices are different for these sectors, so check with your CSP or at https://office365.com.

Taking care of the firstline workforce

If you run a business with deskless workers, shift workers, retail store employees, truck drivers, or similar employees, you probably don't need all the features from any of Enterprise plans. Most of these workers share a PC or work out of a kiosk and have minimal collaboration requirements and limited communication needs. It doesn't make sense for these workers to pay the full price for plans that have more features than they need or exclude them from the benefits of using Office 365.

To solve this challenge, Microsoft designed an offering called Office 365 F1 that is targeted for the "firstline workforce." For $4 per user per month, the F1 plan gives this workforce most of the productivity and collaboration tools focused on these key areas:

>> Schedule and task management

>> Communications and community

>> Training and onboarding

>> Identity and access management

Getting to Know the Security Features in Office 365

When Office 365 was first launched in 2011, most of the pushback from organizations about using the service was around security. People were worried that having their data in the cloud would make them more vulnerable because they don't have full control of the environment. Today, it's exactly the opposite. More organizations are moving to the cloud because of security reasons. They are realizing they don't have the budget, manpower, and expertise to outsmart the attackers who are getting more sophisticated every day, so they rely on companies like Microsoft — with its highly trained engineers and robust infrastructure — to combat cyberattacks.

Especially for small and mid-size companies, it doesn't make sense to invest thousands of dollars to implement an end-to-end security infrastructure, hire top talent, and stay on top of the cybersecurity trends when they can pay for the service at a fraction of the cost.

Every month, Microsoft scans 400 billion emails for malware and phishing attacks from Office 365 and Outlook. 450 billion authentications are processed by Microsoft every month from its 200-plus cloud consumer and commercial services globally. In addition, Microsoft has scanned more than 18 billion Bing web pages and collected data from 1 billion Windows devices. These insights provide Microsoft with visibility into the current threat landscape like no other company can. On top of that, Microsoft is investing $1 billion in cloud security every year. So, if any company is well-positioned to address security challenges in today's computing environment, it would be Microsoft.

Stepping through the anatomy of a modern attack

In Hollywood, con men or women typically are portrayed as well-dressed, suave, and attractive. Whether it's *Ocean's 11* or its all-female version, *Ocean's 8*, the con artists are smart, methodical, and manipulative.

Today's hackers are similar to con artists portrayed in movies with the advantage of not needing to be well-dressed, suave, or attractive. The con does not even require the con artist to be physically close to the target. With social engineering, hackers are able to carry out a con from hundreds of miles away in the comforts of their dorm room — or parent's basement.

The 2015 Data Breach Investigations Report published by Verizon illustrated that attacks can happen very fast. Here's what the statistics tell us in simple terms:

>> If a hacker sends a phishing email to 100 people in an organization,

>> 23 people will open the email,

>> 11 people will open the attachment, and

>> the median time it took users to make the first click is 1 minute and 22 seconds.

If you think you are immune from social engineering, think again. Hackers have gotten so good at this to the extent that your best line of defense is to acknowledge that at some point, you're going to get hacked and therefore, you need to have a plan in place to recover from it. To plan your defense, it's helpful to understand the mindset of a hacker and the anatomy of an attack.

The recon

Just like the Hollywood con movies, a cyberattack typically involves planning and preparation. Hackers have figured out that it's better to focus on human weaknesses than fight security-hardened software or platforms. A starting point for them is usually doing a reconnaissance or *recon* to figure out who the targets are. Believe it or not, there are actually free tools on the Internet to help with this effort, such as Maltego Teeth or a practice called Google Dorking, which is a technique of applying advanced Google searches to discover confidential company information.

From reading the news, we are seeing a rising trend of attack on not just small business but also on local governments. For the most part, the hackers are not necessarily targeting a particular person or public organization but rather, their recon is focused on who is vulnerable. The recent attack on the town of Rockport, Maine in April 2018 that forced the town of 3,400 to suspend operations was due to an attacker inserting malicious software in its network through a vulnerable backup server.

The initial breach

Once the targets are identified, the breach is initiated via phishing scams or other social-engineering methods. Modern hackers have realized that phishing emails are so common that people now know how to deal with them, so they've started putting malicious macros and code within Word or Excel documents or within a PDF file. An example of this may be a hacker posing as a vendor asking an employee to open an "invoice" posted in an organization's file share or document library. As soon as the employee opens the file, the breach is initiated.

The elevation of privileges

Once the attackers gain access to the target's environment, they then use tools to get a dump of all the users in the organization. From there, they then figure out who the administrators are. Admins are the best because they have a lot of power in the IT environment. Once the attackers have the credentials of the admins, they can pretty much do anything they want to do in the environment.

The entrenchment

The entrenchment is the scary part. This is the stage when the attackers typically get really sophisticated. While the duration has gotten shorter as to how long attackers are stealthily and merrily beep-bopping along the breached environment, studies have shown that it still takes an average of 99 days between the initial breach and the detection of the attack. That's three months the attackers have to start impersonating users, delegating permissions, injecting mail-forwarding rules, and more.

The exfiltration

The culmination of an attack is the extraction of the data to be used for further attacks, ransom, sale on the dark web, or to simply embarrass a person or an organization. From leaked celebrity nude photos to ransomware to stolen medical records, there is no shortage of ways hackers can create grief for their targets or make tons of money with the payload from their attacks.

Overview of the built-in security in Office 365

Security in a cloud-computing environment is a partnership between the tenant organization and the cloud service provider. Both parties have responsibilities that, if done right, will enhance the security posture of an organization.

In Office 365, Microsoft, as the cloud service provider, takes care of the physical security of its data centers where all of its customers' data is stored. It has 24-hour monitoring and biometric scanning technologies implemented to secure the access to its data centers. Faulty drives and hardware are not taken out of the data centers — they are demagnetized and destroyed in huge shredding machines.

Microsoft has policies in place to limit human access to customer data. It has dedicated threat-management teams whose sole job is to proactively anticipate, prevent, and mitigate malicious access. The networks are constantly scanned for vulnerabilities and intrusion.

TECHNICAL STUFF

Data sitting on servers at the data centers is encrypted by default. This is called *encryption at rest.* When data moves from one data center to another, for example when sending and receiving email, that data is also encrypted. That is called *encryption in transit.* What encryption does is prevent someone from reading the content of your email even if that person manages to intercept the email during transit.

If your Office 365 plan comes with Exchange Online, you automatically have Exchange Online Protection or EOP. This service is what filters your incoming or outgoing email from spam, viruses, malware, or email policy violations, all to keep your environment safe.

On the customer side, there are tasks a tenant admin can do and actions end users can perform to enhance security. An admin can implement multi-factor authentication (MFA), which requires a user to prove his or her identity using a second factor such as a phone. If you've ever been asked by your mobile banking app to enter a code sent as a text message after you've entered your username and password, you're interacting with MFA.

Office 365 admins can implement policies to prevent users from accidently leaking confidential data. For example, an admin can create a policy that will prevent a user from sending an email if the email contains a string of characters that look like a credit card number or social security number.

Mobile device management (MDM) is another way for admins to increase security in the organization. For example, if a user loses his phone or laptop, an admin can remotely wipe the data from those devices so that even if someone finds the device and manages to log in, all the corporate data will no longer be present on the device.

Office 365 also offers advanced security functionalities such as the ability to send encrypted email to recipients outside of Office 365 (for example, to people with Gmail accounts). This feature, called Office 365 Message Encryption, is available in the E3 license. With an E5 license, Exchange Online Advanced Threat Protection is built-in, so if a user inadvertently clicks on a bad link, it won't cause damage because links are first "detonated" in a virtual machine in the Microsoft cloud. In essence, if a link is good, the user will be taken to the site; if the link is bad, the user will be blocked and a notification will display warning the user of the suspicious link.

Managing security and privacy in a single dashboard

The Security and Compliance Center in Office 365 (see Figure 1-4) is your one-stop-shop to manage policies, reports, investigations, security posture, and even compliance with GDPR, a European Union (EU) regulation that took effect on May 25, 2018. GDPR stands for "General Data Protection Regulation" and is designed to serve and protect the personal data of all EU citizens.

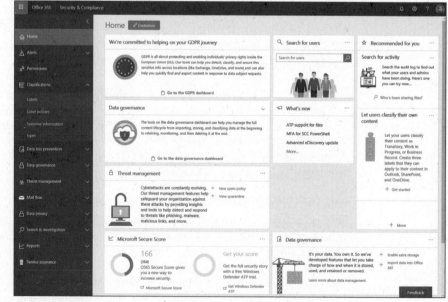

FIGURE 1-4:
The Office 365
Security and
Compliance
Center
dashboard.

The dashboard also provides a link to Microsoft Secure Score, a security analytics tool designed to help you understand what your current risk profile is and how you can improve your security posture (see Figure 1-5).

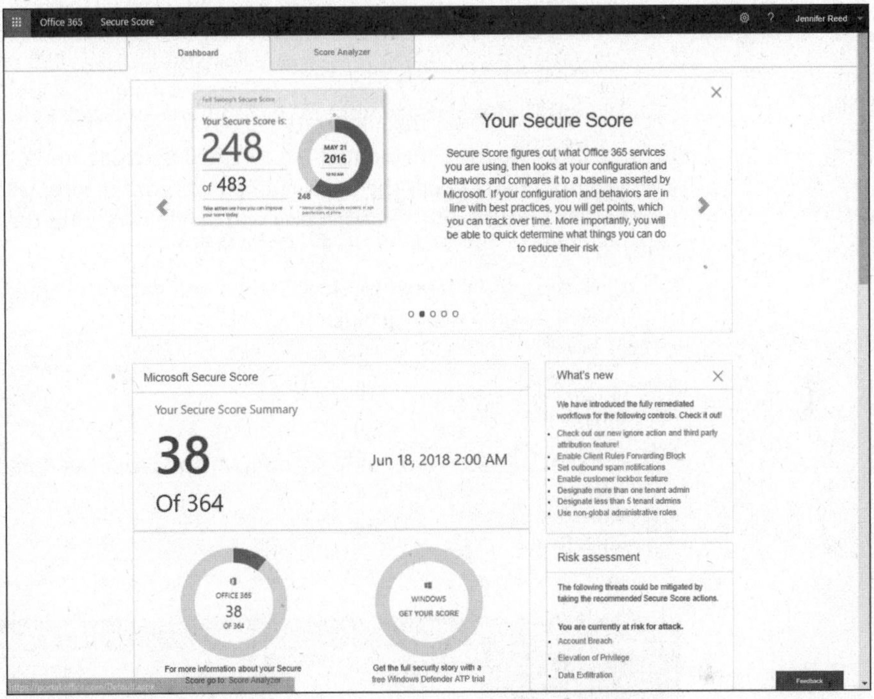

FIGURE 1-5:
The Microsoft
Secure Score
dashboard.

Updating the anti-spam settings

An Office 365 Global Admin can create custom policies or update existing policies in the Security and Compliance Center. If you're an admin and would like to mark a certain user or domain as spam and apply that policy to your entire organization in Office 365, follow these steps:

1. **Navigate to** `portal.office365.com`.

2. **Click the Admin icon.**

3. **From the left pane, expand the Admin Centers group by clicking the arrow pointing down next to the label.**

4. Click Security & Compliance from the list of options.

You are taken to the Security and Compliance Center dashboard.

TIP

You can also go directly to the dashboard by following this link: https://protection.office.com. However, it is recommended that you log in to the Office 365 portal first because this link may change as Microsoft works to consolidate its numerous portals and online assets.

5. Expand Threat Management in the left pane and click Policy (see Figure 1-6).

6. Click the Anti-spam card.

7. Scroll down and expand the Block Lists group.

8. Click the edit icon next to Block Sender and enter the email address of the sender you want to block.

This will prevent this sender from sending email to your entire organization.

9. Click Save.

10. Click the edit icon next to Block domain and enter the domain you want to block.

11. Click Save.

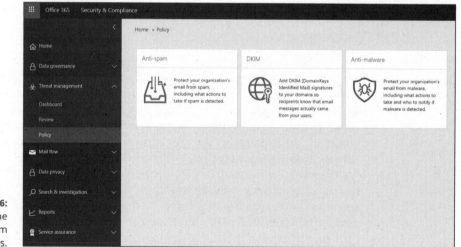

FIGURE 1-6:
Updating the anti-spam policy settings.

Chapter **2**

Moving to the Office 365 Cloud

As we mention in Chapter 1, *cloud computing* is simply using a software application over the Internet. Microsoft Office 365 is a grouping of Microsoft products that are hosted and managed by Microsoft. You sub-scribe to the service on a monthly basis. This model of using software is often called software as a service (SaaS). With the Office 365 offering, Microsoft takes care of all the installation and management of the complicated server products, such as SharePoint, Exchange, Teams, Dynamics, and Power BI (Power Business Intelligence). Your organization simply signs up, starts paying the monthly fee, and uses the software over the Internet (meaning "in the cloud"). The burden of the installation, patches, upgrades, backups, and maintenance (among other stuff) is all taken care of by smart Microsoft employees. To make you feel more comfortable, Microsoft has a 99.9 percent uptime guarantee that is backed by a legal contract called a service-level agreement (SLA).

In this chapter, you get a high-level view of the software products that Microsoft includes in the grouping of software products known as Office 365 and which are delivered over the Internet. These products include SharePoint, Exchange, Teams, Dynamics, Power BI, and Office. You also get some of the basics under your belt including why the cloud and Office 365 in particular are generating such buzz. After all, when Microsoft invests billions of dollars, it must be something worthwhile.

Discovering Office 365 Features and Benefits

Moving to the Office 365 cloud comes with some key features and benefits. Namely, your organization gets to continue to use the software you have been using for years, but you now get to shift the burden of running the servers that serve the software onto Microsoft. In addition to shifting the burden to Microsoft, we describe other key benefits in the following sections.

Generating greater productivity

Productivity is a great word that management-consultant types love to use. In the real world though, *productivity* can be summed up in a simple question: Can I do my job easier or not? Microsoft has invested heavily and spent a tremendous amount of time trying to make the user and administrator experiences of Office 365 as easy and simple as possible.

The idea is that increasing simplicity yields greater productivity. Whether it is an administrator setting up a new employee or a business analyst working with big data and writing game-changing dashboard and data mining in Power BI. When the technology gets out of the way and you can focus on your job, you become more productive. Don't believe me? Try using a typewriter instead of a word processor. Whoever thought copy and paste would be such a game changer?

Accessing from anywhere

Accessing your enterprise software over the Internet has some big advantages. For one, all you need is your computer — desktop, laptop, tablet, or phone — and an Internet connection or phone coverage. Because the software is running in a Microsoft data center, you simply connect to the Internet to access the software, as shown in Figure 2-1.

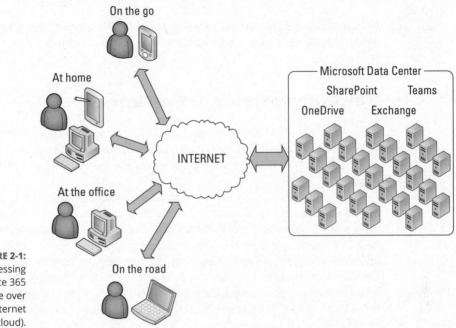

On the go

At home

INTERNET

At the office

Microsoft Data Center

SharePoint   Teams

OneDrive   Exchange

On the road

Another benefit of accessing centrally located data is that you always have a single source of the truth. If you make a change to a document from your tablet at home and then your colleague views the file from her phone, she will see the most up-to-date document. Gone are the days of emailing Excel documents between machines with long file names, such as Forecast_Q1_2019_KW-Reviewed_ Rosemarie-Edited-2-1-19_Revised_2-14-19_KW_final_RW-More_edits_ now-really-FINAL.xlsx.

With SharePoint Online and OneDrive (part of the Office 365 package), a single file, say Forecast_Q1_2019.xlsx, lives out in the cloud (meaning in Microsoft's globally distributed billion-dollar data centers). Because the document lives in the cloud, the security permissions can be set up to allow anyone in the organization, regardless of geographic location, to view the document. Permissions can be as strict or as lenient as desired. For example, you may want everyone in the organization to be able to see a company policy document but only want a select group of individuals to edit the document. In addition, SharePoint takes care of all the versioning and even lets you check out a document to edit so that nobody else can edit it at the same time.

TIP

OneDrive for Business has taken on a life of its own, but it is still powered by SharePoint. Think of OneDrive for Business the same way you think of Dropbox or Box. It is personal cloud storage for your files. And remember that OneDrive is powered by SharePoint. In essence, OneDrive for Business is your personal file store, while a SharePoint library is shared across your organization.

Need to collaborate on the document in real time? No problem. You can do that by using nothing more than your web browser as you find out in later chapters of the book.

Working with what you know

Humans aren't very keen on change. We like to drive the same route to work for years before we figure out there is a better route that avoids all of those snarly traffic snafus. Why would it be any different with the software you use on a daily basis?

Microsoft does not always come out with the best software. Remember Windows Vista and Windows 8? Shiver! Rather than running far away and never looking back at Windows again, users simply held their collective breath until Windows 7 and then Windows 10. And thank you for hurrying Microsoft! Microsoft Word, Excel, and PowerPoint have been in use for more than 30 years, and even though new analysis software comes out all the time, Excel is still the one to best. You know that you can do what you need to do without much headache.

One thing Microsoft did incredibly right is recognize that users don't want to give up the things that make them comfortable. "Don't take away our Word, Excel, and PowerPoint!" we shouted. And Microsoft listened. Office 365 hasn't changed our favorites one bit. The only difference is that now they are seamlessly connected to the enterprise software living out in the cloud. In other words, our favorite applications are cloudified.

One of the coolest features about SharePoint and Office is that you can work with SharePoint and OneDrive without ever having to leave the Office applications. For example, you can fire up Word, check out a document stored in SharePoint or OneDrive, make some changes, check it back in, review versions, and even leave some notes for your colleagues. All without even having to know SharePoint is handling the content management functionality behind the scenes.

Robust security and reliability

With Microsoft taking on all the responsibility for security and reliability, your IT team can rest on their laurels. After all, they spent their entire careers keeping the systems up and running. Shouldn't they get a break? All kidding aside, letting Microsoft do the heavy lifting frees up the IT team to do more important things. No, not playing computer games, but helping users get the most out of enterprise software. Ever wonder why nobody could ever find time to implement a company-wide blog and discussion board? Now they can finally be a reality.

Microsoft understands if you aren't fully comfortable about letting it do the heavy lifting. In my opinion, it is the best scenario. After all, who better to handle managing software products than the same people who built them? To address some of the questions, however, Microsoft has extensive service level agreements to help put your mind at ease.

IT control and efficiency

If you have ever met an IT person, you might have generalized one thing about him or her. IT people are control freaks. They like to know exactly what everyone is doing with their systems at all times. If something goes wrong, then it is probably due to user error. Our systems do what they are supposed to do. Microsoft has gone out of its way to create an unprecedented level of control for administrators. But that is not all. Not only do administrators have control over the environment, but it is actually designed to be simple in nature and, get this, *intuitive*.

Getting Familiar with Office 365 Products

The Office 365 product is actually a package of products rented on a monthly basis. In particular, these include Office, SharePoint Online, OneDrive for Business, Exchange Online, Teams, Dynamics, and Power BI.

The online part just means that you access these server products over the Internet. If your IT team were to buy these products and install them for your use in the company data center, then they would be called *on premise*.

Microsoft Office

Finding someone who doesn't use some aspect of Microsoft Office on a daily basis is difficult. Whether it is Outlook for email, Word for creating and editing documents, Excel for manipulating and mining data, and PowerPoint for creating and making presentations, these old standbys seem to dominate the life of the modern-day information worker.

The newest version of Office came out in 2019. When you have Office 365, you pay on a monthly basis and can always be assured you have the latest version of Office installed on your device.

Microsoft Office includes much more than these old stalwarts, though. In particular, Office includes the following applications:

>> **Access:** A database application used to collect, store, manipulate, and report on data.

>> **Excel:** An application used for data analysis and numeric manipulation.

>> **OneDrive for Business:** A cloud-based, file storage service that is part of Office 365.

>> **OneNote:** An application used for capturing and organizing notes.

>> **Outlook:** An application used for email, contacts, and calendaring including scheduling meetings, meeting rooms, and other resources.

>> **PowerPoint:** An application used to create and deliver presentations.

>> **Publisher:** An application used to create and share publications and marketing materials, such as brochures, newsletters, post cards, and greeting cards.

>> **SharePoint:** A web-based platform that lets you easily create an Intranet for your organization. An Intranet is just an internal-only website where you find content, see company policies, and find other such internal tasks.

>> **Word:** An application used for word processing, such as creating and editing documents.

The list of apps available with Office 365 continue to grow. Microsoft has introduced a range of apps to help its users be even more productive. Following are additional options to help you get more from your Office 365 subscription:

>> **Bookings:** An online appointment scheduling application for small businesses. Customers can schedule appointments and automatically get confirmations, reminders, updates, and cancellation notices.

>> **Business Center:** A three-in-one business application for appointment scheduling, invoicing, email marketing, and managing your business' online presence.

>> **Delve:** An application that helps you handle the deluge of digital content. A newcomer to Office 365, Delve is an extension to SharePoint and OneDrive. Delve shows you content it thinks you want to see, and learns from your behaviors as you work. For example, you might see the latest content your immediate coworkers have updated or updates to content you have had interest in previously.

If you're tech savvy, you will quickly recognize that OneDrive for Business is powered by SharePoint.

TIP

- **Dynamics 365:** An application that combines enterprise resource planning (ERP) and customer relationship management (CRM) software available in the cloud, easing communication and sharing of information between the field, sales, project service automation, and customer service teams.

- **Flow:** An application used to create workflows between apps, files, and data to automate time-consuming tasks without knowing a line of code.

- **Forms:** An application that lets you easily create surveys, quizzes, and polls in minutes.

- **Planner:** An application that helps you get organized on your next project. Create new plans and assign tasks, share files, and chat about the status of the project.

- **Power Apps:** An application that lets anyone in your organization build mobile and web apps with the data your organization already uses.

- **Power BI:** An application that helps you make sense of the mountains of data from all over the place through reports, dashboards, and other analysis tools. ("BI" stands for *Business Intelligence,* but Microsoft simply refers to the product as *Power BI*.) Power BI is not necessarily a part of the traditional Microsoft Office, but it falls squarely within the Office 365 suite of critical applications. It was born in the cloud and has only ever lived in the cloud.

- **StaffHub:** An application that is used to manage work schedules online. Request time off, swap shifts, and communicate directly with your coworkers and supervisors.

- **Stream:** An application that is used to share videos of classes, meetings, presentation, training sessions, or other videos with people in your organization.

- **Sway:** An application that is used to create and share engaging reports, presentations, personal stories, and more.

- **Teams:** A chat-based team workspace application in Office 365. Formerly called Skype for Business, Teams allows you to connect with others using features such as instant messaging and conferencing including screen sharing, polling, and shared presentations. Using Teams, you can also communicate with legacy Skype for Business users who haven't yet upgraded to Teams.

- **To-Do:** An application that is used to manage, prioritize, and complete the most important things you need get done each day.

- **Yammer:** An application that helps you connect to the right people, share information across teams, and organize around projects with coworkers.

Pay-as-you-go flexibility

With pay-as-you-go licensing your organization is able to turn on or off licensing, depending on the number of users that require Office 365. In addition, Microsoft has added flexibility for you as a user by allowing you to activate the licensing on up to five different computers at a single time, depending on your plan. For example, when your organization adds you as an Office 365 subscriber, you can activate the software on your workstation at work, your laptop, your home computer, and your home laptop. When you buy a new computer, you will find a simple user screen where you can update the computers that Office is activated on. This flexibility makes managing your Office applications and licensing as easy and straightforward as possible.

Native apps experience integrated into web apps

In addition to running Office applications such as Word, Excel, PowerPoint, and Outlook on your local computer, Office 365 also includes a web version of these applications called Office Online and mobile versions called Mobile Online. When working with the Office Online apps, you simply open your web browser and browse to your SharePoint portal that contains your document. You can then open or edit your document right in the web browser. Likewise, when using the Mobile apps, you open up the mobile version of the Office app, such as Word, on your mobile device and edit it, just like you would on your laptop or desktop computer.

Microsoft has gone to great pains to make the Office Online apps and Office Mobile apps experience very similar to the traditional Office experience. For example, when you are checking email in Outlook, writing a Word document, or reviewing or editing an Excel document or PowerPoint presentation, you expect certain behavior. Microsoft has tried hard to retain the familiar feel of the Office you love. We cover Office Online apps in great detail in Part 4 and touch on the Office Mobile apps throughout the book.

Latest versions of the Office apps — always

Because Office 365 uses an SaaS model, you are always instantly up to date. When Microsoft releases a new version of Office, your licensing is instantly upgraded. You don't need to wait for the IT team to finally get the new product purchased and rolled out. When Microsoft flips the switch, everyone has the latest and greatest instantly available.

Severing Ties to Your Desk

If you are used to using Outlook for your email, then you won't experience any changes when your organization moves to Office 365. The only difference will be that Microsoft is now hosting your email instead of your local IT department. Should you decide to look a bit further, however, you can find a great deal of extra functionality just waiting to make your life easier. For example, the new Outlook Mobile apps are integrated with Exchange in order to push email directly to your phone whether you use iPhone or Android. Prefer a different email app? No problem. Almost every email app on the market can be set up to receive Office 365 email.

Using Outlook Online

Office 365 provides the ability for you to check your enterprise Exchange email using nothing more than a web browser. Instead of using Outlook on your local computer you simply browse to a web address, such as `http://mail.myorganization.com`, and then log in and check your email. The experience is very similar to other web email services, such as Google's Gmail or Microsoft's Hotmail or Live mail. What's exciting about Outlook Online, however, is that you finally get access to your enterprise email, calendar, and contacts from any computer with an Internet connection and a web browser.

REMEMBER

Outlook and Exchange are both email-related products, but one is for users and the other is server software. Exchange is a server product that sits on a server in a data center and manages all of your email. Outlook is an application that you install on your local computer and then use to connect to the Exchange server to check and manage your email, contacts, and calendaring. With Office 365, you still use Outlook (installed on your local computer or smartphone) but instead of connecting to an Exchange server managed by your IT team, you connect to an Exchange server managed by Microsoft.

Grouping conversations in your inbox

Like it or not, email has become a primary means of communication for the modern information worker. It is common for many people to send and receive a truckload of email on a daily, if not hourly, basis. Keeping track of different email on different topics with different people can be a daunting task. Outlook 2019 includes a feature called Conversations that is geared toward helping you keep track of all that email. The feature automatically groups conversations by subject, as shown in Figure 2-2. Notice that "Update" is the subject of the emails and the entire conversation is grouped for easy reading. You can even see your response emails and any meetings associated with this conversation. No more digging through your Sent box looking for how you responded to a particular email.

TIP

You can turn on the Conversations feature by clicking the View tab in Outlook and then checking the Show as Conversations checkbox, as shown in Figure 2-2.

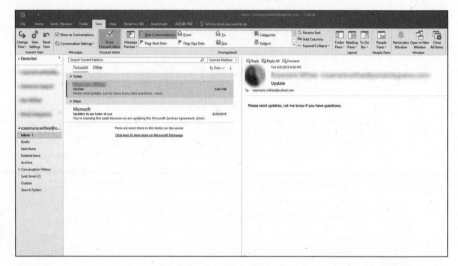

FIGURE 2-2:
Grouping conversations in Microsoft Outlook 2019.

Getting organized with Office 365 Groups

Office 365 is constantly adding features, and a relatively new one is called Office 365 Groups. The Groups feature is aptly named, because it allows you to create public and private groups.

Outlook 2019 is one component of Office that takes advantage of Office 365 Groups. Other apps that work with Office 365 Groups include OneDrive for Business, Teams, and OneNote. Microsoft has plans to integrate most of the Office 365 apps with Groups, so if you have a favorite, check whether Groups is already available.

When a new member joins a group, they can see the history of the group and quickly get up to speed. Everyone in the group can chat with each other, share files, schedule meetings, share notes, and use Teams for real-time communication.

Archiving just got personal

Exchange Online gives you access to your own personal email archiving system. Your personal archive shows up as another mailbox right next to your regular mailbox. You access your archive just like you access your regular mailbox. On top of that, when you need to search for an old email, you can choose to search your archive in addition to your regular mailbox.

Collaborating made easy

In the last decade, SharePoint has taken the world by storm. As consultants, we had a large property management client ask us about SharePoint the other day. We were curious what was driving their decision because they knew very little about SharePoint. Our client told me that when he talks with his peers in the industry, they all tell him they use SharePoint extensively. When he asks them about their experience using SharePoint they tell him that they can't imagine running their business without SharePoint. That was enough of a driver for him to find out about SharePoint right away. After all, when the competition moves toward something that increases their advantage, other companies have to move quickly in order to maintain the ability to compete. And thus is the case with the adoption of the technology wave consisting of communication, collaboration, content management, and consolidation, which is all made possible by SharePoint.

The newcomer to the scene is Microsoft Teams. Teams is a one-stop-shop for all your communications needs and integrates closely with SharePoint. Teams replaces Skype for Business for your messaging, communications, and meeting needs, and it also integrates with SharePoint so that all your documents, calendars, and data are in a single place. Upgrading to Teams can be as simple as starting to use Teams instead of Skype for Business. Microsoft Teams is covered in Chapter 15.

TIP

Microsoft Teams replaces Skype for Business and provides a one-stop-shop for all your communications needs. If you and your organization haven't already upgraded to Teams, it is time to check it out.

With Office 365, your organization gets SharePoint and Teams without the hassle of having to work through a complicated deployment. Your IT staff has an administrative interface and can provision sites and set up users with minimal effort. With SharePoint and Teams up and running, your organization can spend its resources on solving real business problems, instead of working through the technical details of an implementation. Using SharePoint is covered in detail in Part 3.

Creating communities for the corporate world

An online community is nothing more than a group of people coming together by using their computers regardless of geographic location. If you have used Facebook or LinkedIn or even AOL or Yahoo Groups, then you have been involved in an online community. SharePoint brings online communities to the corporate world in a secure corporate environment. You can imagine the scenario where you are in the accounting department and the team is working on company financials. The team needs to collaborate with each other, but you wouldn't want to be posting to each other's Facebook walls or Twitter accounts. Some of the online community features SharePoint provides include wikis, blogs, content tagging, document sharing, discussion boards, people search, alerts, and notifications.

In addition to the online community features already discussed, every person who has a SharePoint account also has his or her own personal online file storage that is powered by SharePoint. This feature is called OneDrive for Business; it allows you to store your files and share them with others. If you are familiar with Dropbox, Box, or Google Drive, you already understand the concept of cloud-based file storage. OneDrive for Business comes with most Office 365 subscriptions, so you don't have to go searching for it. You access it on the Office 365 "waffle," along with the rest of your Office 365 apps. The Office 365 waffle icon is shown in Figure 2-3.

Waffle icon

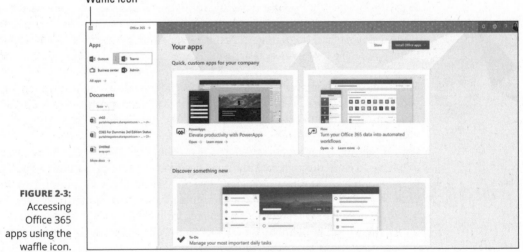

FIGURE 2-3:
Accessing Office 365 apps using the waffle icon.

Depending on the resolution of your screen, the waffle will show up in the upper left or the upper right of your browser screen.

Sharing information with customers and partners with extranet sites

Because SharePoint Online (one of the components of Office 365) is in the cloud, you have the ability to share information with partners that are not part of your local network. These sites that you can make available to people outside your organization are called *extranet sites.* An extranet site is different from a public website because people usually need to log in to see an extranet site. A public website, on the other hand, is open to the world. An example of an extranet site might be a partner network made up of complementary companies. The people in these other companies won't have access to your company network, but you still need to be able to share information and collaborate with them. SharePoint Online offers extranet sites for just such a purpose. SharePoint and extranet sites are covered in more detail in Chapter 5.

Microsoft has gone to great lengths to create a secure, safe, and stable SharePoint environment. In particular, Microsoft guarantees the following:

>> The environment is available 99.9 percent of the time.

>> All content and configuration details are backed up regularly.

>> Virus scanning software for SharePoint constantly scans content for threats.

>> File types that can pose a risk to your SharePoint environment are blocked from upload.

Microsoft Office 365 is truly a global product with data center locations distributed throughout the world. The product supports more than 40 languages including Chinese, Arabic, Spanish, and Portuguese. Need your site to support the Catalan language? No problem, SharePoint Online has you covered.

Going Virtual with Intuitive Communications

Microsoft Teams is the latest iteration of Microsoft's cloud-based communications service. In particular, you can chat through text, talk to people using voice, and even have face-to-face meetings by using your webcam. In addition, Teams allows you to conduct online meetings by using screen sharing, virtual white boards, electronic file sharing, and even online polling. As we previously mentioned, Teams is closely integrated with SharePoint so you won't find yourself having to jump between apps as much as in the past.

Text/voice/video in a single app and service

You can think of the Teams application as a one-stop shop for communication. Because Microsoft has tightly integrated the Office 365 applications, you can move seamlessly between them. For example, you might be reading a post on SharePoint and want to instantly communicate with the poster. Or you might want to start a chat message in a Teams channel and then go off and do other work and check back later to see if you have a reply from anyone in the team.

If you are wondering if someone is available right away, you can view the presence icon. If it is green, the user is available; if it is red, the user is not available. Or maybe you are reading your email and want to see whether the person who sent you the email is available for a chat. From within the Outlook Online App, you can see the Teams status of the user. If it is green, then the person is available and you can instantly open Teams and communicate. The Teams status shown in the Outlook Online App is shown in Figure 2-4. Note the circle presence icon next to Rosemarie's name in the email and the presence icon next to Ken's picture in the upper right corner.

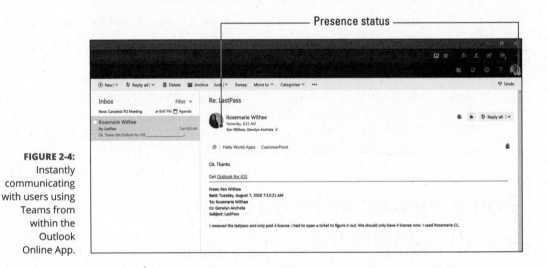

FIGURE 2-4: Instantly communicating with users using Teams from within the Outlook Online App.

As you are chatting with the person who posted, you might decide that you want to share screens and invite others to join the meeting. By using Teams, it is as simple as a couple of button clicks. We cover using Teams for online meetings in Chapters 15 and 16.

From conversations to ad hoc meetings — yes, it's possible

By using Teams, you can instantly connect with others from multiple locations. As previously mentioned, you might be reading a SharePoint post but you also might receive an email and want to meet with that person right away if he is available. You can see his status on the presence icon next to his name in your Outlook email message, as shown earlier in Figure 2-4. If you want to communicate with this person, you can hover over his Teams presence icon to access the menu. You may want to send a chat message to the user, so you click the Chat button. A chat session instantly opens, and Teams takes care of pulling in the subject of the email as the subject of the chat so that the person knows what the chat is about. It's almost as good as walking across the hall to talk to someone, only now that someone can be anywhere in the world.

Online meetings unleashed

An online meeting is nothing new. There are many services that offer the ability to share your screen or co-author documents. What has finally come together with Office 365 is the tight integration between all the different products. You can now see if someone is available for a meeting right from within the applications you use day in and day out, such as Outlook, Office, and SharePoint. Using Teams, it is also possible to set up meetings with those outside your organization. Teams meetings enable you to conduct meetings using chat rooms, audio, video, shared white boards, and even polling. Conducting meetings with Teams is covered in detail in Chapter 15.

Interacting with photos and activity feeds

In addition to instant communication, Teams can also contain personal information, such as photos and activity feeds.

Being able to put a face with a name is nice. Just about anywhere you might connect with another person, be it Outlook, SharePoint, or the author information property from within an Office document, you can view information about the person. The name of a person will have a presence icon next to it. Hover over the presence icon or photo and then click the details screen. Figure 2-5 illustrates viewing the details of a colleague from within the Author property of a Word document.

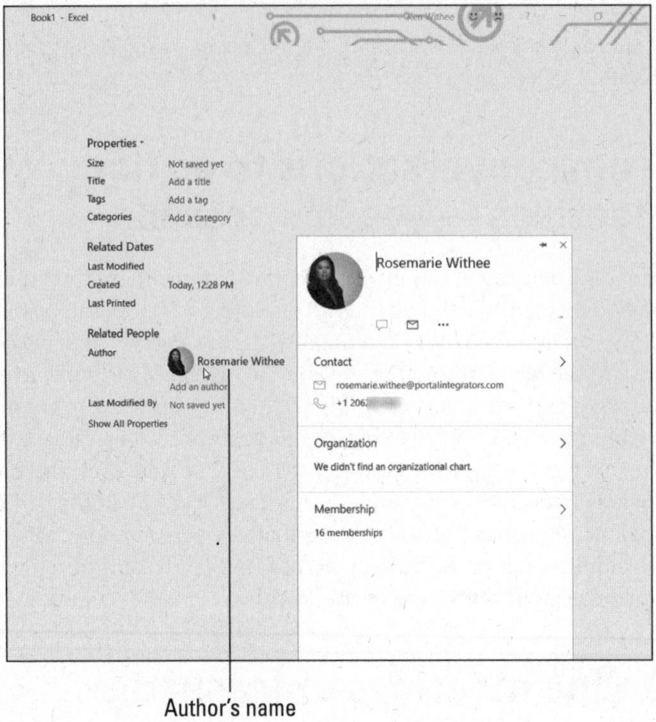

FIGURE 2-5:
Viewing
information
about a colleague
who authored a
specific Word
document.

Author's name

The activity feed is a current status sentence similar to Twitter but on a corporate level. For example, you might be heads down working on a document and update your status with "Working heads down on a document but here if you need me in a pinch!" Other users will see this status message and know that even though you are online at the moment, you are busy working on a document. Of course, another use for the status message could be something along the lines of, "Left over cake in the break room! Get it while it lasts!"

Keeping up with your teammates on your own time

One of the key features of Teams is that it allows for asynchronous chat within a group. This is a simple yet incredibly powerful concept. In Teams you create channels for your groups. If you have ever heard of a product called Slack, then you are already familiar with Teams. Teams is Microsoft's answer to Slack, but instead of just duplicating the features of Slack, Microsoft integrated Teams with the rest of Office 365 and in particular SharePoint. In Chapters 15 and 16 we walk you through some key scenarios to Teams and how you can use it to boost the productivity of the people you work and interact with.

2

Communicating with Exchange Online

Understand the flexibility of Exchange Online.

Dive into how Exchange Online works with both the Outlook client that installs locally on your computer and a web version that provides email from any computer that has a web browser and Internet connection.

Met the bots that allow you to work smarter and faster. Use artificial intelligence to get a no-cost personal assistant.

Communicate with confidence knowing that your email and files are encrypted on their way to the recipient. When you run into trouble, run the troubleshooting tool to fix issues.

Chapter **3**

Unleashing the Power of Exchange Online

I f you are like most people, you couldn't care less about how your email gets into your inbox as long as it does. If your company uses Microsoft products, then chances are you use an application called Outlook to send and receive email. Outlook also has some other nifty features, including a calendar, the ability to reserve conference rooms, invite people to meetings, store contacts, create your to-do lists and tasks, and even read you your email messages or listen as you dictate a message. Although you are probably familiar with the Outlook application, you may not know that it has a behind-the-scenes partner. That partner is Exchange, a server application that handles all the heavy lifting. The Outlook application on your desktop is constantly connecting to the Exchange server to find out what information it should present to you.

Because Outlook and Exchange communicate with each other over a computer network, the physical locations of these two hand-in-hand applications are irrelevant. All that matters is that they can communicate with each other. The Outlook software can be installed on your workstation on your desk, and the Exchange software may be installed on a server under your desk or down the hall (known as *Exchange On-Premises*) or in a data center somewhere out there in the cloud (known as *Exchange Online*).

And because Exchange can be located anywhere, a whole bunch of possibilities open up around who is responsible for managing the fairly complicated server software. If Exchange is running on a server under your desk, then it is highly likely you are the lucky person responsible for it. If it is in your company data center, then you probably have a person, or team of people, responsible for administering Exchange. When you sign up for Office 365, you are letting Microsoft take on all the responsibilities of managing Exchange. Microsoft has Exchange running in its data center, and you simply connect to it with Outlook and use all the functionality.

In this chapter, you find out why letting Microsoft take responsibility for Exchange creates a flexible and reliable option for your email, calendaring, contacts, and task needs. You discover that you can access your corporate Exchange system from almost anywhere at any time and on any device. You also find out about some of the protection and compliance features that take some of the risk out of letting Microsoft take the lead by managing its Exchange product.

Gaining Flexibility and Reliability

Key traits in any good relationship are reliability and flexibility. You look for these same qualities in computer software. When you deploy software, you want the process to be flexible and predictable. After the software is deployed, you want it to be reliable and dependable. Exchange Online falls into the category of service-based software. With service-based software, you don't have to develop, install, or manage the software. You simply sign up and start using it.

Deployment flexibility

When it comes time to roll out software, you have a number of options. You can pay someone to develop software from scratch, which is known as *custom development.* You can buy software, install it, and manage it yourself. Or, you can sign up to use software that is installed and managed by someone else. This third option is called software as a service (SaaS). You sign up to use the software and pay for it as a service on a monthly basis. (See Chapter 1 for more on SaaS.)

Microsoft Office 365 is a SaaS offering by none other than Microsoft. Microsoft has invested billions of dollars building state-of-the-art data centers all over the world. These data centers are staffed by Microsoft employees whose entire responsibility is managing the Microsoft products offered in the Office 365 product.

Because Microsoft is making the service available on a monthly basis, you have the greatest flexibility of all. You sign up for the service and begin using it. No need to go through a deployment phase. Exchange Online is already deployed and ready to go.

REMEMBER

The Office 365 product is actually a bundle of products, and Microsoft is continually adding more. There are Office 365 plans for home users, Office 365 plans for work, and Office 365 plans for education. The products in your bundle depend on the plan you choose. If you sign up for an Office 365 For Work subscription, some of the products you might have in your bundle are the Office productivity suite, SharePoint, Exchange, and Teams. For more about the different plans available, see Part 6.

Deployment predictability

Most decision-makers cringe when they hear the words "custom development." You will hear horror story after horror story when it comes to a custom software development project. If you get really good developers who have been working together as a team and use a solid process (such as Scrum), then you might have extraordinary results and the best software available. On the other hand, you may end up with something that doesn't do what you want it to do and costs 12 times what you thought it was going to cost in the beginning. In short, you can end up with a disaster. For this reason, many decision-makers want to remove the risk and go with packaged software. Because packaged software is already developed and only needs to be installed and managed, the risk associated with adopting the software is greatly reduced.

You will still hear horror stories, however, about the implementation process for packaged software. It generally falls along the lines that someone thought someone else had configured the backups and the person who the other person thought had configured them had already left the company. Oh yeah, and the system was designed to be redundant so that if one key server went down everything would keep working. The only problem is that you only find out if everything works properly when something goes wrong. If the proper procedures were not followed during the implementation, then your organization may find itself in a very bad position.

Those with experience will say that it is often not the fault of any particular person. IT teams are overworked and stretched beyond their capacity to handle everything effectively. For this reason, using a SaaS is popular. With service-based software, another company specializes in managing the software and keeping it available, reliable, and backed up. You pay on a monthly basis and connect to and use the software over the Internet. This last realm removes the risk for chief technology officer–type decision-makers (CTOs). Not only do they not have to pay someone to develop the software, they don't even have to worry about stretching their valuable IT resources beyond the breaking point. And, should the worst-case event happen, another company is liable for the problem based on the service contract signed.

TIP

Because the hosting company is liable for anything that goes wrong with hosted software, making sure that the company is reputable and capable of dealing with a major issue is important. Microsoft is one of the biggest names in the software industry with an established business record and lots of money in the bank. Your cousin's friend who started hosting software in his basement probably doesn't have the same resources Microsoft has in case something goes wrong.

Flexible provisioning

In addition to the predictability of the deployment costs in both time and resources, Exchange Online offers the ability to easily adjust the number of licenses for people using the software. A hiring manager might plan to hire 45 people but find out later in the year that the company needs to hire another 30 as it is growing more rapidly than expected. It is easy to provision new users for Office 365 through the simple administrative interface.

TIP

Another benefit of SaaS software is that CTO–types can find out exactly what the costs will be now and in the future. The CTO doesn't need to explain why the project was eight times over budget or why four more people were required for the IT team to support the new software. The price in resources, people, and time is very transparent and obvious from the beginning. In other words, the costs are predictable, which is what accounting people and executives like to see.

Continuous availability

Although it may seem blatantly obvious that software should be available all the time, you may be surprised by how many enterprise systems are only available during certain business hours. Exchange Online is available all day, every day, without interruption. In fact, Microsoft guarantees a 99.9 percent uptime.

Simplified administration

If you have ever spent time talking with someone who is responsible for configuring Exchange Server, you know that it is not for the faint of heart. In fact, many people are so specialized that their entire careers are spent doing nothing but administering the Exchange Server software. If your organization is lucky enough to employ a full-time team of these rock-star administrators, then you have probably not experienced any major email issues. Everything works as expected and nobody really cares why. The problem, however, is that if one critical person leaves the organization, you might not be as lucky with the replacement.

Exchange Online offers a simplified and intuitive administrative interface. You no longer need extraordinary expertise to get the very most out of the Exchange product. Microsoft handles all the heavy lifting and provides an interface that allows even people with minimal technology skills to administer the company email system by using nothing more than their web browsers. The Exchange Online control panel, also known as the Exchange Admin Center, is shown in Figure 3-1.

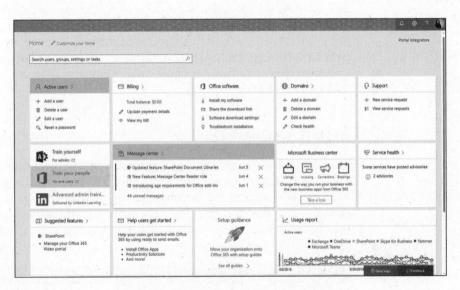

FIGURE 3-1:
The Exchange Online Admin Center is used for administration.

Accessing from Anywhere

Not all that long ago, email was a relatively new thing. We checked our email like we would check the regular mail, and often we could only email people within the organization. Email has come a long way since then. Now you will be hard pressed to find someone who doesn't use email, especially in a work environment. Email is tremendously important for the modern workforce.

Exchange Online provides a continuously available service that can be accessed from just about anywhere at any time. All you need is an Internet connection and a web browser. We recently spent time at a firm that didn't have regular email access for those people not in the office. A couple of years ago, this would have been no big deal. In today's connected world, however, we found it almost impossible to cope with my lack of connectivity when not in the office. With modern smartphones, you can carry around instant email access right in your pocket. There are a number of email apps for every device. Exchange works with almost all of them. Microsoft even has the popular Outlook email client for your iPhone, iPad, and Android devices.

From your Outlook email client

The Outlook application that so many people use day in and day out for email, meetings, tasks, and contacts continues to work the same way with Exchange Online but with some added bonuses. In particular, you get an even tighter integration with the other products that are part of the Office 365 offering. For example, you may have a task list that is part of SharePoint. To integrate your SharePoint tasks with Outlook, you navigate to the SharePoint Online list and click a button that says Connect To Outlook. Bingo. Your SharePoint tasks now show up in your Outlook Tasks folder.

From the web

In addition to accessing Exchange from your Outlook client, you can also use your web browser. When you use your web browser to access Exchange, you are using what has been termed the Outlook Web App (OWA). Office 365 provides a rich experience for working with enterprise email right from the browser. Using the Edge browser to access the Outlook Web App is shown in Figure 3-2.

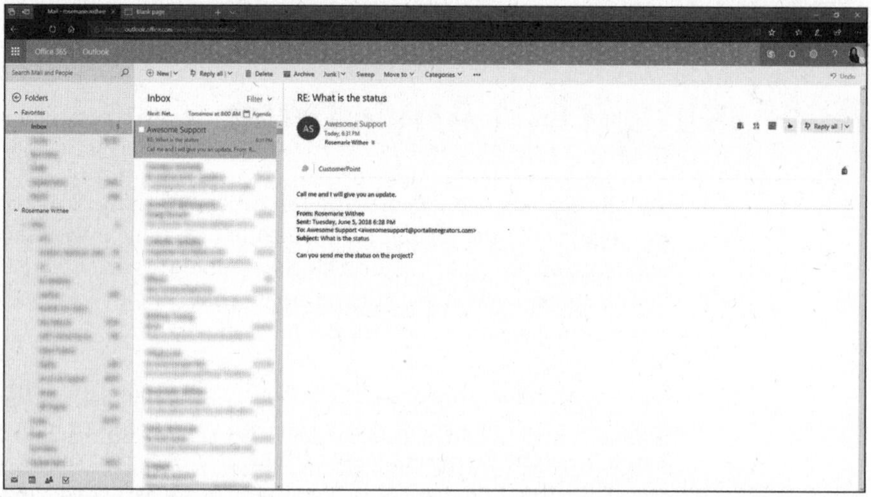

FIGURE 3-2: Using the Edge web browser to access the Outlook Web App.

From multiple devices

Microsoft has released versions of Outlook for all types of devices, including iPhones, iPads, and Android phones and tablets. You don't have to use a Windows PC in order to be productive with Outlook wherever and whenever you want.

In the past, Mac users have faced a difficult decision. Use a Mac and struggle with compatibility with the corporate email system or use a PC and use Outlook for full integration. Exchange Online supports the popular Outlook, which is part of Office 2019 for Mac. Outlook on a Mac provides similar integration to Outlook for the PC. By using Outlook on your Mac, you can access your Exchange Online email, calendars, tasks, and contacts.

From any email client

Exchange Online supports all the standard email protocols, including IMAP, POP, and SMTP. As a result, you can use any email client you like to send and receive email.

WARNING

If you want advanced functionality, such as calendaring and meetings, contacts, tasks, and advanced email features, such as presence information for contacts, then you need Microsoft Outlook as your email client.

Manage inbox overload

The number of email most people send and receive in a given day is amazing! If you are like many office workers, your inbox can quickly become overloaded and your productivity drained just looking at all the unread messages. Exchange Online attempts to help you manage your email by using a number of different features. We cover using Outlook to boost your productivity in Chapter 4.

One of the most important features is that you can access your email any time and from any location that has either cell reception for your smartphone or a computer with a web browser and Internet connection. This feature allows you to stay current with your email on your own time and not just when you are sitting in front of your work computer staring at hundreds of unread emails. Have some downtime while waiting for the bus? Twiddling your thumbs at the doctor's office? Get caught up on your email and find out whether that important proposal has arrived.

Some other features that Microsoft has recently rolled out in Outlook also help you manage email overload. One particularly useful feature is called *Clutter*. The Clutter feature learns which email is important to you and which emails are, well, just clutter. It then moves the annoying email to a folder called "Clutter" and lets you focus on the email you find important.

A cool feature when using Outlook on your iPhone or Android phone is the *swipe* feature. When you look at your email on your phone, you can just swipe an email message left or right to perform an action such as archive. You can configure what swiping a message off to the right or swiping a message off to the left does. For example, you may want to move an email out of your Inbox and into another folder when you swipe left, and delete an email when you swipe right. When you get the hang of it, swiping messages left or right lets you empty your Inbox in no time!

In addition to anywhere access, some powerful productivity features come along with Outlook. For example, you can view all those messages about the same topic in a single email thread known as a *conversation*. You can also quickly set up a meeting with those involved in the topic of the email with a few clicks of the mouse.

Microsoft Teams is closely integrated with Exchange Online and provides even more communication and productivity saving options such as instant chats, voice and video calls, and screen sharing.

You can also include a number of add-ins to Outlook to solve particular needs. For example, one that we use all the time is called Grammarly. It is a form of artificial intelligence that checks your spelling and grammar as you compose messages and offers suggestions. Did we mention we really love artificial intelligence?

Efficient collaboration

Anyone who works with email on a daily basis has experienced the scenario where an email thread goes on and on, and on some more. People are added to the thread, and those people add more people to the thread. At some point, it would be much easier to just set up a meeting and discuss everything in person. With Outlook and Exchange Online, you can do this with directly from Outlook, as shown in Figure 3-3.

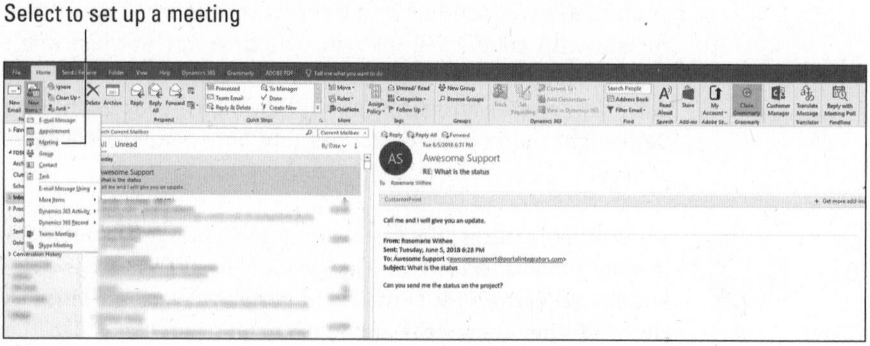

Select to set up a meeting

FIGURE 3-3:
Set up a meeting
with all the
participants in an
email thread.

A meeting is instantly created, and all the email participants are included in the meeting. The subject of the email thread instantly becomes the subject of the new meeting. This major timesaver increases efficiency on a number of fronts.

Enhanced voicemail

A nifty aspect of Exchange Online is that it includes a unified messaging component. Unified messaging means that different types of messaging are tied together. In this case, we are talking about a physical phone. You remember when you used to have to actually wait for a dial tone, right? Yep, that is the type of voice phone we are talking about.

Exchange Online can be used as your voicemail system and automatically transcribe a message that is then sent to your email or texted to your phone. Need to check your email but don't have Internet access? Exchange Online has a dial-in interface for callers. All you need to access your email is a phone. Listening to your email may take longer than glancing at your smartphone but at least it is a possibility. This functionality extends email access to anywhere with a phone.

Protecting Information

One of the most important aspects of any system is the protection of information and compliance with company and government rules. Exchange Online is simple to use and administer, but don't let that fool you. Under the covers, Microsoft has spent a tremendous amount of effort on protecting you from digital threats and making sure that you are in compliance without hindrance.

Archiving and retention

Each person has an email box as well as her own archiving system. An archive shows up in Outlook as another mailbox, as shown in Figure 3-4. The intended purpose of the additional archiving folder is to store older email in a permanent storage location. You can think of your archiving folder as your electronic attic or basement. You can go in there to retrieve stuff if you need to, but it is really a long-term storage location.

TIP

The size of a user mailbox and archive are dependent on the SaaS plan. Some plans have a maximum mailbox capacity and others have unlimited archiving capacity. For more information about the plans that are available and the resources allocated for each plan, check out Chapter 18.

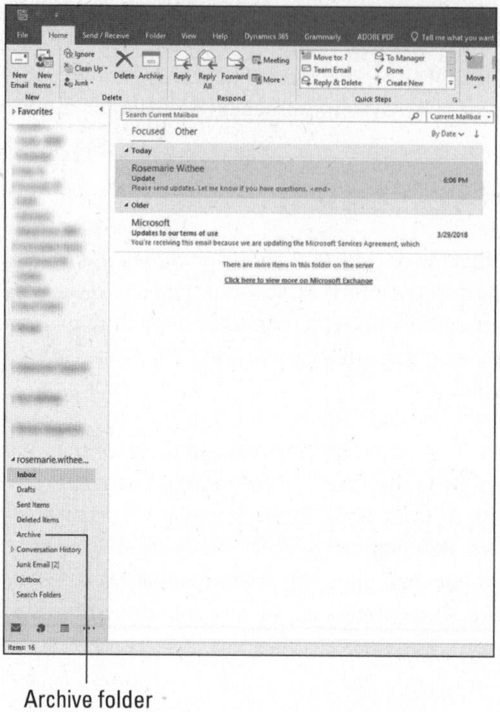

FIGURE 3-4:
The archive folder
shows up as
another mailbox
in Outlook.

Archive folder

Information protection and control

The Exchange Online offering includes antivirus and antispam control without needing to install any third-party or external software. When a new message comes into Exchange Online, it is scanned for risks before being delivered to the intended email box.

TIP

The technology that makes all this protection possible works behind the scenes to make the environment safe and secure. Don't worry, though; you don't have to pay extra or even know how it works. As an end user, you just know that someone is looking out for you so that you don't inadvertently receive spam or virus-infested files.

The government has added many rules and regulations around corporate email. Exchange Online provides the ability to meet these rules with features, such as eDiscovery and legal holds.

TIP

eDiscovery refers to *electronic discovery*, which simply means electronic messages can be searched for relevant communications in the event of a legal process. This might not be a big deal, but if you are in a heavily regulated industry or governmental organization, these features are often required by government regulators.

Chapter **4**

Being Productive, Staying Secure

W e live in a world where the line between our personal and professional lives is becoming more blurred every day. Our personal mobile devices also function as our work phone. We check work email at home from our smartphones. During breaks (and sometimes not) at work, we use our work laptops to tweet. People in the marketing department may use the same device to post corporate news on the company's Facebook page as well as post selfies on their personal Facebook accounts.

The Bring Your Own Device (BYOD) strategy is increasingly being adopted by organizations. As an employee, it's great to be able to use the latest iPhone you stood in line for to get work done instead of fighting with a locked-down company-issued device. For the company, a BYOD policy means more productivity and reduced cost.

While there certainly are upsides to the merging of personal and business use on one device, there are also downsides to be considered. For example, imagine you have an iPhone with two years' worth of family photos that you also use to check corporate email and do light editing of Word documents. One day you're traveling and you lose your phone at the airport. You now have made not only your personal information vulnerable, but also, you've put your company data at risk. If your IT department has some kind of device management solution, it may wipe your entire phone to protect company data. In the process, however, your family photos will also be wiped by your IT department.

When our mobile devices synchronize both personal and work email and are used for our own personal social media activities, the surface for social-engineering attacks increases. For example, consider the following scenario: You have a Facebook friend who is a friend of a colleague at work. You've never met this Facebook friend in person, and you've never interacted with this person in other platforms aside from Facebook. You've never exchanged email. One day out of the blue, you get an email message from this friend with a link to the address for your company picnic. The email seems harmless (you were already aware of the company picnic). Do you click to open the link? Given that you've never received email from this person before, the right thing to do would be to give the link a closer look. It could be a bogus link that could take you to a malicious site instead.

As an end user, it's challenging to keep up with all the tricks attackers are coming up every day. As an organization, it's nearly impossible to think of all the potential breaches and have the right technical solution to prevent them. It's almost a losing battle — you have to pick either increasing productivity or staying secure. You can't have both.

Or can you?

As it turns out, you can. With Microsoft Office 365, you can have the best of both worlds. You can drive productivity and efficiency in your organization while at the same time ensure your company data is secure.

This chapter covers the latest innovations in Exchange Online in Office 365 as well as the Microsoft cloud technologies that integrate with Office 365 to make you more productive. You discover how bots and artificial intelligence can help you work smarter. The chapter also looks at new features available to help you get a handle on your inbox, ways to send secure email, and how to troubleshoot common Outlook problems.

Incorporating Bots to Get More Done

According to Statista, an online statistics and market research tool, by 2021, 40 percent of the world's population will own smartphones — 2.87 billion users! That's a 13 percent increase from the 2.53 billion smartphones in use in 2018. With all those smartphones comes artificial intelligence (AI) in the form of chatbots (or *bots* for short) such as Siri, Google Now, and Cortana.

You may not realize it, but AI has become an integral part of our daily lives. The technology drives our digital assistants to help us get our day started. They tell us what the weather will be like, how long our commute is going to be, and get us up to speed with the latest news. AI can even help us not run over our beloved dog while backing up our car in a hurry through the computer vision recognition in the cameras found in modern cars.

In Office 365, machine learning and AI is already built in to help personalize your experiences and enhance security. The following are examples of how you can incorporate bots in Exchange Online, the technology behind your email, contacts, and calendar.

Your very own AI personal assistant

People who are into gaming will know Cortana as an AI character in the Halo video game series. In Windows and Office 365, Cortana is your personal digital assistant that helps you accomplish simple tasks through programming codes called *skills*. To date, there are a number of Cortana skills available, ranging from money-saving tips from Progressive Insurance, to ordering pizza from Dominos, to controlling your home thermostat's temperature with Nest.

One of the time-saving bots we've found that integrates with Outlook calendar is an AI called Calendar.help. What it does is help us schedule meetings with colleagues, so instead of spending ten minutes rounding up everyone's schedules, all we need to do is simply send an email to a colleague we want to meet with and copy the Cortana bot with instructions for the meeting written as if we were talking to an assistant. The bot does such a good job; a couple of colleagues actually thought Cortana was a real person!

Here's how you can integrate the Calendar.help bot in Outlook to have an AI personal assistant. Please note that the Calendar.help bot is in preview so the name may change by the time this book is published. While in preview, you can sign up and get on the waitlist. In our experience, by signing up with three valid Office 365 accounts, our request was approved within minutes.

1. Go to https://calendar.help.

2. Sign up for Calender.help with a valid Office 365 account.

   You will get an email when the bot is ready to assist you.

3. To schedule a meeting, send an email to the person you want to meet with and add cortana@calendar.help in the Cc: line.

4. **Write your email as if you're communicating with your personal assistant (see Figure 4-1).**

   You will receive an auto reply from Cortana acknowledging your request (see Figure 4-2).

   Once Cortana has found a time that works for all participants, you will get an email confirming the meeting.

5. **Go to your calendar to verify the meeting was added.**

FIGURE 4-1: Asking Cortana to schedule a meeting.

From: Jennifer Reed
Sent: Wednesday, May 2, 2018 3:31 PM
To: Jeff
Cc: Cortana <cortana@calendar.help>
Subject: Jeff/Jenn Meet and Greet

Hi Jeff,
I'm hoping for us to get together for me to get insights from you on how we can partner to support our internal customers and anything you can share to help me with my role. Also, if there's anything I can do to help you, I'd love to know. I hope you don't mind but I've copied my AI calendar bot (Cortana) to find time for us to meet.

Cortana,
Please set up a 30-minute Skype meeting for me and Jeff next week.

Best,
Jenn

FIGURE 4-2: Cortana's auto reply.

Wed 5/2/2018 2:32 PM

C Cortana <cortana@calendar.help>
Re: Jeff/Jenn Meet and Greet

To 	Jennifer Reed

If there are problems with how this message is displayed, click here to view it in a web browser.

Hello Jennifer,

I've received your message, and now I'm going to work with Jeff to get the meeting scheduled. If necessary, I might reach out to Jeff to propose some available times from your Microsoft calendar. You should expect a confirmation email from me when I add the meeting to your calendar.

Getting too many request acknowledgment messages? Unsubscribe

If you have any questions, feel free to email me anytime. Remember you can always check the status of your meeting at https://calendar.help/.

Thank you,

Cortana | https://calendar.help
Scheduling Assistant to Jennifer Reed

Time to leave alerts

The idea behind the Time to Leave Alert bot is that when you schedule an appointment in your calendar and add a location from Bing maps, Cortana will help ensure you get there on time. This bot requires integration with Windows 10 into Office 365. Once the bot is set up, your computer will prompt you when it's time to leave for your appointment. For example, if you have a flight in your calendar, Cortana will recognize your current location and prompt you to leave early because traffic is heavy.

To enable the Time to Leave Alert bot, take the following steps:

1. **In Windows 10, open Cortana and select the Notebook icon (see Figure 4-3).**

Notebook icon

FIGURE 4-3: Opening Cortana in Windows 10.

2. **Click the Manage Skills tab and then select the Commute & Traffic card under Productivity (see Figure 4-4).**

3. **In the Commute & Traffic card, toggle the All Commute and Traffic Updates switch on (see Figure 4-5).**

   That's it! Now that you've enabled the bot, a notification will pop up on your screen based on the appointments in your Outlook calendar, similar to the notice shown in Figure 4-6.

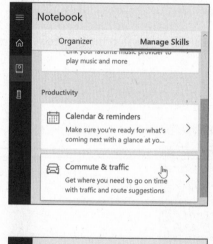

FIGURE 4-4:
Selecting the
Commute &
Traffic card.

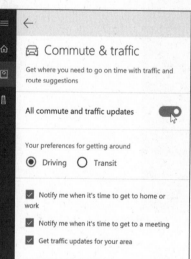

FIGURE 4-5:
Enabling all
commute and
traffic updates.

An Office 365 subscription does not come with a Windows 10 license. You can, however, bundle Office 365 with Windows 10 and an advanced security solutions called Enterprise Mobility + Security (EMS) in a new service called Microsoft 365. For details about this new service, check out *Microsoft 365 Business for Admins For Dummies* by Jennifer Reed.

FIGURE 4-6:
Time to leave alert example.

Integrating Cortana in Office 365

Cortana is built into the Windows 10 operating system. When you integrate Cortana in Office 365, you are giving the AI permission to access your Office 365 data in Outlook. Cortana collects data about your email, calendar, contacts, and communication history from messages and apps to personalize your experience. To learn more about privacy in Cortana, visit the following link:

https://privacy.microsoft.com/en-us/windows-10-cortana-and-privacy

TIP

If you have concerns about using Cortana, you can disable it from the Office 365 portal with these steps:

1. Log on to http://portal.office365.com with a **Global Administrator account** and then click the **Admin** icon.

2. Click **Settings** from the menu on the left panel.

3. Click Services & Add-ins and select Cortana from the list of services.

4. Toggle the switch to Off next to Let People in Your Organization Use Cortana and then click Save.

Securing Your Email

Before the explosion of cloud technologies, organizations had control over their data that resided within the perimeter of their on-premises data centers. The identity of the users, the devices they used, the applications they ran, and the company data were all confined within this parameter and controlled by the IT team.

Nowadays, however, we operate in a boundary-less world. We check email from our personal devices, we do our work at the office or at home — or even at the beach — and we use cloud services outside the perimeter of an organization's data center. We do these things because we want to be productive, but sometimes this productivity can mean sacrificing security.

In Office 365, you can continue to do the things you do to be productive while at the same time stay secure. In Exchange Online (the technology driving your email), for example, you can encrypt your email so that only the intended recipients of the message will be able to read it. You can apply protection to your email so if it's confidential, the email can only be read by people within your organization. If someone accidentally forwards or copies a recipient outside of the organization on email marked confidential, that recipient will get the email but he or she won't be able to read it.

These security features for protecting email are available through the Office 365 Message Encryption (OME) service.

Licensing requirements for Office 365 Message Encryption

Office 365 Message Encryption (OME) is part of the Office 365 subscriptions listed as follows. There is no need to purchase additional licenses for users when the following subscriptions are assigned to them:

» Office 365 E3 and E5 (Enterprise)

» Office 365 A1, A3, and A5 (Education)

>> Office 365 G3 and G5 (Government)

>> Enterprise Mobility + Security E3

>> Microsoft 365 E3

If a user's license is not for any of these subscriptions, you can purchase a stand-alone subscription called Azure Information Protection Plan 1 for $2 per user per month to enable OME as long as the user's current license is any one of the following subscriptions:

>> Exchange Online Plan 1 or Plan 2

>> Office 365 F1 or E1

>> Office 365 Business Premium or Business Essentials

Enabling Office 365 Message Encryption

If you've purchased Office 365 licenses with OME capabilities after February 2018, OME is automatically configured and your users can start using the service.

If you purchased Office 365 license prior to February 2018, you need to enable Azure Rights Management (Azure RMS) from the Office 365 portal. After enabling Azure RMS, Microsoft will automatically configure OME in your Office 365 tenant. Here are the steps to enable Azure RMS:

1. **Log on to** `http://portal.office365.com` **with a Global Administrator account and then click the Admin icon.**

2. **Click Settings from the menu on the left panel.**

3. **Click Services & Add-ins and then select Microsoft Azure Information Protection from the list of services.**

4. **Click Manage Microsoft Azure Information Protection settings from the pane.**

   You will be asked to authenticate with your Office 365 credentials.

5. **In the Rights Management page, click the Activate button.**

6. **Before closing the page, verify that the Rights Management Is Activated notification is displayed with the green check mark next to it (see Figure 4-7).**

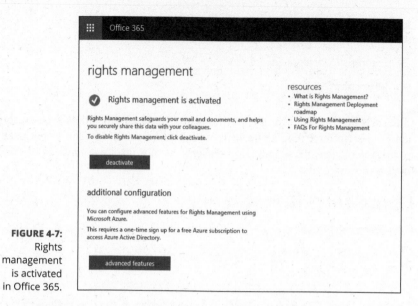

Sending an Encrypted Email

With OME enabled in your Office 365 tenant, users can immediately start sending encrypted email to recipients within or outside the organization based on the default policies available in OME. Depending on your subscription and the functionalities Microsoft has rolled out, you will find two or more pre-configured encryption policies. The two default policies in the Office 365 E3 or the Azure Information Protection Plan 1 subscriptions available as of this writing are Encrypt and Do Not Forward.

To apply these policies to an email using the Outlook desktop app, follow these steps:

1. In the Outlook desktop application, compose a new email and add the recipients.

2. From the ribbon, click Options.

3. Click the Permission button and then select the appropriate encryption policy.

4. Click Send to send your email.

To apply these policies to an email in Outlook Online, follow these steps:

1. **Compose a new email and add the recipients.**

2. **From the ribbon, click Protect.**

3. **Click Change Permissions from the notification bar to display the available options and then select the appropriate encryption policy.**

4. **Click Send to send your email.**

Using the Encrypt policy

When you use the Encrypt policy, the email message will be encrypted on its way to the recipient. Once it reaches the recipient, the message will be decrypted so that it's readable.

Using the Encrypt policy does not prevent the recipient from forwarding the email to someone else. The recipient can print out the email, post it on social media, or frame it on his or her wall. If additional protection is required, the Global Admin for the Office 365 Portal will need to create custom policies.

As of this writing, Outlook Online, Outlook for iOS, and Outlook for Android will automatically display the decrypted message on the screen. For other email applications, the email will provide a link to allow the recipient to read the decrypted message (see Figure 4-8). There are plans underway to expand the list of supported applications in the near future including the Outlook desktop application, which is currently in preview as of this writing.

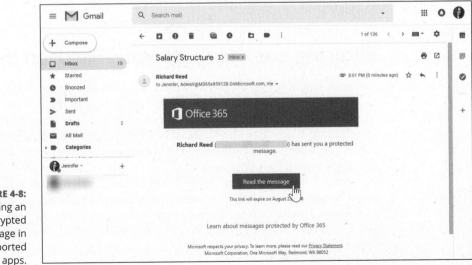

FIGURE 4-8:
Reading an encrypted message in non-supported apps.

Using the Do Not Forward policy

The Do Not Forward policy also encrypts the email message on its way to the recipient, but it has an additional policy restricting the recipients from forwarding the email to someone else. If any of the recipients forwards the email to others, new recipients who try to open the email will get a message saying that they don't have permission to view the message (see Figure 4-9).

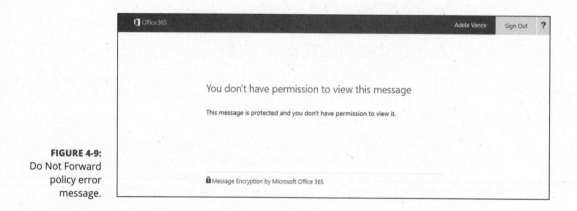

FIGURE 4-9:
Do Not Forward policy error message.

Making Outlook Work for You

As a cloud service, Office 365 has intelligent experiences designed to help you prioritize work so you can be productive. Built-in AI in Outlook allows you to re-focus your energy on what's important. And when Outlook misbehaves, there is a built-in tool to help you troubleshoot common Outlook issues without the need to engage your support team.

Filtering out the noise with Focused Inbox

Exchange Online in Office 365 has built-in spam and spoof filters that block known unwanted and malicious email from reaching your mailbox. Yet even with filters, our mailboxes can still end up being bloated with email from the pizza place, our cable provider, and our favorite shopping site. When you're trying to be productive, it's easy to get distracted by legitimate but unimportant email.

The Outlook desktop application and Outlook Online come with a functionality called Focused Inbox to address that challenge. Focused Inbox helps with mailbox management by acting as an automatic sorter that puts all your important email into the Focused tab and the less important ones in the Other tab (see Figure 4-10).

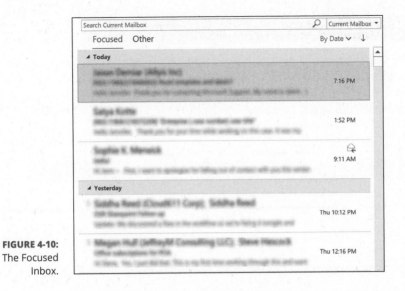

Built-in AI in Office 365 determines what email goes into what tab. Email from the contacts you interact with a lot will go to the Focused tab while bulk email from your shopping site will go to the Other tab to filter out the noise. You can also train the AI to fine-tune the categorization by moving email that ends up in the wrong tab. The more you train the AI, the better it will learn your behaviors to ensure that your inbox feels just right for you.

Diagnosing common Outlook problems with SARA

One of the advantages Microsoft has in running cloud services is its access to error logs and signals from the devices and users interacting with the system. Those logs and signals are transmitted to Microsoft databases where they are monitored and analyzed. Based on those insights, Microsoft is able to improve its service or create self-service solutions for customers.

SARA is short for *Support and Recovery Assistant,* a diagnostics tool built into Outlook. It's a handy tool that automatically fixes common errors users have encountered in Office 365, such as Outlook problems, Office installations, and more. Figure 4-11 lists the common Outlook problems SARA can troubleshoot.

If you are experiencing any of these issues and want to run SARA, follow these steps:

1. **In Outlook desktop application, click File from the ribbon.**

2. **From the backstage left panel, click Support.**

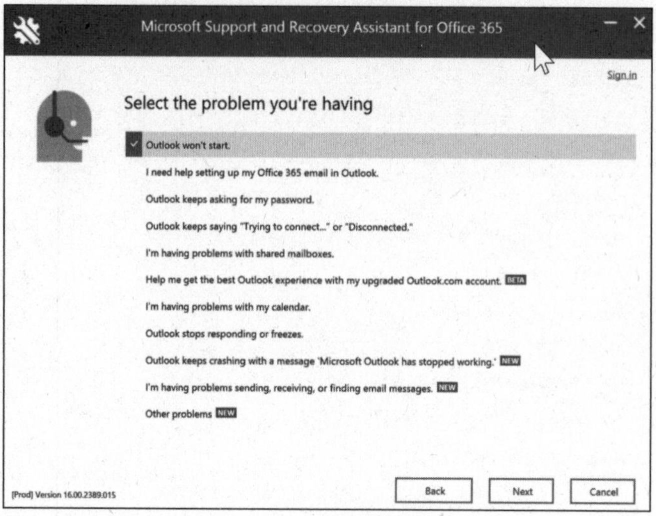

FIGURE 4-11:
Common Outlook
problems SARA
can troubleshoot.

3. **Click Support Tool to install SARA.**

   This action will connect to the Office 365 systems and will download the tool.

4. **Once the tool finishes downloading and starts running, follow the prompts based on the issue you are trying to resolve.**

   Depending on your issue, the process could take a few minutes to half an hour.

Exploring SharePoint Online

IN THIS PART . . .

Explore the worry-free version of SharePoint server.

Use SharePoint Online to collaborate with colleagues, add and manage content, and integrate with your trusted Office applications.

Launch an elegant, fluid, and mobile-friendly SharePoint site with no coding skills using a SharePoint site template.

Whip SharePoint into shape to meet your specific business needs by creating sites, pages, lists, and libraries.

Chapter 5

Collaborating Effectively Anytime, Anywhere

I n 1971, computer engineer Ray Tomlinson sent the first email between two computers set side by side. When asked what prompted him to develop such breakthrough technology, Tomlinson's response was, "mostly because it seemed like a neat idea."

More than 40 years later, and over 269 billion emails sent and received per day in 2017 alone, that neat idea is due for an upgrade. In today's world, where information workers no longer are sitting beside each other but spread out across multiple geographies and time zones, email simply isn't enough to ensure real-time collaboration, self-service information gathering, and robust knowledge management solution.

While email will continue to serve the needs of one-to-one communication and calendaring, SharePoint Online serves as the platform for team-focused and project-focused collaboration needs. The intranet capabilities in SharePoint deliver collaboration capabilities in a way that harnesses the collective knowledge of the people in the organization to not only inform and engage employees but also to transform business processes.

In this chapter, you get a tour of the SharePoint landscape, come to understand features for enhanced collaboration, and learn to build a beautiful, mobile-friendly intranet site without writing a single line of code!

Touring the SharePoint Landscape

SharePoint Online connects the people in your workplace with an intelligent content management solution that drives productivity while keeping your data secure. It is a cloud-based solution that is one of the services in Office 365. Also under the SharePoint umbrella is SharePoint Server, which is a solution similar to SharePoint Online, but it requires buying and maintaining server hardware, installing the software, keeping software or operating system up to date, and hiring people to manage the technology and troubleshoot issues. In SharePoint Online, these tasks are handled by Microsoft.

Getting to know the SharePoint personas

While SharePoint provides a platform for everyone in the organization to share and work together, there are four types of personas who use, interact with, and benefit from SharePoint.

>> **End users:** If you access your organization's portal or intranet on SharePoint to read announcements or any type of communications, you're an end user. The same is true if your project team uses SharePoint for collaboration.

Throughout this book, you find useful instructions to help you quickly become a productive project team member.

>> **Admins:** As you become familiar with the features and functionalities of SharePoint, you may become a super end user and take on administration responsibilities, such as the following:

- *Site collection admin:* This role is responsible for an entire site collection, which may have many SharePoint sites. A site collection admin can control which features are available for the site collection, including workflows, custom branding, and search settings.

- *Site owner:* When you create a new site from the Sites page (instructions are provided later in this chapter), you automatically become the site owner. As a site owner, you can provision sub-sites, manage permissions for the site, change the look and feel, and enable or disable site features according to what's available from the site collection, and more.

>> **IT professionals:** SharePoint has built-in capabilities that cater to professionals in an IT department or IT consultants who serve the needs of their clients. Typically, these IT professionals administer SharePoint Online to ensure the technology meets business needs. They can act as the system or SharePoint admin with access to the SharePoint Admin Center in Office 365 where they configure SharePoint settings, such as

- Enabling/disabling Yammer as the enterprise social collaboration solution

- Allowing external sharing of SharePoint sites

- Configuring compliance and data loss prevention policies

- Restoring deleted sites

>> **Developers:** These are the technical people who create applications and customizations to extend SharePoint functionalities beyond what Microsoft offers. SharePoint has rich features for the hundreds of thousands of developers focused on this platform. There's even a marketplace for these developers to publish and sell their apps and solutions: the SharePoint Store.

Landing on the SharePoint Online home page

SharePoint Online lets you share knowledge, content, apps, and rich, interactive news to a broad audience within your organization. At the heart of the ability to inform and engage employees is the foundational technology that delivers beautiful, modern, and mobile-friend sites and pages.

The SharePoint Online home page gives you a quick list of all the sites you belong to and are following on the left pane. The middle pane displays a card-style list of the latest news in your organization culled from all the sites you have access to as well as a list of the sites you frequently visit (see Figure 5-1).

To access the SharePoint Online home page, follow these steps:

1. **Log in to Office 365 from** `http://portal.office.com`.

2. **Click the app launcher (the icon that looks like a waffle in the top left corner).**

3. **Click SharePoint from the list of tiles.**

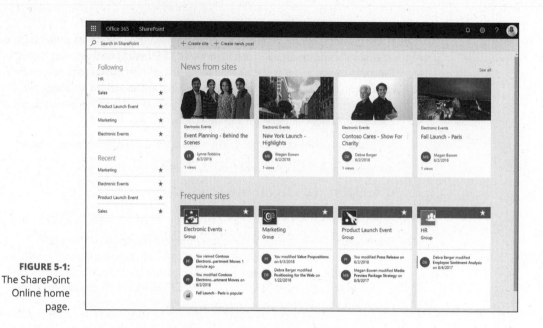

FIGURE 5-1:
The SharePoint
Online home
page.

Be careful what you share!

SharePoint sites and their content can be shared with users outside your organization through a functionality called *external sharing.* By default, external sharing is enabled in SharePoint Online. This means that all sites created from the Sites page can be shared with external users. The Office 365 Global Admin can disable this feature globally for the entire SharePoint Online environment or enable/disable any individual site collection.

External sharing is handy when you want people you work with who don't have an Office 365 license (referred to as *external users*) in your organization to collaborate with you. For example, if you are running a marketing campaign and you're working with an ad agency, you might want to give your contacts in the ad agency access to your project site in SharePoint so you can co-author documents.

WARNING

External sharing can also pose a potential for data leakage, so be careful what you share!

Knocking Down Collaboration Barriers

Great collaboration happens when you give your users the tools and techniques to automate and simplify their work. SharePoint Online is chock-full of features to do just that. It knocks down common barriers for collaboration such as document versioning nightmares, lack of content discoverability, scheduling confusion, and misalignment on project goals and objectives. On top of that, you can do all your work with a modern, clutter-free interface that automatically responds to the size of your screen. You no longer have to be sitting in front of your desktop computer to interact with SharePoint. You can take it anywhere with you — on your smartphone or tablet where you have an Internet connection.

Choosing between Team sites and Communication sites

SharePoint sites are the building blocks for your intranet. The search and discovery features are fantastic so it's easy to find documents across the entire intranet with keyword searches.

With SharePoint, you always have options. If you want to create a site, you have a choice between two templates: Team sites and Communication sites. Both templates are provisioned the same way, but there are considerations for using one versus the other. Figure 5-2 outlines the best uses of each template.

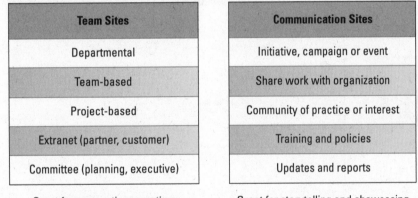

Team Sites	Communication Sites
Departmental	Initiative, campaign or event
Team-based	Share work with organization
Project-based	Community of practice or interest
Extranet (partner, customer)	Training and policies
Committee (planning, executive)	Updates and reports
Great for connecting, creating, and collaborating	Great for storytelling and showcasing work and service offerings

FIGURE 5-2: Team sites versus Communication sites.

Creating a Team site

A SharePoint site using the Team site template has one additional feature the Communication site doesn't have. A Team site includes a group email address so you can collaborate with your team via email. This functionality is called *Office 365 Groups* or *Groups* for short, which is covered in the next section in this chapter.

To create a Team site from the SharePoint home page:

1. **Click the Create site icon.**

2. **Select Team site.**

3. **Enter the Site name.**

   The Group email address is automatically populated based on your entry for Site name.

4. **Enter the Site description.**

5. **Select the Privacy settings and select Next.**

6. **On the next screen, add additional owners and member for the site.**

7. **Select Finish.**

Your newly created Team site will come pre-populated with common elements in a collaboration site. To edit the contents of your landing page, click the Edit icon in the top right corner of the page (see Figure 5-3).

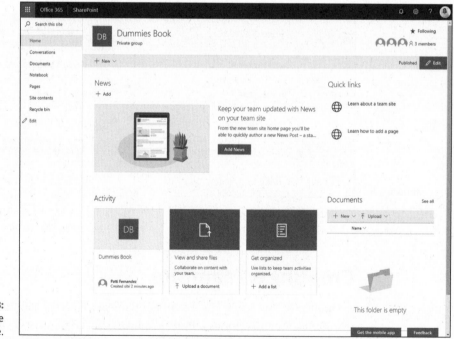

FIGURE 5-3: The Team site landing page.

In editing mode, your landing page will display the content structure of the page comprised of sections and Web Parts. When you hover over the section or the

Web Part, the *edit, move,* and *delete* icons pop up. Selecting any of the icons will display the details pane on the right to give you more options for customization (see Figure 5-4). When you're done editing, click the Publish button in the top right corner of the page.

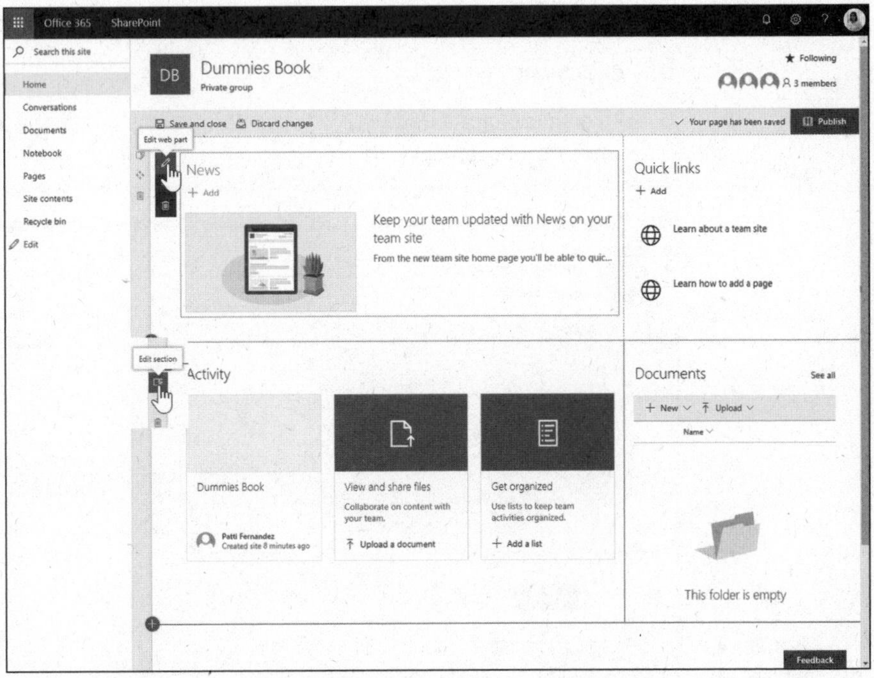

FIGURE 5-4:
Editing the Team
site landing page.

Sharing and co-authoring documents

When you create a Team site, a document library is automatically created. The library is a helpful tool for reducing back and forth emails between team members to work on a document. You can streamline the process by loading your documents in the document library and then working off of the same file with others. This process is called *co-authoring.*

To share a document from the Team site you created in the previous section:

1. **Click Documents from the menu navigation on the left pane.**

2. **Click New from the menu bar at the top to create a new document or Upload to upload and existing document and follow the prompts.**

3. **Select the document by clicking on the row and then click Share as shown in Figure 5-5.**

4. **Choose the permission level you want to assign to the document by clicking People in your organization with the link can edit and selecting the right access level.**

5. **Enter the name or email address of the person you want to share the document with.**

   Include a message if you'd like.

6. **Click Send.**

   An email notification with a link to the document is sent to the people you shared the document with.

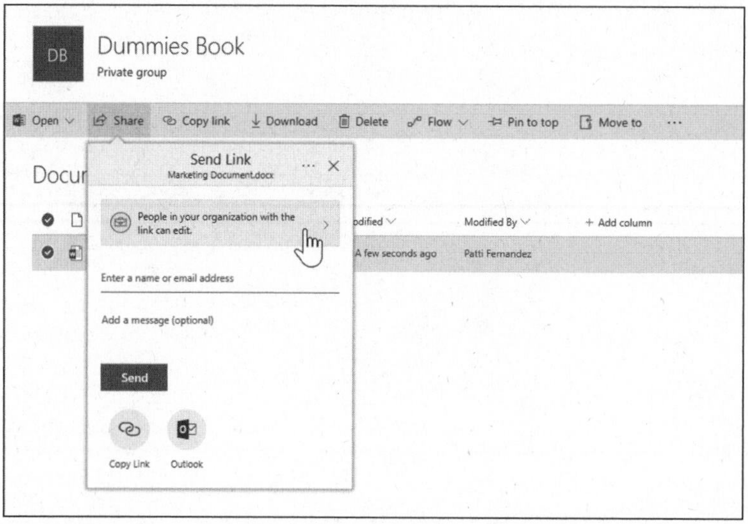

FIGURE 5-5:
Sharing a file
from the
document library.

Restoring a previous version of a document

Version history in document libraries is enabled by default so restoring an older version of the document only takes a few clicks. This is particularly helpful when you want to track the evolution of your document. If for some reason the current version doesn't meet your needs, you can always go back and restore a previous version.

To view the version history and restore a previous version, follow these steps:

1. **In your document library, click the ellipses next to the document name to display additional actions.**

2. **Select Version history from the menu to display the Version history window.**

3. **Hover over one of the dates until you see the down arrow on the right.**

4. **Click the arrow to bring up the View, Restore, and Delete options for the version and make your selection.**

5. **Click OK.**

Getting Social at Work

Working in silos is so ten years ago. The clamor in the workplace nowadays is for people to work better together and collaborate more using social tools similar to what we use in our personal (think Facebook) and professional (think LinkedIn) lives.

Office 365 offers more than one tool for social connections, from Yammer to Communities to Office 365 Groups. There are no hard and fast rules for using all, or one over the other, but generally there are best practices you can apply to ensure you're using the right tool for the right purpose. For each of the tools we cover in this topic, you will find some best practice tips.

Five rules for Yammer success

In SharePoint Online, you can embed a Yammer feed on your site pages to enable two-way conversations without leaving SharePoint. When you want to use the full Yammer functionalities, you can easily navigate to Yammer from the app launcher on the Office 365 navigation bar.

Why Yammer?

>> If you need to collaborate with others, you must Yammer.

>> If you value connections, you must Yammer.

>> If you want to share your ideas and benefit from other peoples' ideas, then you must Yammer.

Like most popular social networking sites, there are basic tasks you must complete before engaging with other users in the network. Yammer is no different. If you'll be using this tool for work, here are five rules to set yourself up for success:

>> **Promote yourself by completing your profile.** List your interests and areas of expertise to let your colleagues know who you are. This will also make you discoverable in searches.

Upload a profile photo — it adds a personal touch when people are conversing with you.

>> **Let them know you're ready to Yam.** Introduce yourself to the network.

By default, Yammer posts a notification whenever a new member joins the network. You can tack your own introduction from that notification by either replying to it or creating a new post.

>> **Start Yamming.** Join a group, follow people and topics, post a message, like a post, reply to messages, and even create your own group! Those are just a few of the things you can do to have an online presence.

Yammer is like a gift that gives back. The more you give, the more you receive. Use Yammer to gather feedback but don't be stingy about sharing great ideas.

>> **Stay in the know.** Stay connected with your Yammer buddies via notifications through the Yammer app.

If you become wildly popular, however, you might end up with a bunch of notifications, so adjust your settings from the edit profile page.

>> **Optimize every conversation.** Similar to Twitter and other social tools, you can use symbols as markers:

- # *(hashtags)* to mark conversations as topics

- @ *(at-mentions)* to alert other users that you've added them to the conversation

Yammer is great for exchanging ideas and two-way conversations around a specific topic. It's an ideal solution for putting a stop to email trees that branch off into multiple replies, forwards, carbon copies, and blind carbon copies just to gather input to arrive at a decision. When you ask a question on Yammer, everyone in the group can see the question, reply to it, and see everyone's replies. You can also conduct a poll as well as praise a colleague on Yammer.

Becoming a groupie with Office 365 Groups

SharePoint Online is great for collaborating with project teams, especially when you have to work with cross-functional teams to meet deadlines. But what happens if you just want to quickly band together with co-workers and need an environment to collaborate without the administration responsibilities that come with a SharePoint site?

The answer is Office 365 Groups, or simply Groups. Groups is a feature in Exchange Online that is deeply integrated with SharePoint Online capabilities. When you create a group, you automatically get a place for a conversation, a calendar, a location to store shared files, and a OneNote notebook.

Groups can be either public or private:

>> In a public group, anyone in your Office 365 organization can participate in conversations, share files, and view the calendar.

>> In a private group, only members of the group can access conversations, files, and calendar.

To create a group, you can either start from SharePoint Online (see Creating a Team Site in the previous section) or Exchange Online. In Exchange Online:

1. Log on to http://portal.office.com.

2. Click the app launcher from the Office 365 navigation bar.

3. Click the Mail tile.

4. From the left pane, click the + sign in the Groups group to create a new Group as shown in Figure 5-6.

5. Enter the required information then click Create.

6. Add members to your group by name and then click Add.

Your Group will be created and the members will receive a welcome email.

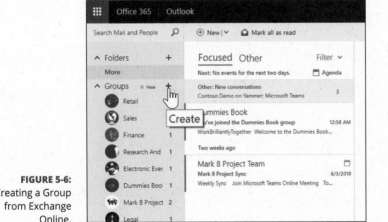

FIGURE 5-6:
Creating a Group
from Exchange
Online.

Chapter **6**

Going Beyond Websites with SharePoint and OneDrive for Business

Finding out what people think about SharePoint is always interesting. Ten different people will often give ten different answers. One thing most people have as a common understanding is that SharePoint focuses on websites. SharePoint definitely handles websites with ease, but there is a whole lot more under the covers.

In this chapter, we explain some of the features SharePoint has beyond websites. In particular, you discover how adept SharePoint is at managing digital content and unlocking the wealth of information contained in that content through the Search feature. Search is the ability to find the digital content you are looking for when you are looking for it. In addition, you find out about the services available in SharePoint Online and get a handle on OneDrive for Business. OneDrive for Business is designed to store your digital documents; under the covers, it's powered by SharePoint.

Managing Digital Content

Imagining a business that functions without using computers is nearly impossible. Computers are used for everything from communication to accounting. Computers definitely speed up business, but this speed has a consequence. The result is that mountains of digital content are produced on a daily, if not hourly, basis. Managing all this content is one of the areas in which SharePoint and OneDrive for Business shine. In the next sections, we examine some nifty SharePoint and OneDrive for Business features, including special online libraries for documents and other media, lists for managing data and tasks, and specialized features, such as Document Sets for working with groups of documents as a single block.

REMEMBER

OneDrive for Business is a place for you to store your documents in the cloud. OneDrive for Business is powered by SharePoint, though. Think of OneDrive for Business as your personal place in SharePoint.

Document libraries

A *document library* is a special folder that you can access through your web browser or directly from within Office applications, such as Word or Excel. If you have ever used SharePoint, then you are familiar with document libraries. With SharePoint Online, these document libraries work the same way they do had you spent the time, energy, and resources of implementing SharePoint yourself. With SharePoint Online, however, you just sign up in the morning and begin using SharePoint in the afternoon.

A document library used to store Word documents, in addition to Excel and PowerPoint documents, is shown in Figure 6-1.

A SharePoint document library takes care of the heavy lifting of managing content, such as the capability to check in and check out a document, versioning, security, and workflow. Each document in a library has a context menu that can be accessed by hovering the mouse pointer over the item and then clicking the drop-down menu that appears to the right, as shown in Figure 6-2.

A familiar theme in Office 365 is integration between products. In addition to working with document library functionality, such as check in and check out by using the browser, you can also do so from within the Office documents, as shown in Figure 6-3.

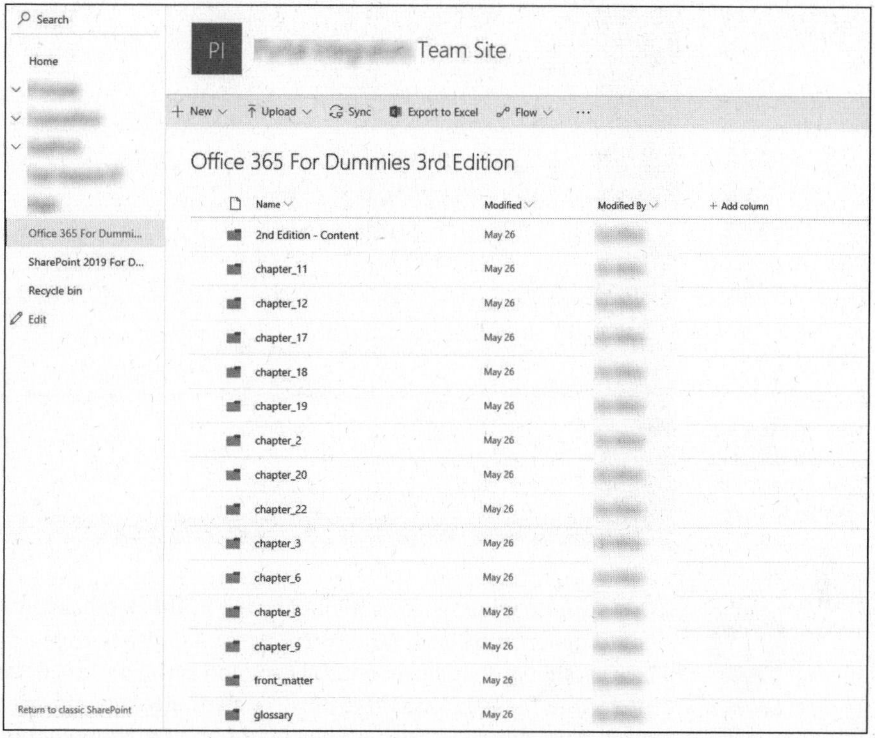

FIGURE 6-1:
A document
library in
SharePoint
Online.

FIGURE 6-2:
Accessing
the content
management
functionality for
a document in a
document library.

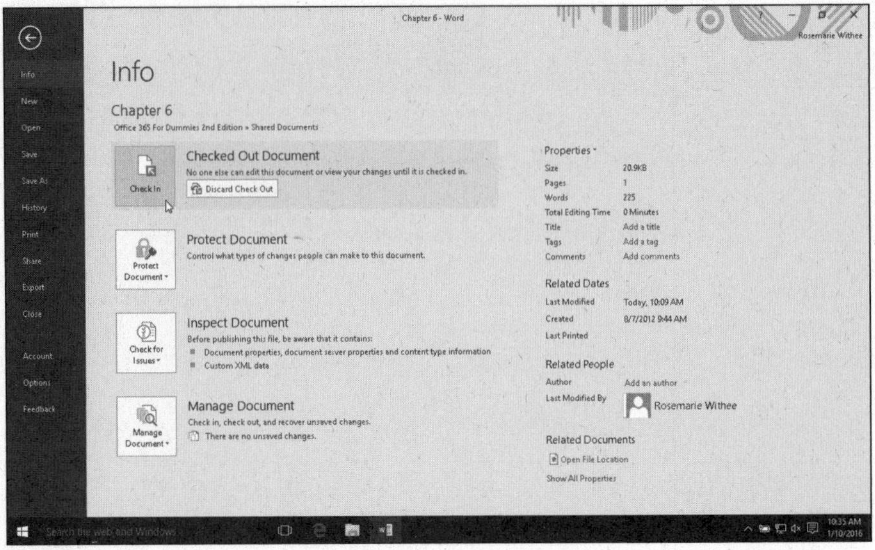

FIGURE 6-3:
Checking in a
document from
within Microsoft
Word 2019.

WARNING

As you can imagine, it takes a lot of space in the database to store multiple versions of documents. Each time you make a change and save a document, you have a new version of that document. One version is the document before you made the change, and the next version is the document after you made the change. For this reason, versioning is turned off by default on new SharePoint document libraries.

To turn on versioning, follow these steps:

1. Open the Document Library and then click the gear icon in the top right of the screen and select Library Settings.

The Settings page for the library appears.

2. In the General Settings list, click the Versioning Settings link.

The Versioning Settings page appears, as shown in Figure 6-4.

3. On the right, select the versioning settings that are required for your scenario:

- You can choose to have No Versioning, Major Versions, or Major and Minor versions. Major versions are created when you check in a document and Minor versions are created when you save a draft.

- You can also configure a number of other settings, including requiring content approval, the number of versions to retain, the number of draft versions to retain, the level of security, and whether the library should require users to check out the document before they can make changes.

4. Click OK to save your settings.

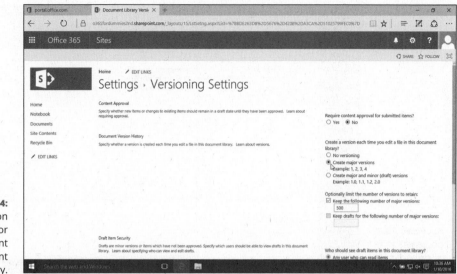

FIGURE 6-4:
Turning on
versioning for
a SharePoint
document
library.

Viewing PowerPoint presentations

As you see in the previous section, SharePoint does a great job of handling and managing documents. In addition to working with documents, a number of other features are designed to make you more efficient.

People give presentations on everything from sales to accounting. If information needs to be presented in a meeting, PowerPoint is often the tool of choice. SharePoint Online includes integration with PowerPoint Online, which is covered in Chapter 13. When you store your PowerPoint presentations in a SharePoint document library, you can open and start presenting them by simply clicking on the title. When you click on the PowerPoint title, your web browser opens the presentation in PowerPoint Online. No need to download the file, save it locally, and open it with PowerPoint on your local computer. SharePoint and PowerPoint Online do all the work for you.

This integration lets you keep your PowerPoint presentations in SharePoint, which acts as a sort of slide headquarters. You have probably experienced the problem of looking for a company slide that you know you saw in the past. You might blast an e-mail out asking if anyone has the particular slide deck that you saw presented last year. You may get a reply, but how do you know that is the most recent version of the deck? After you track down the owner of the deck, you might get the right slides you need for your presentation. Using SharePoint, along with PowerPoint Online, provides a one-stop shop for slides.

To upload documents, such as a PowerPoint presentation to a SharePoint library, you simply drag the files and drop them in the browser, as shown in Figure 6-5.

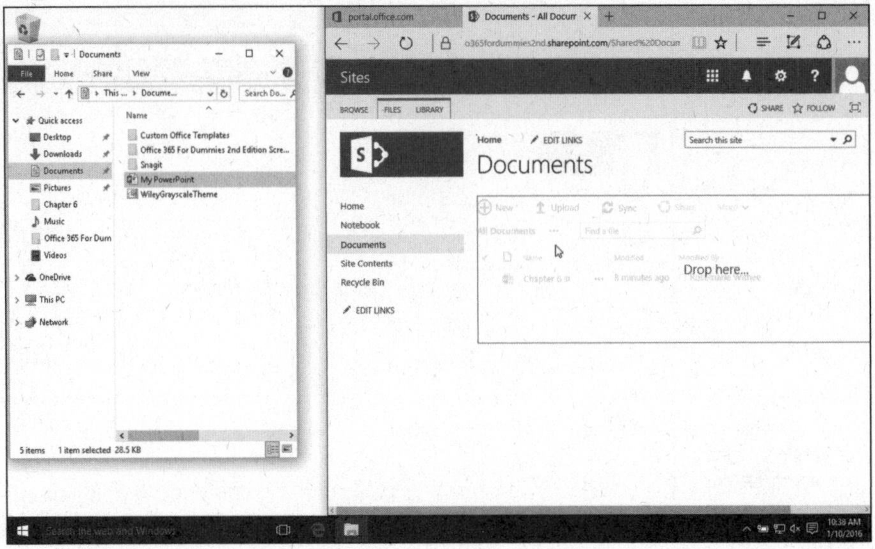

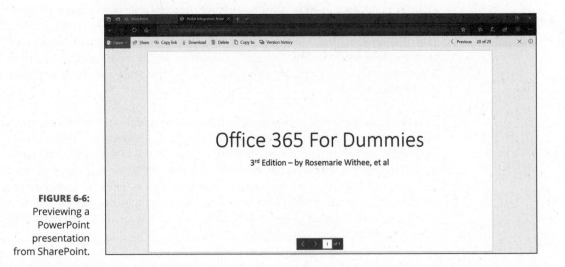

FIGURE 6-5:
Adding a
PowerPoint
presentation to
a SharePoint
library.

In addition to opening a PowerPoint presentation from within your web browser using SharePoint and PowerPoint Online, you can also preview the presentation before you open it. To preview the presentation, click the vertical ellipsis beside the presentation's name and then click Preview. A preview of the document appears in your web browser, as shown in Figure 6-6.

By storing all of your files in SharePoint, you can set up alerts to notify you when anything changes.

FIGURE 6-6:
Previewing a
PowerPoint
presentation
from SharePoint.

TIP

An alert allows you to be notified through either e-mail or a text message whenever changes are made to the file. You can set up alerts to:

» Cover any changes to any file.

» Cover any changes to a single file.

» Cover any changes to any file you have created.

» Cover any changes to any file that you were the last to modify.

A SharePoint library has a number of rich content-management features, such as check-in and check-out, versioning, security, and workflow. Learn more about SharePoint content management features in Chapter 5.

TIP

SharePoint has a specialized library for managing rich media files, such as images, video, and audio files. You can create one of these media libraries by selecting the Asset Library template on the Your Apps page, as shown in Figure 6-7.

REMEMBER

Microsoft also refers to SharePoint lists and libraries as *apps.* You can access the Your Apps page by clicking the gear icon in the upper right corner, then selecting Add an app.

Perform a keyword search to narrow down results

FIGURE 6-7:
Creating a media library by using the Asset Library template in SharePoint Online.

TIP

SharePoint also integrates with other Office products, such as Word and Excel. Just like PowerPoint, you can open a Word or Excel document in SharePoint with Word Online and Excel Online. You can also take a peek and preview a file before you actually open it. To do this, click the Details icon in the ribbon. (The icon is a circle with the letter *i* in the middle.) When you open the details pane, you can see a preview of the document. Word Online is covered in Chapter 11, and Excel Online is covered in Chapter 12. SharePoint integration with Office is covered in detail in Chapter 7.

Document Sets

A feature in SharePoint is the ability to work with documents in a group rather than individually. In a given day, you might be working on documents for a number of different projects. In SharePoint, a *Document Set* allows you to group documents together based on some criteria and then work with the group of documents as a single entity. For example, you may have a project you are working on for marketing and a project you are working on for accounting. You can group your marketing documents together and group your accounting documents together. You can then interact with the accounting or marketing documents as a single group rather than individually. Using Document Sets, you can send all your marketing documents through a workflow in a batch simultaneously or view versioning for all the documents as a set at a given point in time. Versioning is covered earlier in the chapter and also in Chapter 5.

To begin using Document Sets, first you need to activate the feature for your Site Collection. To do so, follow these steps:

1. **Click the gear icon in the top right corner of the screen and then select Site Contents.**

   The contents list for the site appears.

2. **Click the Site Settings link on the right side of the top control bar.**

   The Site Settings page appears showing you all the settings for this particular SharePoint site.

3. **Go to the Site Collection Administration grouping and click the Site Collection Features link.**

   The Site Collection Features page for this specific Site Collection appears.

4. **Click the Activate button next to the Document Sets feature.**

After the Document Sets feature is activated, you can add the functionality to any library. The Document Set takes the form of a Content Type in SharePoint.

A Content Type is the grouping of metadata fields into a single group. For example, you may have a recipe that has a content type that includes metadata such as ingredients, cooking times, and required seasonings. The SharePoint Document Set content type includes all the functionality required to group multiple documents into a single entity.

A common document library in SharePoint is the Documents library. You can add the Document Set functionality to the Documents library by following these steps:

1. **Navigate to the library in which you want to add the Document Sets functionality.**

   In this example, we add it to the Documents Library.

2. **Click the gear icon in the top-right corner of the screen, select Library Settings, and then click the Advanced Settings link.**

   The Advanced Settings page appears and lets you perform advanced configuration for this library.

3. **On the Content Type section, select Yes to allow the editing of content types.**

4. **Click OK to return to the Library Settings page.**

   Notice that a new section appears on the page now called Content Types.

5. **Click the Add from existing site content types link to add an existing site content type.**

6. **Select the Document Set content type, click the Add button, and then click OK.**

Now that the Document Set functionality has been added to the library, you can create a new document set. To create a new Document Set, click the New button and select Document Set, as shown in Figure 6-8. You can provide a name and description and then save it.

A document set shows up in the Shared Documents library just like another document. You can interact with a document set just like you interact with a single document in the library. The difference, however, is that when you click on a Document Set, you open up the grouping of documents rather than a single document. When the Document Set is opened, a new Manage tab will appear on the ribbon. This tab allows you to manage the document set with features such as editing the properties, changing security permissions, sharing the documents, capturing versions, or pushing all the documents through workflow in a batch. Figure 6-9 shows the Manage tab in the ribbon.

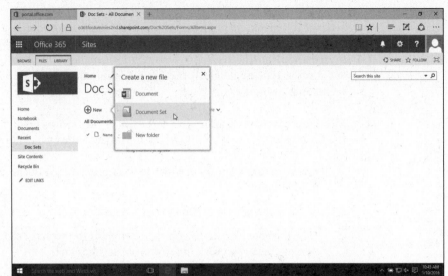

FIGURE 6-8:
Creating a new
Document Set
in SharePoint
Online.

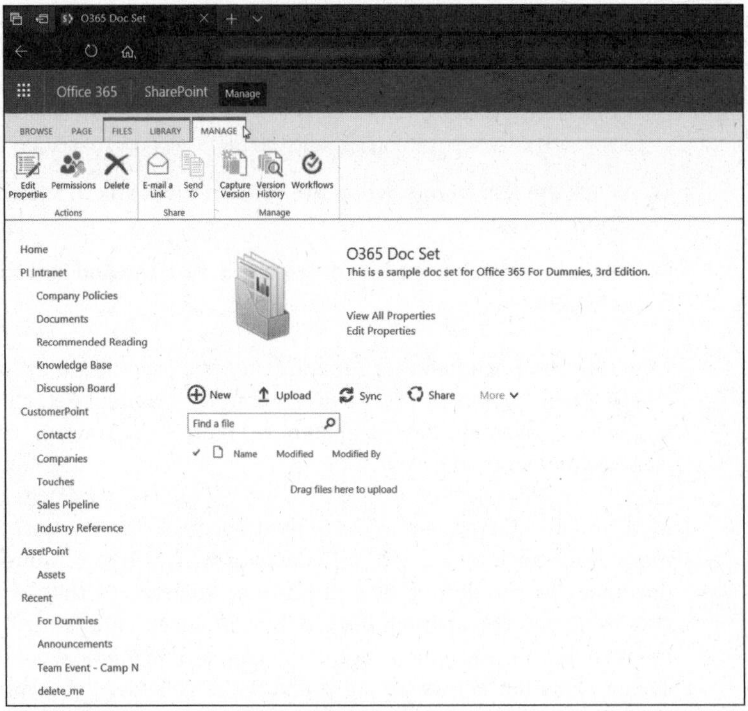

FIGURE 6-9:
The Manage tab,
which is used
to manage a
Document Set.

OneDrive for Business

OneDrive for Business is your personal Office 365 storage location in the cloud.

TIP

If you're already familiar with Office 365 and SharePoint Online, OneDrive for Business is what used to be called SkyDrive Pro; before that, it was called Share-Point My Sites. Along the way, OneDrive for Business integrated a file sync technology called Groove. This winding path took us to OneDrive for Business, and since its initial release a few years ago, Microsoft has continued to improve and iterate on it.

OneDrive for Business is still powered by SharePoint. If you're familiar with other cloud storage services such as Dropbox, Google Drive, or Box, then you're already familiar with the concept behind OneDrive for Business. The OneDrive for Business client is shown in Figure 6-10.

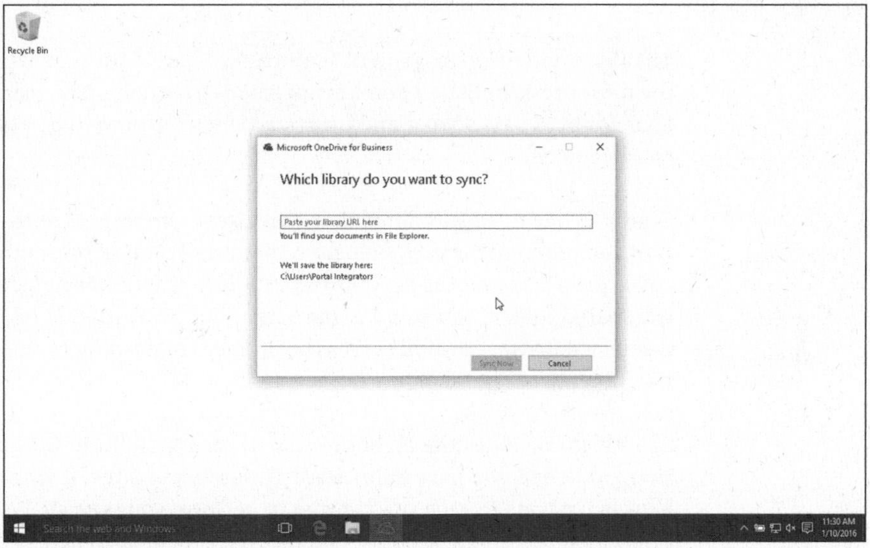

FIGURE 6-10:
Using the OneDrive for Business sync client on Windows 10.

TIP

OneDrive for Business is the aptly named business version of OneDrive. The consumer version is just called OneDrive.

To use OneDrive for Business, you simply configure the sync client. When the client is configured, your files will be synced between your local computer and your cloud-based storage in Office 365. If you've never used OneDrive for Business on your Windows 10 computer, it will walk you through configuration when you open OneDrive for Business. You find OneDrive for Business under your Office 2019 folder on the Start menu.

We really like how OneDrive for Business has improved over the years and now it is easily on-par for ease of use with what has been considered the gold standard, Dropbox. The thing that makes OneDrive for Business stand out is that it is tightly integrated with the rest of the Office 365 products. We find this tight integration dramatically increases our productivity because the entire suite of products feels like one single product and we just use the functionality we need to use when we need to use it.

TIP

If you have Windows 10, you already have the latest version of the OneDrive sync client. If you don't have Windows 10, you need to download and install the latest OneDrive sync client. You download Office 365 software by logging into your account at `https://login.microsoftonline.com` and then clicking Install Office Apps on the main landing page.

Using Search Functionality

The rich content-management features of SharePoint may be what often garner the most press, but SharePoint is not a one-trick pony. The search functionality of SharePoint is very robust and brings a Google or Bing-type experience to corporate documents.

Search is one of those things that don't seem important until you really need to find something. You may vaguely remember seeing a presentation done by your colleague a few months ago but have no idea where to even start to look for it in the shared folder. You could e-mail him, but what if he is not available and you need it right away? Search solves the problem of needing to find specific information in a sea of digital data.

SharePoint includes the ability to search across multiple sites. As your organization grows and you have an increasing number of sites, it would sure be a pain to have to navigate to each site in order to perform your search. With SharePoint, you can search in a single location and the search will span across multiple sites.

Sometimes, it can be difficult to get the exact terminology just right to return the content for which you are searching. SharePoint includes the ability to refine a search based on a number of configurable parameters called *refiners*. For example, you might be searching for that document that Bob presented to a client a while back. You type in the search term "onboarding employees" but receive hundreds of pages of content back. You remember that the presentation was a Word document so you narrow the search to only Word files. You still do not see the presentation right away, so you narrow the search down again further to only those presentations where Bob was the author. Bingo! The presentation you were looking for is right at the top of the list. Use the refiners to narrow a search, as shown in Figure 6-11.

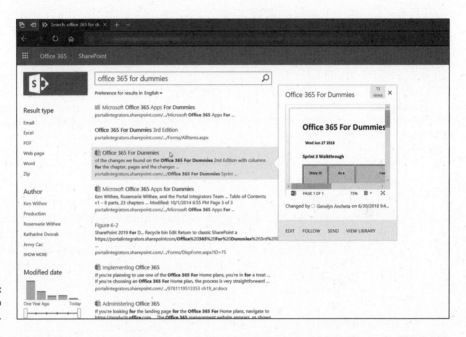

FIGURE 6-11:
Using refiners to narrow a search.

TIP

You can think of a search refiner as a filter. Your search for a broad topic might return hundreds of possible results. The refiner allows you to filter this information down based on the configured criteria.

TIP

The refiners shown in Figure 6-11 are part of the Basic Search Center type site. If you want to implement something similar on your own site, go to Site Contents from the gear menu in the top-right corner of your site, click Add New, and then select the Basic Search Site template from the Enterprise list of templates. The Basic Search Site includes the refiners shown in the screenshot.

Another key aspect of search is finding someone you just met but are not sure how to spell his name. For example, you might meet a coworker in the hall and he mumbles to you that his name is Kain. You register the name as Kain but when you go to search for him online, you wouldn't normally find him if you type in *Kain* because his name is actually Ken. SharePoint phonetic search allows you to still type *Kain* and SharePoint recognizes that this is phonetically very similar to Ken. SharePoint is smart enough to show Ken in the search results, as shown in Figure 6-12. Because SharePoint also shows Ken's mug shot, or should we say company profile picture, in the search results, you can see that you have found the right person you just met in the hall.

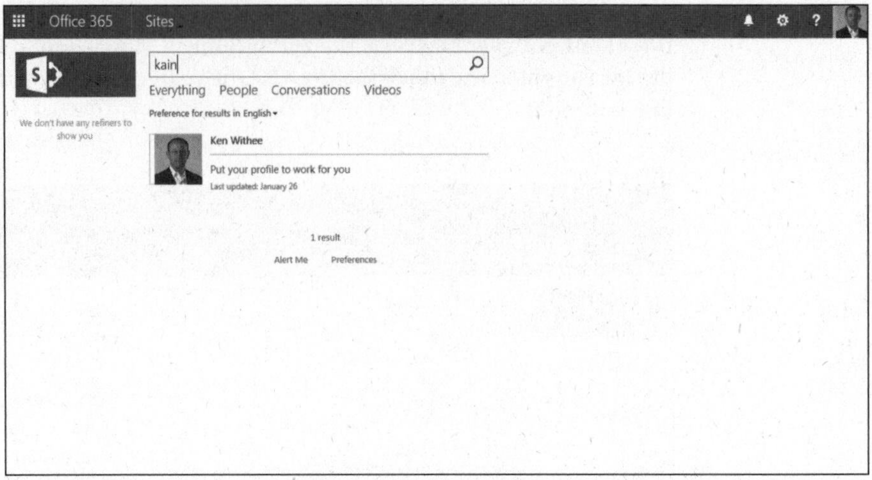

FIGURE 6-12:
Using SharePoint
phonetic search
to find a
colleague.

In addition to Search, SharePoint also includes Business Intelligence (BI) functionality and the ability to develop business solutions without writing a single line of code. BI covers such things as reports, scorecards, dashboards, and key performance indicators. The BI aspects of SharePoint require their own books, but for now you should know that they are important pieces that make SharePoint so valuable.

Using SharePoint with Office Online

SharePoint integrates with Office Online applications, such as Excel Online, Word Online, and PowerPoint Online. All of these services fall under the Office 365 umbrella, so they work together nicely.

Excel Online

The Excel application is a component of Microsoft's productivity suite called Office. Excel is geared toward numbers, lists, and analysis. Excel is widely adopted in the business world and many users probably wonder how they could function in business life without this tool. Excel Online is a service that SharePoint integrates with to cater to Excel spreadsheets. In particular, Excel Online lets you view your Excel data in a SharePoint site.

Using Excel Online, you could have one analyst responsible for the management of the Excel document but share the summary page, graph, or entire document with the rest of the organization. The rest of the members of the organization might not even realize they are looking at an Excel document as the driving force behind the data. From their perspective, they just see a web page on a SharePoint site with graphs, charts, grids of data, and summary data (or whatever part of Excel you decide to include in the page). The person that manages the Excel document doesn't need to learn a new tool. If she has used Excel, then she can simply continue to use Excel with the difference being that her hard work is displayed to the rest of the organization without the involvement of the IT department, developers, or anyone else.

Excel Online is covered in Chapter 12.

Word Online

Word is another application that is part of the Microsoft Office productivity suite. Word provides word processing capabilities. SharePoint integrates with Word Online, which lets you view and edit Word documents from your SharePoint site. When you click a Word document, the Word Online service takes over; you can interact with your document without leaving your browser.

Just as with PowerPoint and Excel, you can preview a Word document that is located in a SharePoint library. To preview a Word document, just click the ellipsis that appears beside the document name and click Preview. A preview version opens up in your web browser. If you are looking at the results from a search in the Basic Search Center site as described earlier, you can also just click the ellipses and see a small preview. And yet another way to preview a document is to open the details pane in a document library. To do this, click the Details icon in the ribbon. (The icon is a circle with the letter *i* in the middle.) When you open the details pane, you can see a small preview of the document along with other details about the document. This provides you with a way to peek inside the document without opening it.

Word Online is covered in Chapter 11.

PowerPoint Online

As shown previously in this chapter, SharePoint can also integrate with PowerPoint. PowerPoint is part of the Office suite, and it's designed for building and displaying presentations. SharePoint works closely with PowerPoint Online, so you can view and edit a PowerPoint presentation in your web browser from your SharePoint site.

PowerPoint Online is covered in detail in Chapter 13.

Chapter **7**

Integrating the Mobile Experience

The era of personal computing is here. We have crossed over from a time where we personalized our computers with our preferences, loaded them with content relevant to us, or bookmarked sites that interest us to an era when our computers are learning so much about us and our working habits that they are able to serve up personalized information to us. Through cloud computing and machine learning, artificial intelligence (AI) agents like Siri, Google Now, and Cortana are making headway in learning our habits, favorite foods, interests, schedules, and even our personalities!

Personal computing is personal because, regardless of the device you're using at any given moment, your personalization is there. It travels with you. It doesn't stay at home in your desktop computer nor is it limited to your mobile devices. And even if your computer crashes or you lose your smartphone, you can have access to your personal content and settings from your devices' automatic cloud backups.

Personal computing then makes you — the user — mobile. It isn't about having mobile devices. Instead, it's about making your *experience* mobile as you go from one device to another. For example, you can start working on a document from your desktop computer at work, make edits to it from your tablet while waiting at the doctor's office, and finalize it from your smartphone while sitting on a bus.

In this chapter, you see the investments Microsoft has made in making the SharePoint experience mobile. First, we walk you through basic SharePoint collaboration tasks and its integration with Office Online applications and then we demonstrate how you can perform the same collaboration tasks from a mobile device. Because the core foundation for being mobile is storing your data in the cloud, this chapter also covers basic data security and privacy in Office 365 and instruction for protecting your documents in SharePoint Online.

Office and SharePoint Integration

The Office Online and the desktop version of the Office suite offer a robust set of collaboration capabilities available on both desktop and mobile devices. These capabilities help remove some of the time-consuming processes in-between creating and finalizing documents by enabling real-time coauthoring for documents saved in a SharePoint document library. For example, if you click on a Word document, the browser will fire up the online version of Microsoft Word to open the file. Within the browser, you can share the document with others and make edits to the document in real time. If you want to use the full functionality of Microsoft Word, you can choose to open the file in the desktop application and continue where you left off.

TIP

These functionalities are also available for documents stored in OneDrive for Business, a 1 terabyte (TB) online storage solution for Office 365 users. OneDrive is an ideal alternative to your computer's hard drive. Storing your files in OneDrive allows you to access those files from other devices, thereby cutting you loose from your desk.

These new productivity-boosting features are just the tip of the iceberg as Microsoft continues to build a suite of integrated apps and services in Office 365 in much shorter cycles than we were accustomed to in the boxed software days.

Creating a SharePoint document library

A document library in SharePoint is like a folder on your hard drive where you store your files. In SharePoint, there are several types of libraries, but the most commonly used type is the library in a Team site. Files stored in the Team site document library lend themselves well to sharing, collaboration, version control, and search.

If you have at least an Edit permission level in a Team site (the site admin can give you that permission), creating a new library is simple. Here's how:

1. **From your Team site, click the settings icon from the Office 365 navigation bar.**

   The settings icon looks like a gear.

2. **Click Add an app.**

3. **Click Document Library from the list of apps.**

4. **Give your library a name, then click Create.**

Upon successful creation, your library will be listed in the Site Contents page. Click the name of the library you created to start adding new or uploading existing documents. To add a new document, click the New icon from the Command bar as shown in Figure 7-1. To upload an existing document from your hard drive, click the Upload button. Figure 7-1 illustrates the various components of a document library. A SharePoint list follows the same structure.

Breadcrumb bar   Command bar

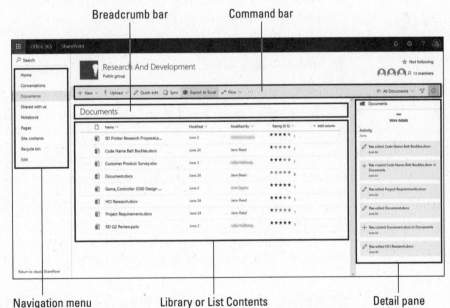

Navigation menu   Library or List Contents   Detail pane

FIGURE 7-1:
Navigating the
SharePoint
document library.

REMEMBER

Version control is enabled automatically when you create a document library. For additional information on how to restore a previous version of a document, refer to Chapter 5.

TIP

You can reduce the number of clicks to access a document in a SharePoint document library by synching the library to your hard drive. When you do, the library is represented as a folder in File Explorer much like you would see a folder in your hard drive.

To sync a document library, click the Sync button from the Command bar. This action will fire up the OneDrive for Business app and will ask you to enter your Office 365 credentials. Follow the prompts to begin syncing your documents to your hard drive.

Encouraging interaction with ratings

Similar to using the "Like" feature in Facebook, SharePoint users can quickly express their opinion of documents in a library through a rating system. *Ratings* — either a like or a star — can be used to create views, such as displaying items with the highest number of stars or likes. If you own the content, the ratings give you insights for improvement.

To set up the rating system in your document library, follow these steps:

1. **From your document library, click the settings icon next to your profile icon in the top-right corner of your screen.**

2. **Click Library Settings.**

3. **Under the General Settings group, click Rating Settings.**

4. **Select Yes under the Rating Settings label.**

5. **Select either Likes or Star Ratings for the voting/rating experience.**

6. **Click OK.**

   Back in the document library settings page, you will notice that three new columns have been added to the library (see Figure 7-2).

When the rating system is set up, the default view of the document library will display either a series of stars or the word Like. Each unique user can vote once. When the vote is submitted, it is averaged with other ratings. Figure 7-3 shows an example of a document library with ratings enabled.

Sharing documents from Word Online

Office Online, the cloud version of the Microsoft Office suite, is great for on-the-go quick editing and collaboration. When you want to use the robust set of features and functionalities in the Office suite, it's easy to switch to the desktop version right from the browser.

Let's say, for example, you're working on a document with your colleagues for your next product release. You've uploaded the document in your SharePoint document library and now you want to share it with your colleagues so you can all work on the document at the same time. Here's what you need to do:

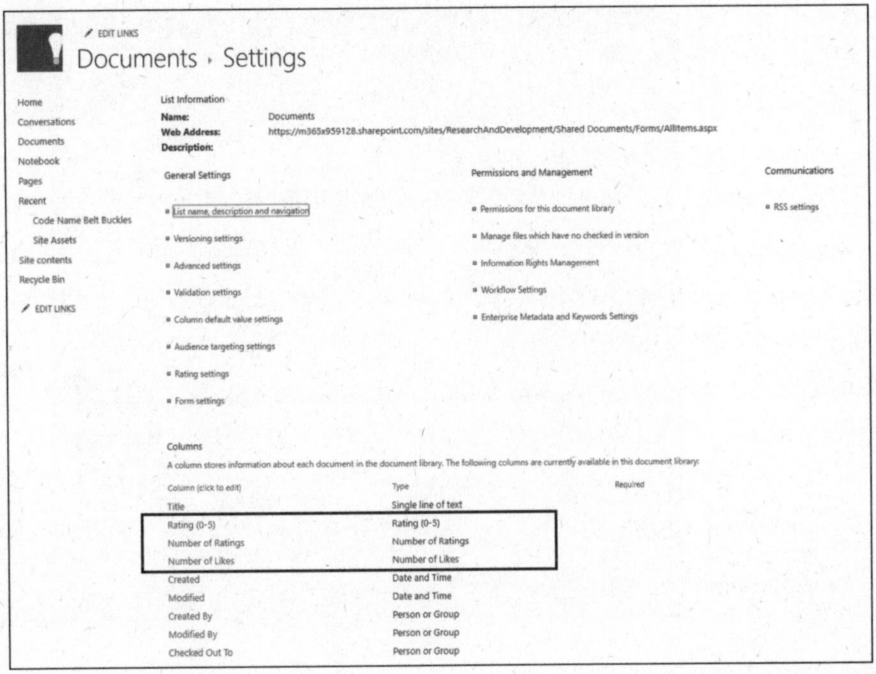

FIGURE 7-2:
Configuring the rating system in a document library.

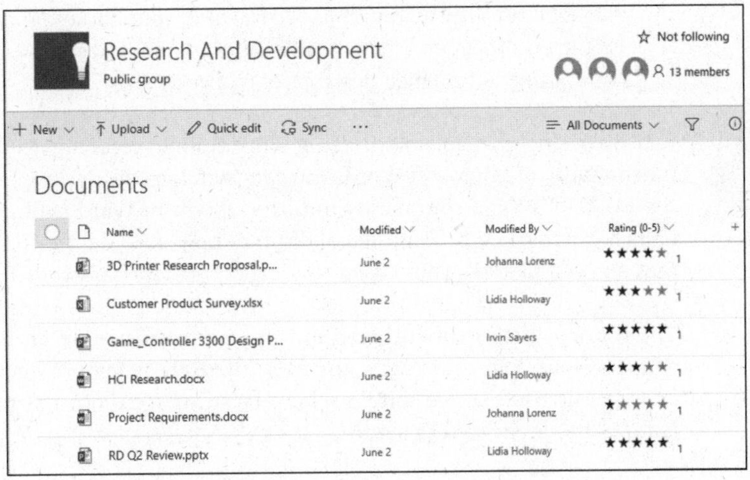

FIGURE 7-3:
A document library with ratings enabled.

1. From your document library, click the name of the document to open it on the browser.

2. In the top-right corner of your screen, below your name, click Share, as shown in Figure 7-4.

3. Enter the name of the colleagues with whom you want to share the document.

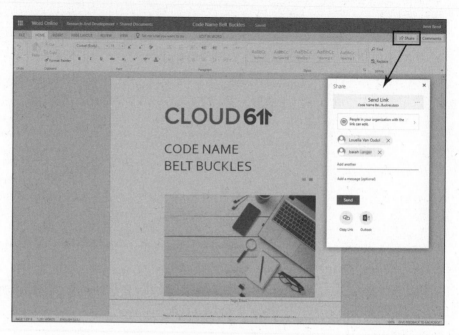

FIGURE 7-4:
Sharing a
document from
Word Online.

4. Add a message if you'd like and then click Send.

A window will display confirming that a link to your document has been shared with your colleagues. When they click the link, they will be able to view and edit the document from their desktops or mobile devices.

TIP

While working on a document using Word Online, you may need to access the full functionality of Microsoft Word. You can switch to the desktop version by clicking the EDIT IN WORD command from the ribbon in Word Online. This action will launch Microsoft Word and depending on how your device is set up, the system may ask you to enter your Office 365 username and password.

The sharing features mentioned in this section also apply to PowerPoint, Excel, and OneNote. Microsoft rolls out new integration features between SharePoint and the Microsoft Office suite, so don't be surprised if one day you discover a new feature that wasn't there before.

Knowing when to use OneDrive for Business

OneDrive for Business with its 1TB of storage is your personal online storage for the workplace. It is different from OneDrive, the consumer version, which is

5 gigabytes (GB) of online storage from Microsoft that anyone can use for free with an Outlook.com, Hotmail, or live.com email account.

While a document library in SharePoint is great if you're working with a lot of people, OneDrive for Business is ideal when you don't plan to share your files with a broad group of people in your organization. Especially when you need to keep your files longer than you would keep project files, OneDrive for Business is the best storage location.

Files you create or save in OneDrive are private by default and available to you only. You can, however, share them with others just like in SharePoint and in Office applications like Word, Excel, and PowerPoint. Figure 7-5 illustrates how a private file is designated with the word *Private* listed under the Sharing column. Shared files include the people icon and the word *Shared* in this column.

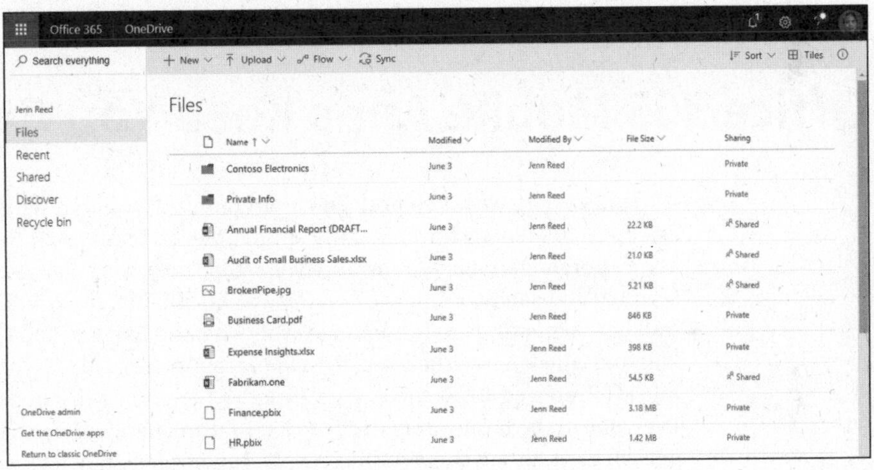

FIGURE 7-5: OneDrive for Business documents and sharing indications.

Similar to SharePoint Online document libraries, you can sync OneDrive for Business files to your computer by clicking the Sync button from the Command bar.

Once the sync is complete, you will see your OneDrive for Business folder from the Quick Access panel in File Explorer. Figure 7-6 shows my two synced OneDrive folders: OneDrive – Cloud611 Corp, which is my workplace account (OneDrive for Business), and OneDrive – Personal, which is my free OneDrive live.com account. Also notice the sync'ed SharePoint document libraries that display a different icon than the OneDrive accounts.

Synced SharePoint document libraries

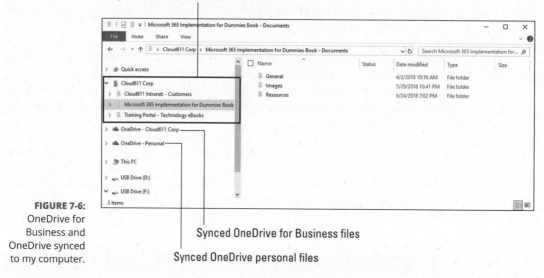

FIGURE 7-6:
OneDrive for
Business and
OneDrive synced
to my computer.

Synced OneDrive for Business files

Synced OneDrive personal files

Office 365 Mobile Apps Keep You Going

A friend of ours with two preteen children recently shared with us that he set up an Office 365 tenant for his family so that he can manage all the devices his wife and children were using, and to ensure that they were using cloud applications securely and safely. From the comforts of his iPhone, my friend literally runs his family's computing environment very much like a Fortune 500 IT department. His kids and wife log into their social media accounts from the Microsoft MyApps portal (also referred to as the Access Panel) where he configured a single sign-on. Everyone in the family only needs to log in using their Office 365 credentials. If he gets an alert for anything suspicious, he can immediately lock an account or reset the password. Neat, huh?

Suffice it to say, in today's world it's no longer enough to be working off of one device. The good news is that in Office 365, you can seamlessly go from desktop to laptop to mobile device when working on documents or interacting with collaboration tools such as SharePoint Online or OneDrive for Business.

Installing the mobile apps

You can find the Office Mobile apps in the App Store (iOS) or the Play Store (Android) by searching for "Microsoft Office." On a Windows phone or a Surface device (acts as both a laptop and a tablet), the apps are pre-installed. Another way to get a summary of the Office Mobile apps available for your device is as follows:

1. **Navigate to** `https://portal.office.com/OLS/MySoftware.aspx`.

2. **From the left pane, click Phone & Tablet.**

3. **Choose your device and click the Get apps button.**

   You are taken to the Microsoft products page specific to your device.

4. **Enter your email address and click Send.**

   You will receive an email with a list of mobile apps available for your device.

5. **Click the Download link to access the download instructions.**

TIP

Be sure to have your Office 365 login information handy during this process. During setup, you will be asked to log in with your Office 365 account.

Collaborating on a Word document from an iPhone

The Office Mobile apps are a great way to pick up where you left off in a document while sitting on a bus, waiting for a doctor's appointment, or cooling your heels in-between your kids' soccer games. They are available for the following platforms: PC, Mac, iOS, Android, Windows Phone, and Windows tablet. The apps are also a great way for workers with no PCs or Office desktop licenses to contribute and interact with documents stored in OneDrive for Business or SharePoint Online.

In this section, we walk through the experience of creating, editing, and collaborating on a document stored in OneDrive for Business using a real-life example experienced by Jennifer, one of the authors of this book, while she was working on chapters. Following are the steps she took to collaborate with our editors:

1. First, Jennifer created a folder in OneDrive for Business and saved the Word documents she needed to share with others.

2. In OneDrive for Business, she selected the folder she wanted to share. She could share each file individually, but she wanted to share the entire folder so that our editor and technical advisor could see all the documents we are working on at any given time.

3. From the Command bar, she clicked Share and entered the email addresses of the people she wanted to share the folder with. She made sure the permission level was set to "Only the people you specify will have access to edit," as shown in Figure 7-7.

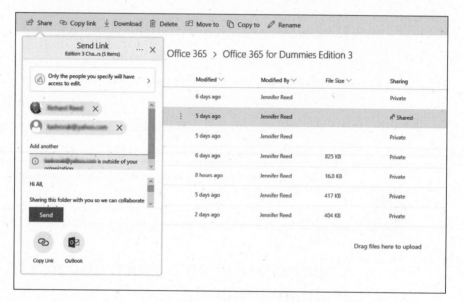

FIGURE 7-7:
Sharing a folder in OneDrive for Business.

4. She clicked Send and a notification went out with a link to the people specified.

5. Jennifer then opened one of the documents from her laptop to start editing it at her home office. A couple of hours later, she had to leave to go to a dental appointment.

6. While she was at the dentist's office, she had remembered a key point she wanted to include in the document. Jennifer was early for her appointment, so she grabbed her iPhone and launched the Word app.

7. From the Word app, she tapped the Recent button (see Figure 7-8).

8. She tapped the first item in the list, which was the last document she was working on (ch01). The app opened the document with Track Changes turned on — the same way she left it in her laptop!

FIGURE 7-8:
A list of recent files in the Word app.

9. She tapped the Edit icon to start editing (see Figure 7-9).

10. The app split the screen to show the formatting commands available in the app. In this view, the app then started to remember where she was at last and displayed a "Welcome back!" notification, as shown in Figure 7-10.

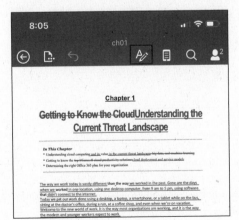

FIGURE 7-9:
The Edit icon in the Word app.

FIGURE 7-10:
"Welcome back!"
notification.

11. Jennifer tapped the notification and the screen jumped to the section she was editing last. From there, she entered her edits. When she was about to close the app (there is no need to save — Office apps automatically save as you work), she noticed there were two people currently editing the document, so she clicked the Share icon, which is shown in Figure 7-11, to see who else was working on the document.

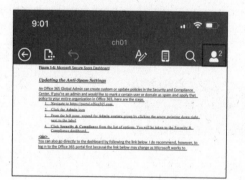

FIGURE 7-11:
The Share icon in
the Word app.

12. In the Shared With screen (see Figure 7-12), she saw that she was editing the document from two devices: one from her laptop and the other one from her mobile device. She then proceeded to add the key point she wanted to add to the document ensuring that others who will view the document at a later date will see her updates.

And just like that Jennifer was able to make best use of the ten-minute wait time she had before her dental appointment to update a document.

FIGURE 7-12:
The Shared With
screen as seen on
an iPhone.

The Scoop on External Sharing

SharePoint Online is a great solution for project team members to stay on the same page by giving everyone a one-stop location for team files, calendar, task list, notebook, and more. But what happens when one of your team members is outside your organization? Let's say you're a manager of a statewide political campaign and you want volunteers to access your SharePoint site so they can see the candidate's schedule and download the latest campaign talking points. In this situation, you probably don't want to get Office 365 subscriptions for all of your volunteers and pay for thousands of licenses.

One way to address this scenario is to use the external sharing feature in Share-Point. Your volunteers in this scenario are considered external users. Simply put, an *external user* is someone who does not have a paid license in Office 365 and does not have an email address with your organization's domain name.

When you invite an external user to your SharePoint site, that user will inherit your permissions. In other words, if you can edit or delete a file, the external user you invited will also be able to edit or delete a file.

If your Office 365 license includes the desktop Office applications (Office ProPlus), however, the external user you invited will not have access to those Office applications. The external user will be able to view and edit Office documents through Office Online, the browser version of the Office ProPlus.

While external users can create new documents and save them back in SharePoint, they can't have their own OneDrive for Business account in which to store files.

When an external user does a search at your site, the search results will be limited to the content they have access to within your SharePoint Online environment only.

There are other advanced features that aren't available to external users, such as accessing site mailboxes, features related to reporting and analytics (Power BI), and opening restricted/protected documents.

TIP

External sharing is enabled by default in SharePoint Online. If you want to disable this feature, refer to Chapter 5.

To share a site, click the Share button on the top navigation bar, enter the recipient's email address, specify the permission, and then click the Share button (see Figure 7-13). SharePoint will display a helpful reminder that the email address you entered is outside of your organization.

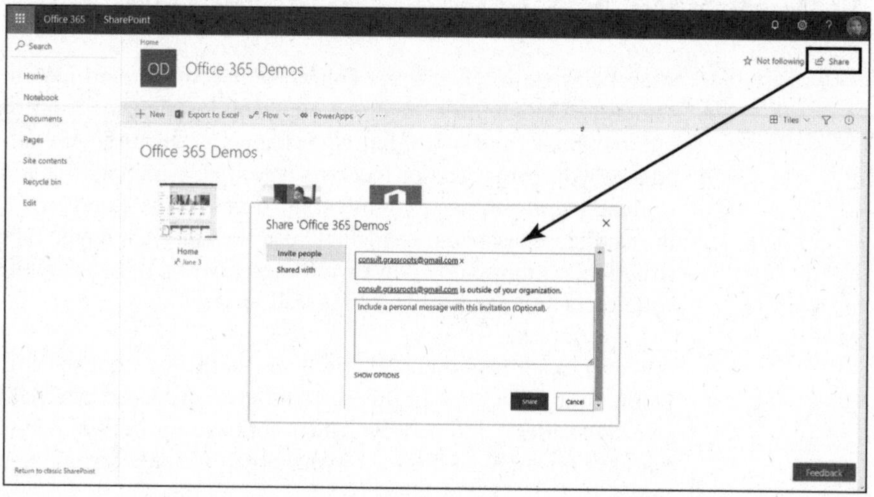

FIGURE 7-13:
Share a SharePoint site with external users.

If your SharePoint site was created with external sharing disabled, you will not be able to share the site and will instead get an alert to let you know external sharing is not allowed.

REMEMBER

Chapter **8**

Demystifying SharePoint Online Administration

I f you are working for a small business or a nonprofit organization, or you are a sole proprietor, you likely wear many hats. It's not easy to function as your organization's CEO, CMO, COO by day and at the same time be the IT department also by day! Getting bogged down with data security and protection, patch management, network stability, and a host of other IT–related daily tasks takes time away from your efforts to move your business forward and achieve your goals.

The folks at Microsoft understand those issues and as a result, they've made it so that administering Office 365 and SharePoint Online is not an onerous task.

Office 365 administration is designed to be easy and intuitive. Setting up a globally distributed organization with a dozen people can be done in 20 minutes. For $12.50 per user per month (as of the date this was written) on an Office 365 Business Premium plan, your business will get Exchange Online, SharePoint Online, Teams, Office Online, and 1 terabyte of online storage per user. Best of all, you'll get premium anti-virus and antispam security, 99.9 percent uptime guarantee, and 24/7 support from the Microsoft IT department. Sounds great, right? The one downside is that SharePoint can have a steep learning curve as there can be ten different ways to achieve the same result. SharePoint is definitely a journey, as anyone with experience will tell you. But getting in at the high level is fairly straightforward and a good way to get started.

In this chapter, you find out how to share the workload with other team members by delegating some administrative tasks, such as enabling access for external users and allowing site collection owners to configure and manage their sites. You explore the similarities and the differences between the roles and responsibilities of the SharePoint Online Administrator and the Site Collection Administrator.

In case you're ever in a SharePoint conference or gathering, we also include some basic information about such SharePoint-speak as farms, tenancies, and multitenancies. The intent is not to turn you into a SharePoint geek, but rather to make you a knowledgeable SharePoint technology user.

Appreciating the Concept of a SharePoint Farm

For the end user, the SharePoint Online experience centers around using the technology to collaborate effectively, secure and share information, upload and download files, track tasks, manage content, and stay connected with the team in other ways. Although you may not think much about what happens to create the SharePoint Online experience, a series of services and applications are running on multiple servers on the backend to give you just the right experience.

Servers are similar to desktop computers but with a lot more power. These powerful computers *serve* up requests from network users either privately or publicly through the Internet, hence the term "server." When SharePoint servers and SQL (a programming language used to communicate with databases) servers come together, they provide a set of services, such as serving up HTML so you can view formatted text on your browser (Web Server), or executing search queries (Query Server), or performing Microsoft Office integration, and much more!

In essence, the infrastructure responsible for your experience as the end user is supported by a collection of servers, each responsible for a set of tasks. That collection of servers is what makes up a SharePoint farm. Everything that happens in SharePoint is administered at the highest level in a SharePoint farm.

REMEMBER

Don't let SharePoint jargon deter you from exploring and using the great benefits this technology has to offer. At its core, SharePoint Online is what allows your organization to round up most — if not all — of your organization's data collection and storage efforts, business processes, collaboration activities, and much more in one web-based application. After you get past the confusion of how farms, tenants, and silos ended up in this technology's dictionary, you'll be on your way to a successful SharePoint coexistence.

Administering the SharePoint farm and why you don't want to do it

SharePoint farm administration is not for the faint of heart. If you look at the list of typical SharePoint farm administration tasks, your eyes will probably glaze over. Don't fret though. In Office 365, Microsoft manages SharePoint farm–level administration. This is the value of having SharePoint Online as a service hosted in the cloud. In a sense, "putting up the farm" in SharePoint is a risk-free exercise.

The following list covers the SharePoint farm administration tasks:

» **Backup and recovery:** A backup is a copy of a set of data as insurance in case of system failure. You use a backup to restore and recover lost data. Recovery in SharePoint farms enables administrators to quickly restore the farm in the event of a disaster.

» **Database management:** This administration task includes adding, attaching or detaching, and moving content databases, moving a site collection between databases, and renaming or moving service application databases.

» **Security and permissions:** Your organization's SharePoint sites most likely will contain data that you don't want to be publicly available. To restrict access, security and permissions need to be configured. At the highest level, this configuration is done in a SharePoint farm.

» **Service application and service management:** When resources are shared across a SharePoint farm, service applications are deployed. Services that are deployed are named service applications. Service applications are tied to web applications by service application connections. Some services can be shared across farms.

» **Web application management:** In order to create a site collection, such as My Site, a web application must be created first. A web application isolates one site's content database from another's. It also defines the authentication method for connecting to the database.

» **Health monitoring:** As with any IT systems, it is important to monitor how the SharePoint server system is running in order to determine issues, analyze problems, and repair those problems. The monitoring feature in SharePoint collects data in a log, which in turn is used to create health reports, web analytics reports, and administrative reports.

» **Farm administration settings management:** Configuring and customizing the default SharePoint farm settings are part of the farm administration settings management tasks. In addition, these tasks include enabling some key features that are turned off at the initial installation, such as diagnostic logging, e-mail integration, and mobile account connections.

>> **Farm topology management:** At some point, a SharePoint farm will need to be updated to address current needs. Farm topology management tasks include adding or removing a web or application server, adding a database, renaming a server, and managing the search topology.

Multitenancy explained

In a multitenancy (multiple users on the same server) environment, a SharePoint farm is architected in such a way that it serves the needs of multiple client organizations. This means that the farm is sliced into subsets that are deployed individually for clients and tenants who then manage their own tenancy. This model gives you, as a business owner, the ability to run your business the way you want to and leave the IT–related tasks to Microsoft.

For example, as a tenant, you have full control to manage how your content, product, service, marketing collateral, and any other information that you want to manage on the Tenant Administration level (see Figure 8-1), are categorized or classified. In SharePoint-speak, this process defines your *taxonomy*. A taxonomy is just a fancy name for how you organize the terms you will use throughout your site. Defining your taxonomy upfront establishes naming standards to achieve consistency and content discoverability.

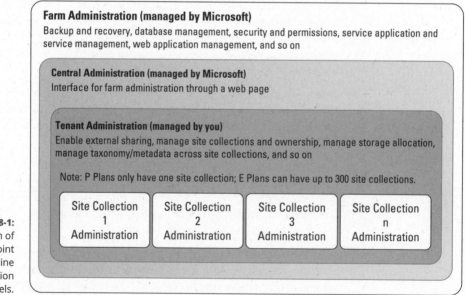

Farm Administration (managed by Microsoft)
Backup and recovery, database management, security and permissions, service application and service management, web application management, and so on

Central Administration (managed by Microsoft)
Interface for farm administration through a web page

Tenant Administration (managed by you)
Enable external sharing, manage site collections and ownership, manage storage allocation, manage taxonomy/metadata across site collections, and so on

Note: P Plans only have one site collection; E Plans can have up to 300 site collections.

| Site Collection 1 Administration | Site Collection 2 Administration | Site Collection 3 Administration | Site Collection n Administration |

FIGURE 8-1: Breakdown of SharePoint Online Administration levels.

After you enter your taxonomy in the Term Store, tagging content becomes easy and intuitive. For example, if you're tagging content from a SharePoint site and you type in the letters *p r o*, terms listed in your taxonomy starting with *pro* (for example, program, project, prospect, and so on) appear, giving you the ability to select the one that fits your needs.

The great thing about this is that all the site collections under your tenancy can now consume company-approved, corporate-driven keywords from your taxonomy. This doesn't mean, however, that tagging is limited to the keywords in your taxonomy. Users can always add new tags, which the admin can then add to the Term Store, if appropriate.

In a multitenancy environment, each tenant is separated from all the other tenants with secure "walls" so that one tenant cannot access another tenant's assets. In other words, you might be sharing a physical server with other people, but you will never know they are there. You cannot see other tenants and other tenants cannot see you. Therefore, if you do a keyword search from any of your site collections, the search results will only pull data from within your tenancy.

Delegating administration tasks

Delegated administration is pervasive throughout Office 365 and bodes really well for businesses knowing that their cloud solution is not hinged on one person. Can you imagine what it would be like if only one person had the power to grant access, enable features, and block users and then one day that person is somehow not available?

With Office 365 and SharePoint Online specifically, you can delegate administration up and down. By delegating administration and sharing the workload, you can empower the person who knows his business unit best to control who gets access, how much storage to have, and what custom solutions to install in his site collection.

At the top level, the Tenant Administration level, Office 365 enterprise plans offer the following roles in the Office 365 Admin Center:

>> **User:** This role doesn't provide any administrative access.

>> **Global Administrator:** This role is the top-level administrator for your company who has access to all the features in the administration center. Global administrators can assign other administrator roles, including granting someone a global administrator role.

>> **Customized Administrator:** This role allows you to create a customized administrative level so that roles can be divided among multiple people.

The Customized Administrator role can be refined to the following administrative roles:

>> **Billing Administrator:** This role is limited to making purchases, managing subscriptions, support tickets, and service health.

>> **Exchange Administrator:** This role is designed to manage the Exchange email service for Office 365.

>> **Password Administrator:** This role can reset passwords for users (but not other admins), manage service requests, and monitor service health.

>> **Skype for Business Administrator:** This role is used to manage the Skype for Business service in Office 365.

>> **Service Administrator:** This role is limited to managing service requests and monitoring service health.

>> **SharePoint Administrator:** This role is used to manage the SharePoint service.

>> **User Management Administrator:** This role can do everything password and service administrators are empowered to do plus the ability to manage user accounts and user groups. The exception is that this role cannot create or delete other administrators or reset passwords for billing, global, and service administrators.

From the Office 365 Admin Center, the Global Administrator can go down one more layer to the SharePoint Online Administration (Admin) Center where further tasks can be delegated. The SharePoint Online Admin Center is where site collection administrators are assigned, who in turn can go down one more layer to assign site collection owners.

Understanding SharePoint Online Administrator Responsibilities

The SharePoint Online Admin Center is the hub of activities for the SharePoint Online Administrator, who may be the same person as the Global Administrator. To get to the SharePoint Online Admin Center, expand the Admin Centers node and then click the SharePoint link on the lower-left side of the Office 365 Admin Center.

As a SharePoint Online Administrator, you have control over site collections, Info-Path forms, user profiles, Business Connectivity Services (BCS), the Term Store, records management, search, secure store, apps, settings, and configuration for hybrid environments (see Figure 8-2).

FIGURE 8-2:
The SharePoint
Online Admin
Center.

Turning on external sharing

If you anticipate that any of your site collections or business units that use Share-Point Online have a need for external sharing, the first step as a SharePoint Online Administrator is to turn on external sharing. By turning on this feature (if it was not already on by default), users outside of your organization can be invited to SharePoint Online. This one-time action enables the site collection administrators to grant external access to their individual sites without going through the Share-Point Online administrator.

TIP

Enabling external sharing turns on the feature for all existing and future sites within the site collection for which you activate it. This does not, however, mean that all your SharePoint sites are now publicly accessible. The site collection admin-istrator has to grant someone outside of the company access to a SharePoint site.

WARNING

Microsoft is constantly fiddling with the user interface for Office 365. As of 2019 you can turn on a preview for the new SharePoint Online Admin Center. You will find it in the upper part of your screen with a button that says "Try the preview." If you don't see that button, you might already be in the new portal. The proce-dures we outline will be the same, but the interfaces will look different. If you do decide to try the preview, then be warned — Microsoft changes it constantly based on customer feedback. If you are open to trying it and giving feedback to make the product better, then it is a great way to learn and influence the future!

To enable external sharing for a site collection, follow these steps:

1. **Click the SharePoint link in the Admin Center node in the Office 365 Admin Center.**

The SharePoint Online Admin Center screen appears.

2. **Click Site Collections in the left pane of the SharePoint Online Admin Center screen that appears.**

   You see a list of all of the site collections in your Office 365 instance.

3. **Select the check box next to the site collection for which you want to enable sharing, then click the Sharing icon in the ribbon, as shown in Figure 8-3.**

   The Sharing window appears.

4. **Select one of the radio buttons to allow sharing to external users who accept sharing invitations and sign in or to allow sharing to all external users by using anonymous links.**

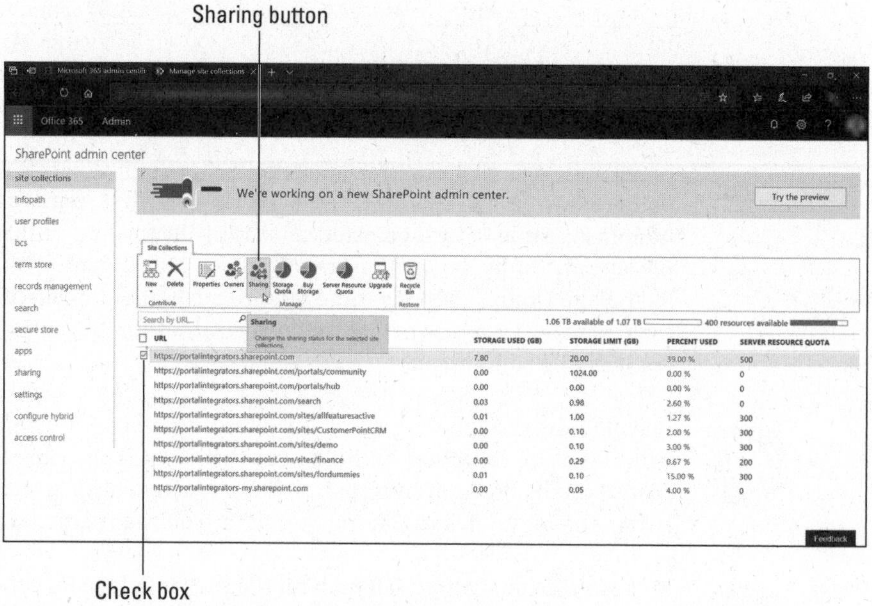

FIGURE 8-3:
Selecting a site collection and then clicking the Sharing button.

Creating a new site collection

A site collection contains a single top-level site and multiple subsites below it that share common navigation, template galleries, content types, Web Parts, and permissions.

To create a new site collection, follow these steps:

1. **Click the SharePoint link in the Admin Center node in the Office 365 Admin Center.**

   The SharePoint Online Admin Center screen appears.

2. **Click Site Collections in the left pane.**

You see a list of all of the site collections in your Office 365 instance.

3. **Click the New button in the ribbon and then select Private Site Collection.**

The New Site Collection window appears.

4. **Enter the required information.**

5. **Click OK to go back to the SharePoint Online Admin Center dashboard.**

When you create a new site collection, you are prompted to enter a value for the Server Resource Quota, as shown in Figure 8-4. The value you enter in the box represents resource points that measure the effectiveness of custom applications running inside your site collection. For example, say you uploaded a custom Web Part that does a lot of calculations and uses up a lot of computing power. Share-Point Online monitors how many resources your custom Web Part uses. The resource points that you assigned will authorize SharePoint Online to either leave it alone if it's performing within the quota, throttle it if the code is poorly written and starts to hog all the resources, and ultimately kill the Web Part or make the application stop running if it goes haywire and starts to cause problems. Fortu-nately, the killing only happens within the affected site collection and has no impact in other site collections within the tenancy.

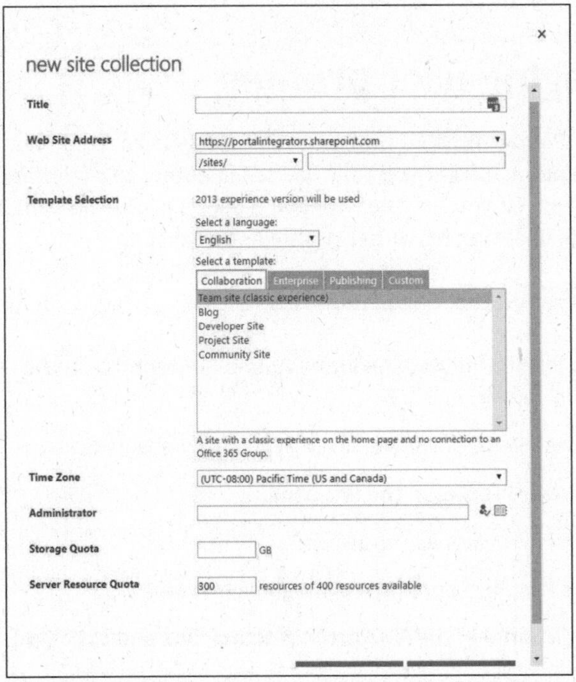

FIGURE 8-4:
Adding a Server
Resource Quota.

Assigning a new site collection owner to the new site collection

The idea behind delegated administration is to share power so that you, as the SharePoint Online Administrator, can be relieved of business-unit-specific tasks, while at the same time empowering members of your organization to make the call on tasks related to SharePoint for their business units.

To assign one or more site collection administrators to your site, follow these steps:

1. **Click the SharePoint link in the Admin Center node in the Office 365 Admin Center.**

    The SharePoint Online Admin Center screen appears.

2. **Click Site Collections in the left pane.**

    You see a list of all of the site collections in your Office 365 instance.

3. **Select the check box next to the site collection for which you want to assign administrators, then click the Owners drop-down in the ribbon and select Manage Administrators.**

4. **Enter the name or names of the site collection administrators.**

5. **Click OK to go back to the SharePoint Online Admin Center dashboard.**

Managing user profiles

As a SharePoint Online Administrator, you may need to edit a user profile to identify the relationship between one user and another to encourage or enhance social collaboration. Or you may need to edit a user's profile on behalf of someone having trouble updating his or her profile in Office 365.

To edit a user profile, do the following:

1. **Click the SharePoint link in the Admin Center node in the Office 365 Admin Center.**

    The SharePoint Online Admin Center screen appears.

2. **Click User Profiles in the left pane.**

    The User Profiles page appears.

3. **In the People group, click Manage User Profiles.**

4. **Enter a name in the Find profiles search box and click Find.**

5. **On the name you want to edit, hover the mouse pointer over to the right of the entry and click the down arrow to display additional commands.**

6. Select Edit My Profile (see Figure 8-5).

7. Enter your edits in the page that displays and then click Save and Close to go back to the SharePoint Online Admin Center dashboard.

Importing a new custom taxonomy into the Term Store

As a content management system, SharePoint Online provides great out-of-the-box metadata management capabilities through the Term Store. If your organization uses taxonomy to organize data, then you can simply use what you have by importing your custom taxonomy into the Term Store. If you are a small business, using taxonomy to tag content could mean better governance of how things are described in your company, as well as help build the social fabric of your organization.

For example, say that you require SharePoint users to enter certain information about files they upload to the document library. They have to enter the title, author, business unit, audience, and subject for each file. You can leverage taxonomy so that when a user enters metadata in the Audience field, they can choose from keywords already in the Term Store, such as Internal or External. If the user selects Internal, additional options display to choose from, depending on whether the internal audience is for executives or managers. Under Subject, users can select from keywords, such as HR, Legal, or IT. You can also allow users to enter their own keywords to describe the subject. As you see a pattern emerging of frequently used keywords, it may signal you, as the SharePoint Online Administrator, to move those keywords into the main Term set. Not only that, but it may prompt your organization to start thinking about creating a new name for a product according to what words best describe it to your people and what those words mean to them.

To import a custom taxonomy to the Term Store, follow these steps:

1. **Click Term Store from the left navigation in the SharePoint Online Admin Center.**

   Make sure that your name is listed under Term Store Administrators.

2. **Under Sample Import on the right pane, click View a Sample Import File.**

3. **Download the comma-separated values (.csv) file and make edits to it in Excel to fit your taxonomy.**

4. **In Excel, arrange the terms in hierarchies up to seven levels deep.**

5. **Save the file in its original .csv format.**

6. **Back at the Term Store from the SharePoint Online Admin Center, hover the mouse pointer over the group where you want to load the Term set and then click on the arrow that appears on the right (see Figure 8-6) to display additional commands.**

TIP

If you don't see the arrow when you hover the mouse pointer over the group, make sure you've added yourself as a Term Store Administrator and saved the setting.

View a sample import file

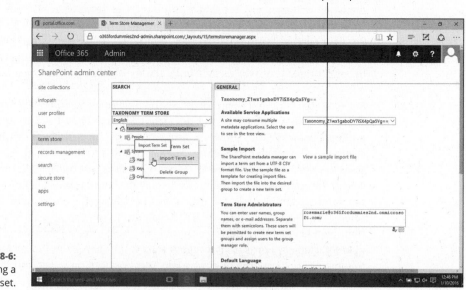

FIGURE 8-6:
Importing a custom Term set.

7. Select Import Term set.

8. From the Term set import window, click Browse.

9. Navigate to the .csv file you saved in Step 5, select the file, and then click Open.

You are taken back to the Term set import window.

10. Click OK.

You are taken back to the SharePoint Online Admin Center portal, where you'll see the Term set you just imported listed under the group you selected in Step 6.

Exercising the Powers Vested on the Site Collection Administrator

As a Site Collection Administrator, you have the highest level of permissions in your site collection that allows you to perform tasks that may have routed to your IT team in the past. You also have the power to enable or disable features that are used in subsites within your site collection. Moreover, you have access to all the subsites regardless of whether you've been added as a user to the site.

Sharing your site externally

When the SharePoint Online Administrator enables external sharing from the SharePoint Online Admin Center, this does not mean that all site collections are automatically shared externally. You, as a Site Collection Administrator, also need to share the site.

To share the site, click the Share button in the upper right of any site. Once the Share dialog appears, you can share the site with others by entering their email address.

If the external users you invite to your site already have an Office 365 account, they can log in by using that account. If not, they will be asked to log in with a Microsoft account. Also, you can share the site with anonymous users using a special link, if the SharePoint Administrator for Office 365 has allowed it for the site collection.

Creating a new team subsite and/or new document libraries

A subsite is merely a SharePoint site under a site collection. It uses the same navigation as the top-level site and has the capability of using all the site collection features that have been activated at the site collection level. Sometimes, it is referred to as the *child site*, whereas the top-level site is called the *parent site*.

To create a subsite, first go to your main SharePoint site by clicking the waffle icon and selecting SharePoint (not the Site Collection Admin interface mentioned earlier but the SharePoint site itself), and follow these steps:

1. **Go to Site Actions (gear icon) ⇨ Site Contents.**

   The site contents page appears.

2. **Select the New drop-down menu in the ribbon and click Subsite.**

3. **Enter the title of your site in the Title box and enter the URL for your site in the box below it if you want a URL different from the title and then select a template.**

4. **Complete the rest of the settings as needed and then click Create.**

   After the request is processed, you are taken to your new site.

About content and content types

One of the many cool features SharePoint Online offers is not only the ability for users to upload documents, but also to create a new Word document right from the document library by clicking Documents from the Library Tools on the ribbon and then clicking New. This action opens a new blank document in Microsoft Word that will be saved online after you give it a filename.

What most new SharePoint users don't know is that you can actually "upload" a link to a document in another library or create new Microsoft Office documents other than Word. In the case of the former, this eliminates duplicate documents that could become a nightmare to sync. For the latter, it streamlines creation of form-based documents.

Uploading a link instead of a file is made possible by SharePoint content and content types features. Think of content as the Word document you uploaded or the new file you created from the document library. The way you defined the settings for your documents is the content type. The geek way of defining content type according to Microsoft TechNet is covered in the next two sections describing scenarios that you're likely to encounter.

Keeping one version of a document in multiple sites

Suppose you manage two separate SharePoint sites and you have a document you want to share between the two sites. If you create two documents to upload one for each site, you have to update two documents when something changes.

To avoid the extra work, you can upload one document in one site, and "upload" a link to the document in the other site. To do so, follow these steps:

1. **Navigate to the document library where you want to add the link to, click the gear icon on the top right of the page, and then select Library Settings.**

2. **Under General Settings, click Advanced Settings.**

3. **Under Allow Management of content types, select Yes and then scroll down and click OK.**

   Under Content Types, you see that Document is already listed as the default content type. This returns you to the Settings screen.

4. **Click the Add from existing site content types link that appears below the Document content type.**

5. **On the Add Content Types page, select Link to a Document in the Available Site Content Types: box.**

6. **Click the Add button in the middle to add the selected content type into the Content types to add: box on the right.**

7. **Click OK.**

   You are taken back to the Document Library Settings page.

Now that you've added Links as a content type, let's see it in action. Exit out of the library settings view and go back to your document library. To do so, follow these steps:

1. **Click the New drop-down menu and then select Link.**

2. **On the New link to a document window that appears, enter the document name and the URL or just select it from the list of Recent documents.**

3. **Click OK.**

   You are taken back to your document library.

Voila! Now you can see the link listed as if it were a real document in the library. When you update the original file, the link will always open the latest version of the file it's linked to.

Adding an Excel template in the content type

Suppose you want to be able to create not just Word documents from your library but also Excel files. The Excel file you want to use when you create new Excel files is a form template for an invoice that you created. To achieve this, first you need to add your invoice template as a new content type in the site collection. The second step is to then add this new content type to your document library following Steps 1 through 7 in the preceding section, but replacing Link to a Document with the new Excel form template.

To add your invoice template as a new content type in the site collection, follow these steps:

1. At the parent site, click the gear icon, select Site Contents, and then click Site Settings on the ribbon of the Site Contents page.

2. Under Web Designer Galleries, click Site content types and click Create.

3. Give it a name (Invoice Template), enter a description if needed, and select Document Content Type under Select parent content type from.

4. Select Document under Parent Content Type and choose from one of the existing groups or create a new group for your new content type and then click OK.

5. Click Advanced under Settings, select Upload a new document template, browse for your template, and then click OK.

Your new template now displays as an option when you create new documents at your document library.

Managing the look and feel

Sometimes the default look and feel of the site may not suit your needs for one reason or another. You can easily customize your site with out-of-the box features that do not require coding. You can edit the title, description, and icon for your site, give it a new theme, reorder the left navigation, and customize the top link bar (or the horizontal navigation). Click the gear icon, select Site Contents, and then click Site Settings in the ribbon of the Site Contents page. The commands are available under Look and Feel.

Managing the web designer galleries

As a site collection administrator, you have the ability to manage the web designer galleries in your site collection. These galleries include site columns, site content types, Web Parts, list templates, master pages, themes, solutions, and composed looks. You access the web designer galleries by going to Site Settings again as mentioned in the previous section.

As with content types, you can create a new site column to represent an attribute or metadata for a list item or content type. When created, the site column can be reused in multiple lists, in multiple sites within the site collection.

One of the handy links in the Web Designer Galleries group is List templates. When you see a SharePoint list that you like and may want to reuse, save the list as a template and then add that template in the gallery. After the template is added, an icon for the list will be displayed as one of the options when you create a new list.

To save an existing list as a template and add to the gallery, follow these steps:

1. **Go to an existing list.**

2. **Click the gear icon in the top-right corner of the page and select List Settings.**

   If you don't see List Settings, you will need to navigate by selecting the List ribbon and then clicking Settings and choosing List Settings.

3. **Under the Permissions and Management group, click the Save list as template link.**

4. **In the Save as Template page, enter the file name, template name, and description.**

   If you want to include the content of the existing list in the template, check the Include Content box. Note that the more data you have in your template, the bigger the file size will be and may cause issues loading the template. We recommend leaving this option unchecked.

5. **Click OK.**

   When the saving process is complete, a notification will be displayed confirming successful completion of the operation.

6. **Click OK.**

   You are taken back to the List Settings page.

When you go to the gear icon in the upper right of the screen and choose Add an app, you will see the new template you added as an option.

If for some reason you do not like the master page template that's applied to your SharePoint site, you may need to hire a designer to create a new master page. You then load the new master page into the Master Page Gallery as if it were a document in a document library.

Web Parts, themes, solutions, and composed looks require technical know-how to create, but after you have them, you can easily add them to the Gallery as if they were list or document items.

Managing permissions and groups

To maintain security and integrity of your site, assign the right level of permission or privilege to the users of your site. As a best practice, create a SharePoint group first, assign a permission level to the group, and then start adding users to the appropriate groups.

An example of a SharePoint group could be the "Executive" group with Contribute access where all your C-level executives are members. Another example is a "Site Owners" group with Full Control privileges, comprised of a few members of your team who are technically advanced.

TIP

Grouping your users with similar access needs minimizes the administrative burden of individually adding or removing users from sites, libraries, and lists. Doing this allows you to use those groups in workflows, such as assigning tasks to a group rather than an individual.

In SharePoint, you can assign permissions on the site collection level and have those permissions be inherited or not inherited on the subsite level. You can also further customize the permission on document libraries or lists so even if users may have access to the site, they may or may not have access to certain contents within the site. You can take it even farther down to the granular level by customizing the permission for items in a list or contents in a library so that even though a group may have access to a document library, only certain individuals have access to certain files:

>> To manage your site's permissions, go to the gear icon and select Site Contents. On the Site Contents page, click Site Settings in the ribbon and then follow the links under User and Permissions.

>> To manage permissions on a list, library, or item, look for the Share or Shared With buttons. When you share, you can choose to either allow only view permissions or also allow edit permissions.

Chapter 9

Customizing SharePoint Online

After you get the hang of SharePoint, you may want to dive deeper into the technology. SharePoint is a web-based product (meaning that you use it with your web browser). Being a user of SharePoint is just the beginning, however. You can develop real-world business apps by using nothing more than your web browser. You don't need to be a programmer and you don't even need to be very technical. You just need some time to find out how to drag and drop components and enter content.

This chapter walks through SharePoint development using a web browser. You also find out about key SharePoint development concepts, such as sites, lists, libraries, pages, and apps.

Going Over SharePoint Development

SharePoint development doesn't mean you need to be a programmer or have any understanding of programming. If you can tweak your Facebook page or update your LinkedIn profile, then you can be a SharePoint developer. SharePoint development begins with nothing more than your web browser.

When you use your web browser to develop new functionality or customize existing functionality, the result is called an *app*. For example, let's say you create a blank SharePoint list, then add some columns and workflow behavior to it and call it an expense manager. You have just created your very own SharePoint app called Expense Manager. Of course, this is a very simple example. Apps can get incredibly complicated. But the idea is the same, regardless of how complex your apps become.

When you customize a SharePoint list or library, you're creating your very own SharePoint app. Apps are covered in detail later in the chapter.

TIP

Using a Web Browser as a Development Tool

To a user, browsing a SharePoint site looks like a regular website — with some fancy SharePoint capabilities. Those SharePoint capabilities enable easy collaboration, access to business information, and a boost to business intelligence, all through the web. In SharePoint terms, a site is a container for SharePoint pages. This entire ball of functionality, also called a *platform* (because you can build on it), is the Microsoft product called *SharePoint.* One of the things that makes SharePoint so exciting is that you don't even have to drop out of your web browser to tell SharePoint what to do. As long as you have access to SharePoint and a current browser, you're ready to start developing a site.

When you're first starting out with SharePoint development, you need a site that you can use to practice. When you create a new site, you start by choosing a *template site* that already has some stuff built into it — such as lists, libraries, and Web Parts (also known as *apps*) developed and configured to do particular tasks. Those templates are available on the Create screen when you create a new site. For example, you may get a request to create a Document Center site in order to manage documents from a central location. Rather than try to configure a Team site to be optimized for document management, you can use a template specifically designed for this task. In this scenario, the template site you would use is called the Document Center and is shown in Figure 9-1.

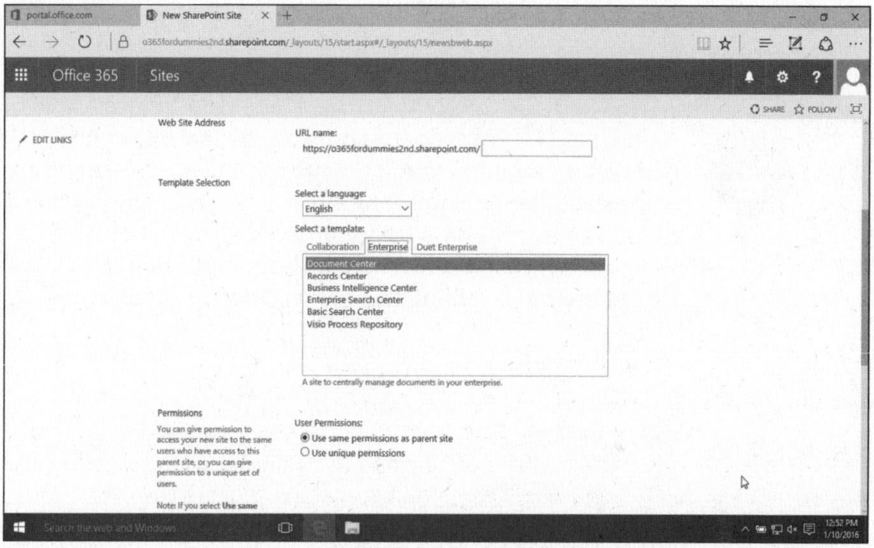

FIGURE 9-1:
The Document
Center site
template.

Developing SharePoint sites

When you need to develop a SharePoint site to solve a problem, be sure that you start with a solid understanding of the available site templates. It's often much easier to start with a site template that almost does what you want, and then develop it from this starting point, than to develop everything from scratch.

TIP

Before you start building custom applications for SharePoint, having a solid working knowledge of its various components is a good idea. (After all, you wouldn't try to design a house without having some knowledge of how the plumbing works, right?) The best way to get to know SharePoint is to start with a basic Team site, then further develop it so you understand what the templates are doing. Then you can expand to explore other templates as you build your SharePoint knowledge.

Creating a new site is as simple as clicking Site Actions (gear icon) ⇨ Site Contents from the parent site and then clicking the New button and then clicking Subsite on the drop-down menu. On the New Subsite page, you provide a title and a URL and select a template (in addition to some other configuration options). The template you choose determines how your new site will be preconfigured. A parent site is simply a site that holds another site.

Site templates are included in SharePoint Online:

>> Some templates are used only for creating a Site Collection (a container for subsites).

>> Some templates are used only for creating subsites.

>> Some templates can be used for both.

REMEMBER

A site collection is a special SharePoint site that allows you to separate key aspects of the sites contained within the site collection. For example, you turn on features at the site collection level, which makes those features available to all sites within the site collection. On a technical level, SharePoint separates site collections by using different databases. This allows for separation of security and users, because two different site collections use two different databases.

Templates for subsites only:

>> **Publishing Site:** A site used to publish content. The site template is used for subsites that need the publishing functionality provided by the Publishing Portal template.

>> **Publishing Site with Workflow:** A site for publishing web pages on a schedule by using approval workflows. It includes document and image libraries for storing web-publishing assets.

>> **SAP Workflow Site:** A site designed to work with SAP, an enterprise resourcing planning software program that aggregates all business tasks for users.

Templates for site collections only:

>> **Community Portal:** A site that can be used to contain community sites. In other words, an aggregation of communities.

>> **Community Site:** A site where members of the community can come together to discuss topics and interact with each other.

>> **Compliance Policy Center:** Contains policies that are used to manage when documents can be deleted after a certain period of time.

- >> **Developer Site:** A site where developers can create, publish, and test apps designed for Microsoft Office.

- >> **eDiscovery Center:** A site designed for legal matters and investigations where the preservation and search ability of content is critical. The site is also designed for exporting of content for legal compliance.

- >> **My Site Host:** Used to host the personal sites functionality of SharePoint, also known as OneDrive for Business, as well as the personal profile pages of users.

- >> **Publishing Portal:** This template offers a starter site hierarchy (grouping of SharePoint sites) for an Internet site or a large intranet portal. You can use distinctive branding to customize this site. It includes a home page, a sample press-releases site, a Search Center, and a logon page. Typically, this site has many more readers than contributors; it's used to publish the Web pages by using a process for approving new content known as an approval workflow.

  By default, this site enables content-approval workflows to provide more control over the publishing process. It also restricts the rights of anonymous users: They can see content pages but not application pages.

- >> **Team Site — SharePoint Online configuration:** A Team site that is preconfigured to allow users to share content with external users.

Templates for both subsites and site collections:

- >> **Basic Search Center:** This site provides SharePoint search functionality, including pages for search results and advanced searches.

- >> **Blog:** This site works like an Internet blog; a person or team can post ideas, observations, and expertise that site visitors can comment on.

- >> **Business Intelligence Center:** A site that can be used to present content focused on business intelligence.

- >> **Community Site:** A site where members of the community can come together to discuss topics and interact with each other.

- >> **Document Center:** You can manage documents centrally for your entire enterprise from this site.

- >> **Enterprise Search Center:** This site provides the SharePoint search capability. The Welcome Page includes a search box that has two tabs: one for general searches and another for searches for information about people. You can add tabs, delete them, or customize them with different search scopes or specified result types.

>> **Enterprise Wiki:** You can use this site for publishing knowledge that you capture and want to share across the enterprise. Use this site to edit, coauthor, and discuss content, as well as to manage projects.

>> **Project Site:** A site used for managing, discussing, and collaborating on a project.

>> **Records Center:** A site for managing digital records. The site is optimized to handle the routing of documents and determine whether documents can be deleted or modified or must be retained with their original content.

>> **Team Site:** A site on which a team can organize, generate, and share information. It provides a document library as well as lists for managing announcements, calendar items, tasks, and discussions.

>> **Visio Process Repository:** A collaborative site on which teams can view, share, and store Visio process diagrams. It provides a document library (with version control) for storing process diagrams as well as lists for managing announcements, tasks, and review discussions.

TIP

Microsoft is constantly updating SharePoint Online with new features and removing old features. If you see a template not listed here, then Microsoft might have recently added it. Similarly, if you see a template here that you can't find, then Microsoft might have removed it.

TIP

When you create a new Site Collection, you can also choose the Custom grouping that allows you to choose a template for the new site collection later after you have already created it.

Adding apps (lists and libraries) and pages

To develop a SharePoint site (using your browser no less!), you need to understand some of the key components. In particular, these include list apps, library apps, and pages.

When you have an idea of the type of app you want to add, you can add it by clicking the gear icon in the upper-right corner and then selecting Add an app, as shown in Figure 9-2. You will then see all of the list and library app templates described shortly.

Knowing your list app options

SharePoint Online comes with a collection of standard lists and libraries. Microsoft has already taken the time to develop these in order to make your life as a developer easier, so you may as well use them. The following list introduces the standard SharePoint list apps and provides brief descriptions:

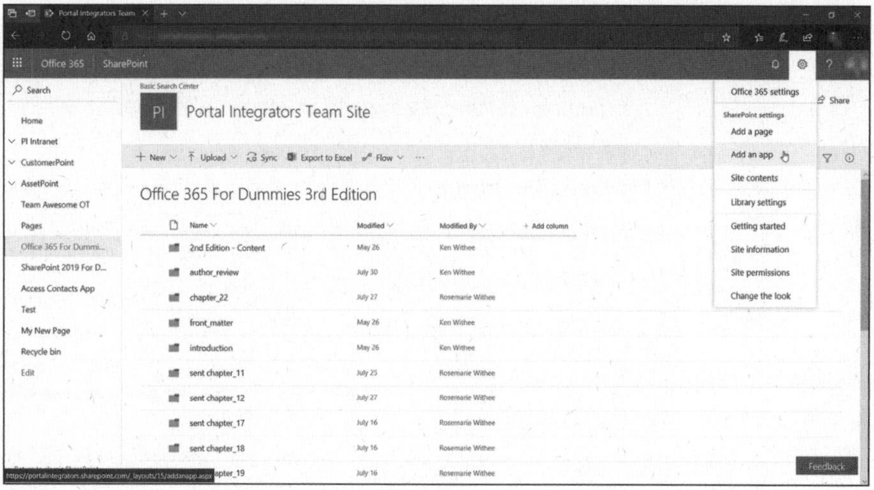

FIGURE 9-2:
Opening the Your
Apps page to add
a new app to a
SharePoint site.

>> **Announcements:** This app is for brief news items, quick status checks, and other quick, informative stuff.

>> **Calendar:** This calendar is strictly business — deadlines, meetings, scheduled events, and the like. You can synchronize the information on this calendar with Microsoft Outlook or other Microsoft-friendly programs.

>> **Contacts:** If you're a regular Outlook user, you may have developed a list of contacts. If you haven't, here's your chance to list the people relevant to your team (such as partners, customers, or public officials). You can synchronize the SharePoint Contacts app with Microsoft Outlook or other programs that play nice with Microsoft products.

>> **Custom List:** If you're trying to develop a list app but none of the standard list app types does what you have in mind, you can start from scratch with a blank list and drop in the views and columns you want.

>> **Custom List in Data Sheet View:** Here's a familiar twist on the blank list app: SharePoint shows it as a spreadsheet, so you can set up a custom list app as easily as you would in Excel, specifying views and columns as needed. Note that this list type requires an ActiveX control for list datasheets; fortunately, Microsoft Office provides such a control. (Coincidence? I think not.)

>> **Discussion Board:** If you're a seasoned netizen from the heyday of the newsgroup, this list app will be a familiar place for online discussions. Naturally, you want to keep the discussion businesslike, so this list app type helps you manage those discussions (for example, you can require posts to be approved before everybody can see them).

>> **External List:** Use this list app type to create a list of data identified as an External Content Type. An External Content Type is a term used to describe groupings of data that live outside of SharePoint. An example might be data that lives in a backend system, such as SAP.

>> **Import Spreadsheet:** If you have data contained in an existing spreadsheet (created in Excel or another Microsoft-compatible program) that you want to use in SharePoint, you can import it into a list app of this type. You get the same columns and data as the original spreadsheet.

>> **Issue Tracking:** If you want to organize your project team's responses to a problem associated with (say) an important project, this is the type of list app you use to set priorities, assign tasks, and keep track of progress toward resolving the issue.

>> **Links:** This list app type helps you organize links. The user can consult a list of web pages and similar online resources — and simply click to go to any of them.

>> **Promoted Links:** You can use this list app type to create a list of items using visual buttons instead of boring old text.

>> **Survey:** This list app type is for gathering information, specifically by crowd-sourcing. Here's where you put a list of questions you want people to answer. A survey list app helps you formulate your questions and can summarize the responses you get back. The responses to the survey are stored in the list and can then be analyzed, charted, or exported.

>> **Tasks:** This list app type is essentially a to-do list for a team or individual.

Checking out the available library apps

When you need a way to organize files so that they're accessible via a SharePoint site, you find a selection prebuilt for the most common types of library apps in SharePoint Online. Take a gander at the following standard library apps and the brief descriptions of what they do.

TIP

If you do not see these options in the Add an App page, you need to activate the Site Feature called *Wiki Page Home Page*. You can do this by clicking the gear icon in the top-right corner of your page and then clicking Site Settings. On the Site Settings page, click the Manage Site Features link located in the Site Actions section. Activate the Wiki Page Home Page feature. Remember that features are also available at the Site Collection Administration level, which can also be accessed on the Site Settings page.

>> **Asset Library:** Here's where you store information assets other than documents — ready-to-use information in the form of images, audio files, video files — to make them available and regulate their usage.

>> **Data Connection Library:** This library app type is where you can put and share files that specify and describe external data connections. For example, you might want your users to be able to pull data from a data warehouse. Setting up a connection to the data warehouse and getting all the server names, usernames, and connection information just right can be tedious. Using a Data Connection Library app, an administrator could set up the connections and store them in the library. The users would then just use the connection to the data warehouse whenever they want to pull data and analyze it.

>> **Document Library:** You run across — and create — a lot of these in SharePoint. Such library apps are for storing documents, organizing them in folders, controlling their versions, and regulating their usage with a check-in/check-out system.

>> **Form Library:** Here's where you store and manage electronic versions of blank business forms for everyday documentation, such as purchase orders and status reports. To create and maintain library apps of this type, you need a compatible XML editor. Keep in mind, however, that the form library app is just a place to store the data that has been entered into the form. To build the actual form, you need the XML compliant form editor.

>> **Picture Library:** This library app type is for storing and sharing digital images. The difference between the Assets Library and the Picture Library can be subtle because they both store images. The key distinction lies in the name. The Picture Library is designed specifically to store pictures, and the asset library is used to store images. If you think of a picture as a photo and an image as something like a logo or graphic, the differences start to emerge. For example, the pictures in a Picture Library app show a thumbnail image when they show up in searches, but the images in an image library do not.

>> **Record Library:** You store business records in this library app. When you create a Record Library app, you're adding some functionality that allows SharePoint to create record management and retention schedules. This type of functionality is important when you want to make sure that you are doing your due diligence in keeping track of your business records by letting SharePoint do the heavy lifting.

>> **Report Document Library:** This library app type is used to store and manage report documents. This library app is similar to the Report Library; however, there are some differences. Explore the Report Document Library and the Report Library apps to see which one you like better and which one best fits your reporting needs.

>> **Report Library:** This library app type is dedicated to web pages and documents that keep track of performance (and other such metrics), progress toward business goals, and other information used in business intelligence.

>> **Site Mailbox:** This library app type is useful to keep email and your documents closely connected because this app connects your site to an Exchange mailbox. Once connected, you can view your email in SharePoint and view your documents in Outlook.

>> **Wiki Page Library:** Library apps of this type have interconnected web pages containing content, such as text or images and functionality in the form of Web Parts that multiple users can edit easily.

Making information available with pages

You can create and develop pages to share information with others. A *page* is nothing more than a web page, and SharePoint Online has made a lot of progress in making page creation and development easier than in previous versions.

In the past, you had to understand different types of pages, including content pages, Web Part pages, and publishing pages. These page types are still available behind the scenes, but the on ramp for getting started has been dramatically reduced. You can now create a page and publish it without ever needing to understand the page types. To create a new page and add content:

1. **Open your web browser and navigate to the SharePoint site where you want to add a page.**

2. **Click the gear icon in the top-right corner of the page and select Add a Page.**

   A template page is displayed and you can start entering content as shown in Figure 9-3. You can add a title and then click the plus signs in order to add content. The plus sign on the left allows you to change the number of columns on the page, and the plus sign for each column allows you to add content to the column.

3. **When you are ready to publish your page, click the Publish button in the top-right corner of the page.**

   The Publish dialog box appears and you can add the page to your navigation, copy a link, post the new page as news to the site, or email the page to others. The Publish dialog box is shown in Figure 9-4.

PI
Portal Integrators Team Site
Not following
Share
Save as draft
Page details
Publish
Name your page

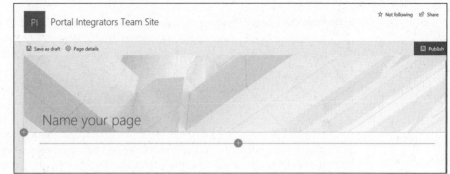

FIGURE 9-3: Adding a new page to a new page to a SharePoint site.

Help others find your page
Add page to navigation
Post as News on this site
Email
Page address
https://portalintegrators.sharepoint.com/SitePages/My-New-Page.aspx
Copy address

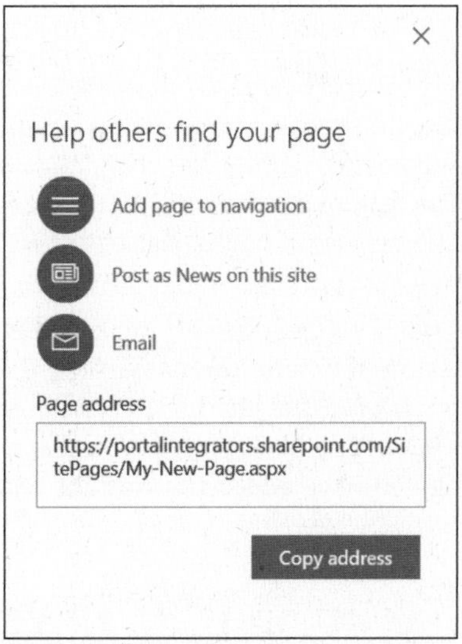

FIGURE 9-4: Publishing a new page to a SharePoint site.

If you want to dig deeper you can look into the guts of SharePoint to see the three primary types of SharePoint pages (in your browser, no less!) — each with a distinct function:

- **Content page:** Also known as a *wiki page*, this is the Swiss Army knife of SharePoint pages. A content page provides not only a place to put content but also a kind of workshop for collaboration, development, and customization — multiple users can wield a full-featured text editor built right into the browser. A content page is easy to develop and is an extremely powerful and intuitive tool for collaborative authoring, data capture, and documentation. For example, if you're in the business of manufacturing consumer products, then you might have a content page that allows customer service reps to capture common questions that users have regarding your products. The page could be dynamically updated, without the need to call in a programmer, as the reps encounter new questions.

>> **Web Part page:** This type of SharePoint page provides Web Part zones where you can drag and drop various Web Parts (reusable pieces of functionality) right onto your pages from the SharePoint Web Part gallery. Although a set of Web Parts comes standard with SharePoint, you can also custom develop Web Parts to meet your specific business needs. Imagine developing a Web Part for your company that ventures forth to become an everyday tool for nearly all the users in your organization — on their own sites — and to get the tool, all they have to do is simply drag and drop the Web Part right onto their pages. For example, you may have Web Parts that you have developed for your call center reps. When new Web Part pages are developed, the Web Parts that are used by the call center can be added to the page. This lets a programmer package up web functionality into a reusable component (Web Part) that can be reused on multiple pages.

>> **Publishing page:** This type of SharePoint page is designed to serve two functions: managing content and managing the look and feel of the page. A publishing page lives in a document library that provides version control and the SharePoint workflow feature. It's designed for the management and distribution of content — the essence of publishing content to SharePoint.

To start exploring these page types you just need to make sure you have the Publishing Infrastructure feature turned on and then you can either add the content types to an existing library or look for the existing Pages library already on your site. Selecting New from the ribbon of a library gives you the option to create one of these page types (assuming you have added the content type to the library as was described in Chapter 8).

TIP

For more information on developing in the SharePoint environment, check out *SharePoint 2019 For Dummies* by Rosemarie Withee and Ken Withee.

4

Diving into Office Online

IN THIS PART . . .

Harness the power of Office with nothing more than your web browser.

Gain fundamental knowledge about what an online app is and how it differs from the desktop version of Office.

Dive into each component individually by looking at Word Online, Excel Online, PowerPoint Online, and OneNote Online.

Chapter **10**

Introducing Office Online

O ffice Online is the cloud version of Microsoft Word, Excel, PowerPoint, OneNote, and Outlook. The apps allow users to create high-quality documents, simultaneously make changes to the documents with coauthors, share these documents from a browser without the need for the desktop application, and more. With Office Online, you're no longer tethered to your office desk to be productive. As long as you have an Internet connection, you can use any of the popular browsers from most common devices to access your documents and even quickly pick up from where you left off in your last session.

And don't worry; you don't have to give up beauty when you create documents on Office Online. Your visual-rich documents look identical to documents created with the Office desktop application. Formatting styles, graphs, charts, and data are retained when you open and share documents from Office Online. Flat, boring documents have no place in Office Online. The most common features and functions are available in Office Online from the ribbon similar to the desktop version.

In this chapter, we show you the new updates to the Office Online experience and touch on recently added features and functions to enhance your security posture.

Benefitting from Office Online

Office Online is great for everyday work, especially for millennials who are accustomed to using a variety of Internet-connected devices running on different platforms. It runs on all major operating systems and web browsers.

If you're a company that wants to foster a culture of collaboration and cooperation (who doesn't?), then Office Online is a great solution to add to your toolkit.

TIP

You can also save on licensing costs with Office Online. If you have workers out in the field or assigned at retail stores who don't need the full-fledged version of Office, you can assign them a cheaper license for access to just Office Online such as Office 365 Business Essentials or Office 365 E1. You can even save money on company-issued devices by allowing your employees to use their own devices to run Office Online.

Security features in the Office desktop applications such as SafeLinks are also available in Office Online. SafeLinks is a feature that proactively protects users when they click on malicious hyperlinks inside an Office document.

Boosting team collaboration, intelligently

You always start at `https://office.com` to access Office Online. From there you can run any of the online apps: Word, Excel, PowerPoint, OneNote, and Outlook.

Core authoring features in Word include table of contents, spell check, grammar check, picture editing (rotate, crop, drag and drop), numbered lists, bullet lists, and more. You can even have smileys as your bullets as shown in Figure 10-1!

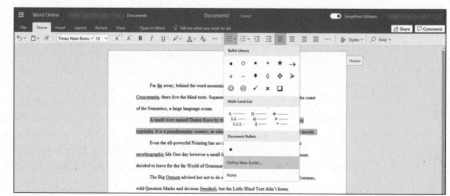

FIGURE 10-1:
Use smileys as
your bullets.

In Excel, conditional formatting, pivot tables, shapes, freeze panes, clear formatting, cross-sheet copy/paste, find and replace, and improved printing are supported.

Creating professional presentations no longer requires the desktop version of PowerPoint. The online version supports copying and pasting slides across presentations, image effects, format painter, the ability to select multiple slides and add charts from Excel, contextual spelling, animation markers, animated GIFs, improved tables, and more.

Office Online has also gotten smart. Unlike the previous version, your documents in Office Online now open in Editing Mode so you can immediately start working on the document. And the Share dialog box in Office Online works the same way as the desktop version (see Figure 10-2).

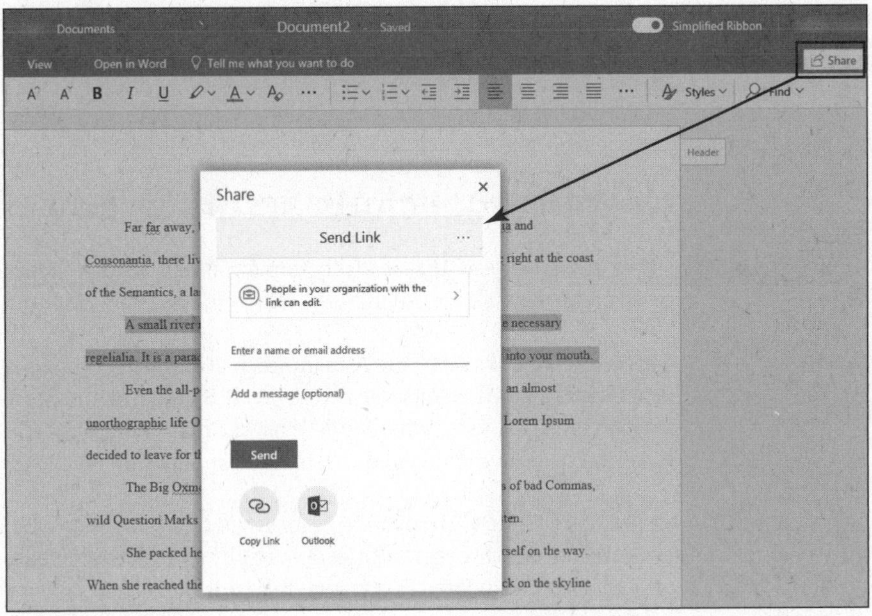

FIGURE 10-2:
The Office Online
Share dialog box.

Intelligent services delivered through artificial intelligence (AI) and machine learning have always been available in Office Online. These services save us time and make us not just seem smart but actually become smarter. For example, spell check is something available and commonly used in Word. And Microsoft's addition of grammar checking was a great boon for non-native English speakers.

Recently, Microsoft added writing assistance so not only does the intelligence service check for spelling (indicated by a red squiggle) and grammar (shown with a blue double underline), it also checks for clarity and conciseness (shown with a dotted underline in Figure 10-3).

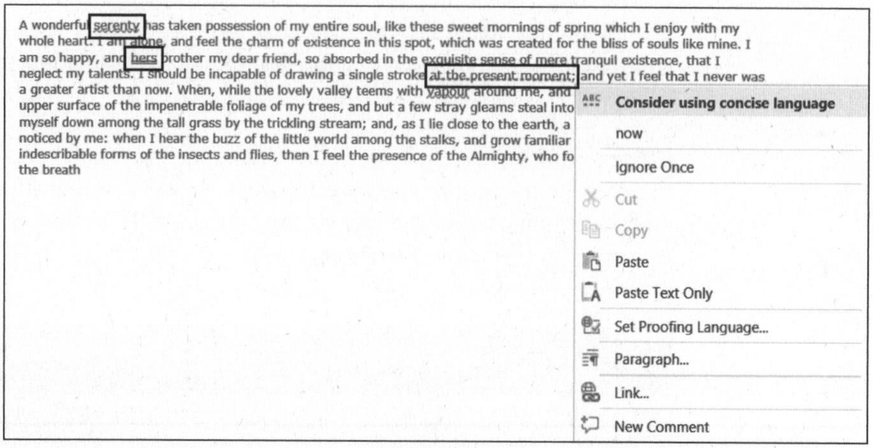

A wonderful serenity has taken possession of my entire soul, like these sweet mornings of spring which I enjoy with my whole heart. I am alone, and feel the charm of existence in this spot, which was created for the bliss of souls like mine. I am so happy, and hers brother my dear friend, so absorbed in the exquisite sense of mere tranquil existence, that I neglect my talents. I should be incapable of drawing a single stroke at the present moment; and yet I feel that I never was a greater artist than now. When, while the lovely valley teems with vapour around me, and upper surface of the impenetrable foliage of my trees, and but a few stray gleams steal into myself down among the tall grass by the trickling stream; and, as I lie close to the earth, a noticed by me: when I hear the buzz of the little world among the stalks, and grow familiar indescribable forms of the insects and flies, then I feel the presence of the Almighty, who fo the breath

Consider using concise language

now

Ignore Once

Cut

Copy

Paste

Paste Text Only

Set Proofing Language...

Paragraph...

Link...

New Comment

FIGURE 10-3: Intelligent services in Office Online help you improve your writing.

Keeping malicious actors at bay

Office 365 Advanced Threat Protection (ATP) is a security feature in Office 365 E5 or A5 plans. If you have other plans, Office 365 ATP can be purchased as an add-on.

Office 365 includes ATP Safe Attachments and ATP Safe Links to help protect your organization from malicious actors. ATP Safe Attachments ensures that email attachments are safe, whereas ATP Safe Links makes sure links to websites in email messages or embedded in Office documents do not result in a breach.

In Outlook Online, you may receive an email from someone who is trying to harvest your credentials through an infected attachment. With ATP Safe Attachments, that attachment is detonated in a virtual machine before it reaches your mailbox. If it's a safe attachment, then you will see it in your email. If not, the attachment will be removed automatically from the email with a notification to inform you that a malicious attachment has been removed. This all happens very quickly, within minutes and even seconds, so it doesn't impact your productivity. If Microsoft needs more time to analyze the attachment, your email will still be delivered immediately with a notification that the attachment is still being analyzed.

ATP Safe Links, on the other hand, protects you by checking web addresses (URLs) in real-time every time you click on a link in your email or in an Office document. Verifying the web address at the time of click is important because hackers can redirect a once-safe URL to a bad URL. Just as ATP Safe Attachments detonates attachments, ATP Safe Links detonates URLs in a virtual machine when you click on them to determine whether or not the destination is safe. If it is, then you are taken directly to the website. If it's not safe, you will be blocked and presented with a notification as shown in Figure 10-4.

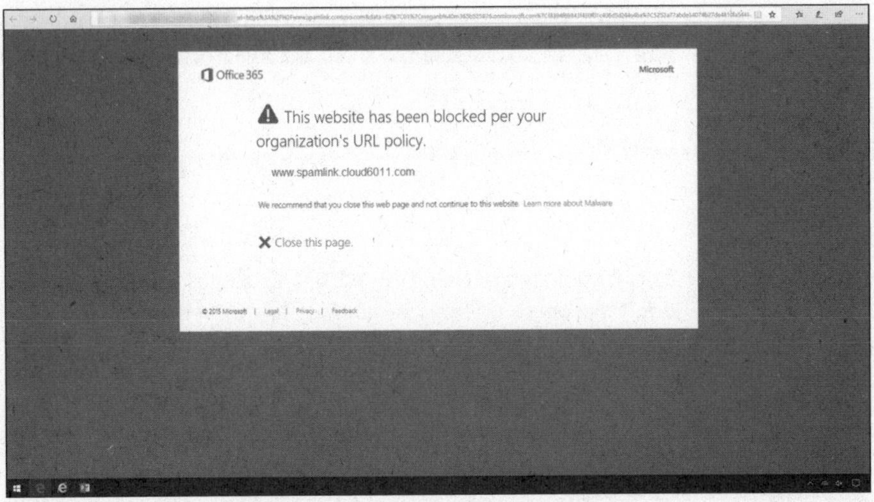

FIGURE 10-4:
ATP Safe Links
blocks bad
websites.

TIP Don't confuse Office 365 ATP with Windows Defender ATP, which is a separate set of security features in Windows 10. Using the power of AI, machine learning, and behavior analytics, Windows Defender ATP helps prevent, detect, and respond to attacks. If used together with Office 365 ATP, your organization will gain a much more enhanced security posture.

Experiencing Office Online

Since it first debuted in Office 2007, the ribbon interface has gone through several updates. In June 2018, Microsoft rolled out yet another update designed to adapt to the needs of users who need to collaborate in today's cloud computing environment. These updates include:

» A simplified ribbon that displays one row of buttons instead of multiple rows. Features and commands you use most are readily available while giving more real estate on your screen for content. If, however, you prefer the previous version, a toggle is available to revert to the classic ribbon interface (see Figure 10-5).

>> New colors and icons designed to scale based on the size of the screen so they stay crisp and clear across different types of devices.

>> Search powered by AI and machine learning, which displays recommendations as soon as you click the search box.

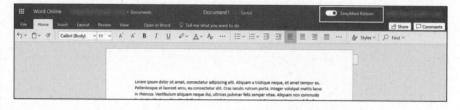

FIGURE 10-5:
The Office
Online ribbon
interface toggle.

These updates are being rolled out in stages starting with Word Online. If you don't see these updates in your Office 365 environment, don't worry; they will eventually be rolled out to all Office 365 tenants.

REMEMBER

Office Online as a cloud service is a browser-based productivity solution that includes the core Office apps: Word, Excel, PowerPoint, OneNote, and Outlook. It's a free service, but it requires a cloud storage account for storing documents such as OneDrive (consumer version), OneDrive for Business, and SharePoint Online.

Getting the most out of Office Online

The advantage of software as a service (SaaS), such as Office 365, is that SaaS vendors can roll out enhancements and updates in shorter cycles and require minimal actions from the end user. If you visit the Office 365 Roadmap page (see https://products.office.com/business/office-365-roadmap), you'll notice a number of features and updates in development to the service. When Microsoft launches these items, they may just show up in the service or application without the user installing anything. So, don't be surprised if you're using Office Online one day and come back the next day to find new features to help you get the job done.

Here are some tips to get the most out of Office Online:

>> **Use SharePoint Online and OneDrive for Business as your online storage solution versus a third-party solution.** The deep integration between Office Online and other Office 365 services can save you a lot of time by avoiding integration issues. Additionally, built-in AI and machine learning in Office 365 will capture computing behaviors in your environment to drive better security and collaboration.

>> **Install the free Office apps on your mobile devices so you can access files on to go.** When you open a document in your mobile app, you will automatically be taken to the last spot you were working on so you can easily pick up where you left off.

>> **Sync your OneDrive for Business and SharePoint Online document libraries to your hard drive.** This way you can access documents when you're offline using your Office desktop applications. Any changes you make while you're offline will automatically be saved and synced when you're back online.

Getting your voice heard

Microsoft is eager to get your feedback on Office Online and other services. If you would like to help improve Office, there are many ways to make your voice heard.

In Office Online, at the bottom right of the screen, you will see a link that says GIVE FEEDBACK TO MICROSOFT. Clicking on that link will open a quick feedback form, which you can then submit (see Figure 10-6).

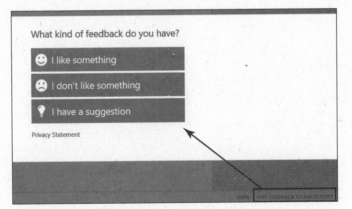

FIGURE 10-6: The Help Improve Office feedback form.

If you want to actively engage with other users who are providing feedback to Microsoft, you can also visit the following forums:

>> Word Online UserVoice: https://word.uservoice.com

>> Excel Online UserVoice: https://excel.uservoice.com

>> PowerPoint Online UserVoice: https://powerpoint.uservoice.com

>> OneNote UserVoice: https://onenote.uservoice.com

Chapter **11**

Getting into Word Online

O ffice 365 includes a version of Word that runs as a web application in your web browser — Word Online. Microsoft has put a lot of effort into making Word Online a valuable experience, which is a result of competing directly with Google Docs.

In this chapter, we explore some of the basic concepts of Word Online, such as using the web interface to create, read, edit, and delete documents. We also look at some of the advanced features of Word Online, including working with styles and tables.

Comparing Word Online and Word

Unless you have been living under a rock, you have probably used or heard of a program called Microsoft Word. Word is an aptly named word-processing application. In fact, we wrote this this book with Word. Word is a *thick client*, meaning that you run it from your local computer. In Windows 10, you fire up the Word program from the Start menu. Word then runs on your computer. A web-based application, on the other hand, runs on a computer in a data center, and you access it over the Internet. If you use Outlook.com or Gmail for email or browse a web page, then you are using a web application. You access a web application by using a web browser, which is a program installed on your computer.

Although Word Online is still Microsoft Word, there are some differences between the two. The biggest difference is that Word runs on your local computer, and Word Online runs in the cloud and is accessed by using your web browser.

When you fire up Word on your local computer and create a document, that document can either stay on your local computer or be saved to the cloud. When you click the Save button and save the document, you are prompted for the place where you want to save the file. For example, you can choose to save in a cloud location (such as OneDrive or Dropbox) or you can choose to save the document on your local computer in a location such as the Documents directory or your Desktop. In any case, your creation is a file located on a cloud-based storage location or your local computer.

GOING BEHIND THE SCENES

The cloud is just a fancy way of describing the act of accessing software and computer resources over the Internet. For example, when you create a Word Online document, it is not some mystical and magical fog that is conjured up from the mists of the Internet. To track down where the actual Word file lives requires a bit of detective work, but it is entirely possible.

Office 365 is nothing more than server software that Microsoft has installed on computers in their data centers around the world. For example, if you are on the West coast, then the physical data center that your Office 365 software is running in might be in the state of Washington. You access this server software over the Internet. Because you don't know, or even really care, where the actual data center is located, you can say it is running "in the cloud."

Now, to track down that file you created with Office Online, you need to think about where you saved it. If you saved it to SharePoint, then you saved it into a document library app. We know that SharePoint uses a database product called SQL Server to store all of its content and configuration information. So, when you are saving something to SharePoint, you are actually saving it to an SQL Server database. That SQL Server database is running in the Microsoft data center in the state of Washington (or Hong Kong, or Germany — or wherever the closest Microsoft data center is located).

Opening your web browser, pointing it at SharePoint Online, and clicking on a Word document to open or print it is actually very easy to accomplish. Behind the scenes, however, SharePoint Online (running in a Microsoft data center) is contacting the SQL Server program (also running in the Microsoft data center) and requesting the specific Word document. SharePoint then sends that to your web browser, and you see it magically appear.

When working with Word Online, however, you do not have a local file. When you create a document and save it, your document lives out in the cloud. In the case of Office 365, your document lives within a SharePoint Online document library app or OneDrive.

You can create a document using Word on your local device, save it to the cloud, and then edit it using Word Online. Word Online works even if you are at a computer that does not have Word installed locally, because Word Online only needs a web browser. You can even save a Word Online document to your local device using the Download a Copy button on the File menu.

Getting the Basics

You need to know some basic things about Word Online, such as how it differs from the traditional Word application that runs on your desktop or laptop. You also want to become familiar with the Word Online interface and discover how you can easily work with documents right from your web browser.

Using the Word Online interface

The Word Online interface is similar to the regular Word interface, except that it runs within your web browser. The interface contains a Ribbon at the top of the screen, which contains such tabs as File, Home, Insert, Layout, Review, and View.

In 2018, the ribbon for Word Online changed to a simpler and easier-to-use interface. At least this was the goal of Microsoft. Keep in mind you might see the older interface or you might see the new interface depending on when Microsoft flips the switch for your Office 365 instance. In the screenshots that follow we use the new interface, but if you still see the older interface, don't worry; the concepts are still the same. The ribbon may just look slightly different.

The Home tab on the Word Online ribbon contains common functionality in groupings, such as Clipboard, Font, Paragraph, Styles, and Editing, as shown in Figure 11-1.

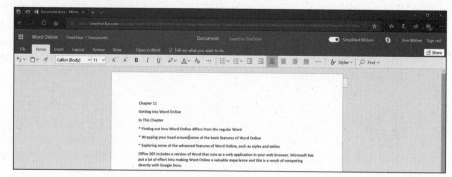

FIGURE 11-1:
The Home tab on the Word Online ribbon.

You use the Insert tab to insert objects into your document, such as a table, a picture, add-ins, links, comments, and notes. The Insert tab is shown in Figure 11-2. You learn more about how add-ins work with the Office products in Chapter 12.

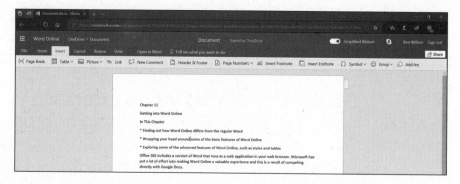

FIGURE 11-2:
The Insert tab on the Word Online ribbon.

The Layout tab is where you can change the formatting of the document. You can change things like the margins widths, orientation (portrait or landscape), the paper size, indentation, and line spacing. The Insert tab is shown in Figure 11-3.

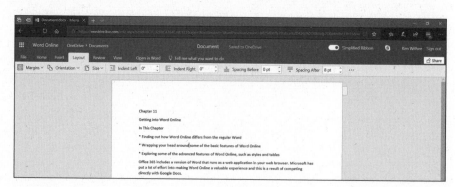

FIGURE 11-3:
The Layout tab on the Word Online ribbon.

The Review tab includes such functionality as spell check and comments. You can use the Review tab to add comments and collaborate with others on the document without actually changing the contents of the document itself. The Review tab is shown in Figure 11-4.

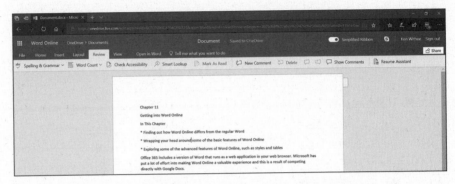

FIGURE 11-4:
The Review tab
on the Word
Online ribbon.

The View tab allows you to flip between Editing Mode and Reading View. When in edit mode, you can work with the Home and Insert tabs to modify and develop your document. In addition, you can also find the capability to zoom in on the document and change the view to show page ends and the header and footer. The View tab is shown in Figure 11-5.

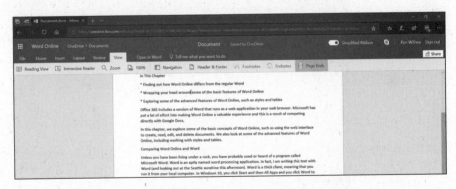

FIGURE 11-5:
The View tab
on the Word
Online ribbon.

In addition to the standard tabs in the ribbon, specialized tabs show up when you are working with certain objects. For example, when you select a picture by clicking on it, you will see a new tab — Picture, as shown in Figure 11-6. The Picture tab contains functionality for working with a picture, such as adding alternate text or resizing the image.

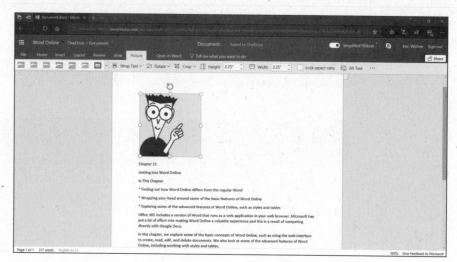

FIGURE 11-6:
The Picture tab
on the Word
Online ribbon.

In addition to the ribbon tabs, the interface also includes a File menu. The File menu allows you to save the document, open it by using the traditional Word application located on your computer, or close the document and return to the document library app that houses the document. The File menu is shown in Figure 11-7.

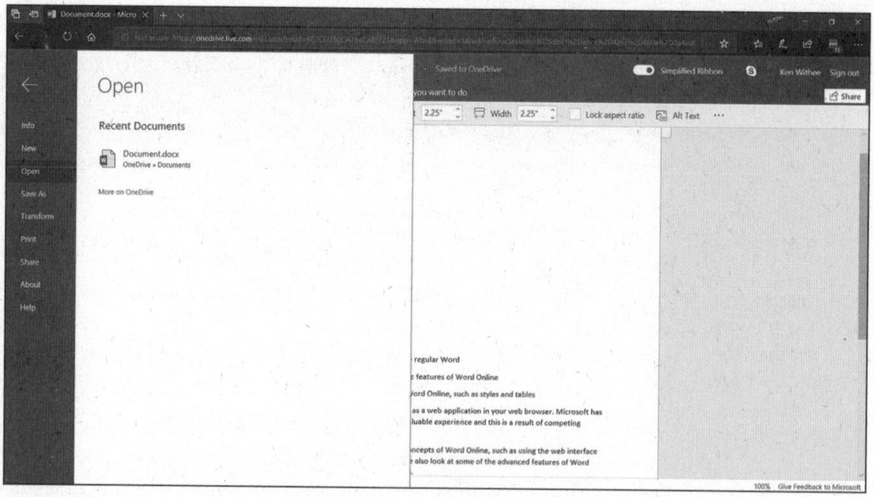

FIGURE 11-7:
The File menu
on the Word
Online interface.

Working with documents

Creating a new Word document in a SharePoint document library app is straightforward:

1. **Browse to the Documents Library in your SharePoint site.**

2. **Click the New button at the top.**

3. **Choose the Word document type, as shown in Figure 11-8.**

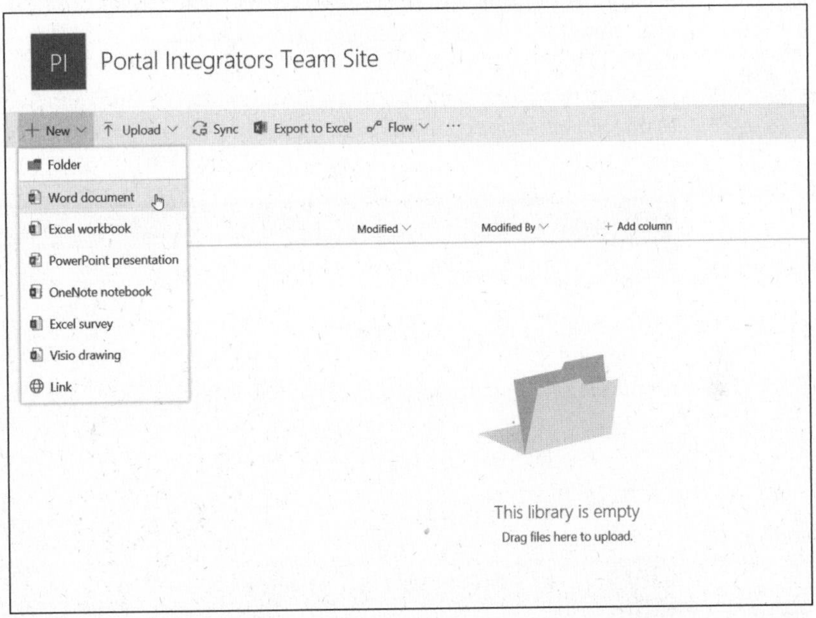

FIGURE 11-8:
Creating a new Word document in a SharePoint document library app.

When you create a new document, SharePoint is smart enough to create the new document using Word Online, but you can also open the document by using Word installed on your local computer or device.

One of the advantages working in the cloud is that your documents are auto-saved. However, it is best practice to name your file as soon as starting it. After you have finished developing your document, you can save it. Doing this automatically saves it to the document library app in which you created it. You can then click on the document to view it and then edit it further by using either Word Online or the local Word app running on your computer, phone, or tablet.

Editing Mode and Reading View

The preceding section discussed working with Word documents in Editing Mode. There may be times, however, when you simply want to read the document and not edit it. When you want to only read the document you can switch to Reading View, which looks very similar to a document that is printed on paper.

In addition, in Reading View you can access Immersive Reader. The Immersive Reader mode provides a focused view of the document that walks you through the document by reading it to you out loud. You can adjust the text size, volume, and view of the document in Immersive Reader mode.

A document in Immersive Reader mode is shown in Figure 11-9. The Reading View and Immersive Reader is found on the View tab.

TIP

As we developed this book using Word, we often found ourselves using Immersive Reader to have the chapters read back to us as we worked through edits.

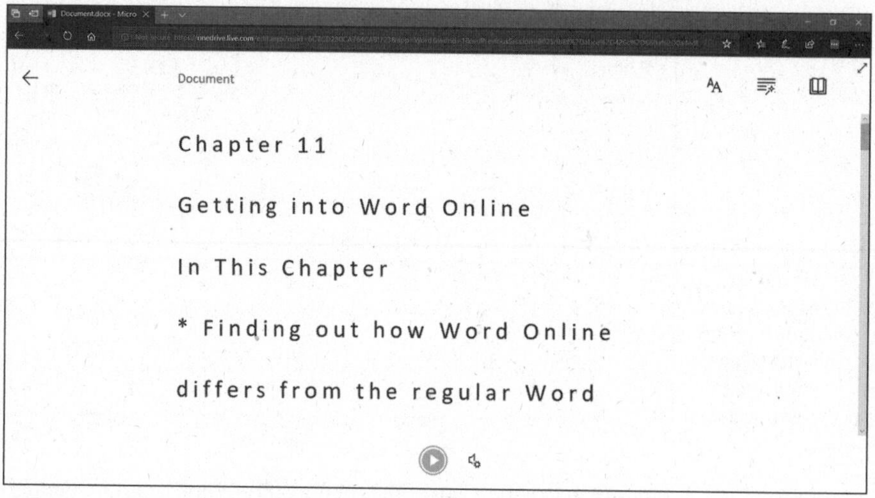

FIGURE 11-9:
A Word document in Immersive Reader mode in Word Online.

Document

Chapter 11

Getting into Word Online

In This Chapter

* Finding out how Word Online

differs from the regular Word

Working with Advanced Functions

Word Online contains features beyond just adding and modifying text-based content. In particular, you can:

>> Manage styles in order to standardize the look and feel of your document.

  • You find the styles functionality on the Home tab.

>> Insert Word objects, such as pictures, tables, add-ins, and links.

  • You can insert items on the Insert tab.

Styles

The styles let you consistently format a document by selecting a predefined style rather than going through a manual process. For example, you may want your headings to be larger font and a different color. You can, of course, type the text and then highlight the text and make it bigger, and also change the color, but using this method is a lot of work for every heading. A style allows you to simply click the Heading style to make the change, as shown in Figure 11-10.

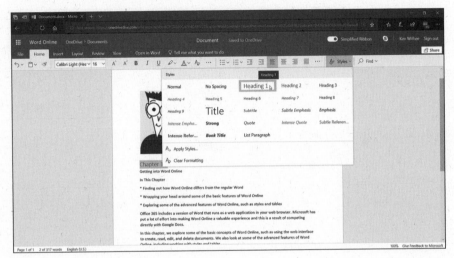

FIGURE 11-10:
Selecting a heading style in Word Online.

Tables

A table provides a mechanism for organizing content in your document. A table is divided into vertical columns and horizontal rows. You can insert a table with Word Online by following these steps:

1. **Click on the Insert tab.**

   The Insert tab displays the Ribbon that allows you to insert items into your document.

2. **Select the Table button.**

   When you select the Table button, you are presented with a grid that allows you to visually choose the number of rows and columns you want to include in your table, as shown in Figure 11-11.

3. **Highlight the number of rows and columns you desire for the table and then click the left mouse button.**

The table is automatically inserted into the document.

After the table is created, you can add content to the cells of each column. The table provides a lot of flexibility in the look and feel and layout of the content in your Word document.

FIGURE 11-11:
Inserting a
table into a
document by
using Word
Online.

Chapter **12**

Getting into Data with Excel Online and Power BI

Excel Online is a version of Excel that is part of the Office 365 offering. This version of Excel runs as a web application in your web browser. Working with Excel as a web application has a number of benefits, including the simple fact that you don't need to have the full version of Excel installed on the computer you are using to edit your workbook. All you need is a web browser and access to your SharePoint site, OneDrive, or another cloud-based storage location (such as Dropbox). You might be on a cruise or using a computer in a café or working from a shared computer at your organization. You can still work with your spreadsheets without having to have Excel installed on the computer you are using.

Power BI is a fairly new product from Microsoft and is included with the Office 365 E5 subscription. Using Power BI you can pull data from all types of sources and show it in standalone reports or integrate it into other Office 365 products such as SharePoint.

In this chapter, you explore some of the basic, as well as the more advanced, features of Excel Online and discover how it differs from the traditional version of Excel. You also get familiar with Power BI and learn how to pull data and build some basic reports.

Comparing Excel Online and Excel

Microsoft Excel is one of the most popular data analysis tools on the planet. Using Excel, you can enter numbers into a spreadsheet and use functions to manipulate them and perform analysis. In addition to analyzing numbers, Excel is often used for tracking and managing other data, such as customers, for example. In many organizations Excel has turned into a database-type application where all types of information is stored.

Excel is what is known as a thick client in that it runs from your local computer. In Windows 10, click the Start button (the Windows icon in the lower-left corner of the screen) and browse the listed applications. When you see Excel, click the icon to fire up the program. Excel then runs on your computer. A web-based application, on the other hand, runs on a computer in a data center that you access over the Internet. If you use Outlook.com or Gmail for email or browse a web page, then you are using a web application. The way you access a web application is by using a web browser, which is a program installed on your computer.

You will find that Excel Online is still Microsoft Excel, but it does have some differences. For one thing, Excel runs on your computer while Excel Online runs out in the cloud and you access it by using your web browser.

When you create a workbook on your local computer with Excel, that workbook traditionally has been stored locally on your computer. When you click the Save button to save a workbook, you are prompted for the location in which to save the file. You may save the file to a cloud-based storage location (such as SharePoint, OneDrive, or Dropbox) or to your Desktop or any other folder on your local computer. In any case, your creation is a file located in cloud-based storage or on your local computer.

When working with Excel Online, however, you do not have a local file. When you create a workbook and save it, your workbook lives on a computer in one of Microsoft's data centers. Because you don't know exactly which computer in which Microsoft data center, you can just say that the workbook lives out in the cloud. In the case of Office 365, your workbook lives within a SharePoint Online document library app.

TIP

You don't have to be a paid subscriber to Office 365 to work with Excel Online. You can use it for personal use for free with a free Microsoft Office 365 account or Outlook.com account.

Covering the Basics

Working with Excel Online is easy after you find your way around the interface. If you have used the traditional Excel application, then you can recognize that it is extremely similar and you won't have any trouble at all using Excel Online. If you've never used Excel, then you shouldn't have much trouble at all getting up to speed with Excel Online.

Using the Excel Online interface

The Excel Online interface is different from the traditional Excel application in that the web app runs within your web browser. The ribbon at the top of the Excel Online interface screen contains tabs, such as Home and Insert.

WARNING

Microsoft is rolling out a new ribbon for all the Office products. The rollout is happening in stages and, as of this writing, Word Online includes the new ribbon. (You can take a look at it in Chapter 11.) Excel Online, however, still has the regular ribbon, which we showcase in the following figures. You might see the old or the new ribbon in your Office 365 environment as it is being rolled out in stages. You can toggle the new ribbon on and off with a button once the new ribbon is available to use.

The Home tab contains common functionality in groupings, such as Clipboard, Font, Alignment, Number, Tables, Cells, and Editing, as shown in Figure 12-1.

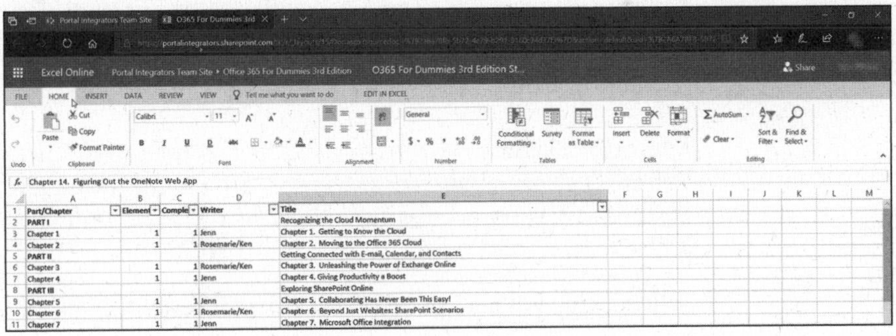

FIGURE 12-1:
The Home tab on the Excel Online ribbon.

Table 12-1 describes the sections of the Home tab on the Excel Online ribbon.

The Insert tab allows you to insert objects into your Excel Online workbook, such as functions, tables, add-ins, charts, hyperlinks, and comments.

TABLE 12-1 **Features of the Home Tab**

Home Tab Section	Description
Clipboard	Allows you to cut, copy, and paste data between cells within the spreadsheet
Font	Allows you to adjust the font size and style
Alignment	Sets the alignment of the data in the cells and allows text to wrap
Number	Changes the formatting of numeric data
Tables	Sorts and filters tables or access the table options
Cells	Inserts or deletes cells in the spreadsheet

A *function* performs some calculation, such as summing the values of cells. There are many different functions to choose from in Excel Online. Many would say that the functions are what make Excel so valuable. Adding functions is explored later in this chapter.

A *table* allows you to manipulate data with functionality, such as sorting the data in ascending or descending order or filtering the data based on specific criteria.

An Office *add-in* is like an app that extends the Excel environment. There is an online store that lists all of the Excel Online add-ins. You access the store by clicking the Office Add-Ins button in the ribbon of the Insert tab.

A *chart* is a visualization of data. You can insert many different types of charts into your spreadsheet. Some of the most common types include bar charts, column charts, line charts, and pie charts.

A *hyperlink* allows you to create clickable text that, when clicked, opens up a new website. For example, you can create a hyperlink with text that says "Learn More" — clicking it takes the viewer of the Excel Online workbook to a news article.

The *comment* field allows you to insert a comment into the spreadsheet. A comment is *metadata* because it isn't part of the actual data in the spreadsheet. The comment is data about the data in the spreadsheet, which is why it's called metadata. Comments are useful so that you can leave notes about the spreadsheet without actually modifying the spreadsheet data.

The Insert tab is shown in Figure 12-2.

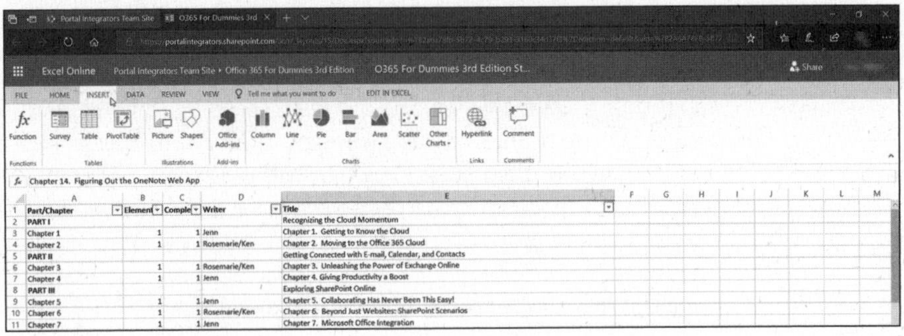

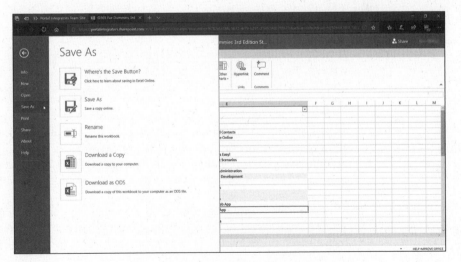

FIGURE 12-2:
The Insert tab on the Excel Online ribbon.

The Data tab includes data specific functionality, such as connections to data, calculations about data, and sorting of data. After the Data tab are the Review and View tabs. These tabs are designed to provide you various views into your spreadsheet. On the Review tab, you can view and edit comments. On the View tab you can switch between the Editing Mode and the Reading View. The Reading View gives you a preview of how the spreadsheet will look when printed. If you're just reviewing a spreadsheet and not editing it, the Reading View can be much less distracting, which will let you focus on the contents instead of the editing details. The Reading tab is also where you can turn on and off grid lines and headings.

In addition to the ribbon tabs, the interface also includes a File menu. The File menu allows you to perform functionality, such as saving the workbook with the same or a different name, opening the workbook in the traditional Excel application located on your computer, downloading a snapshot of the workbook or a copy of the workbook to the local computer. The File menu is shown in Figure 12-3.

FIGURE 12-3:
The File menu in the Excel Online interface.

Working with workbooks

Creating a new Excel Online workbook in a SharePoint document library app is easy. On the header of the document library app, click the New button and then select Excel Workbook, as shown in Figure 12-4. If you don't see the Excel type on the New drop-down menu then the library has been customized and you will need to add the appropriate Document content type and templates. If you create a brand-new Document Library app, you will see the standard Office types like Excel, Word, PowerPoint, in the drop-down menu.

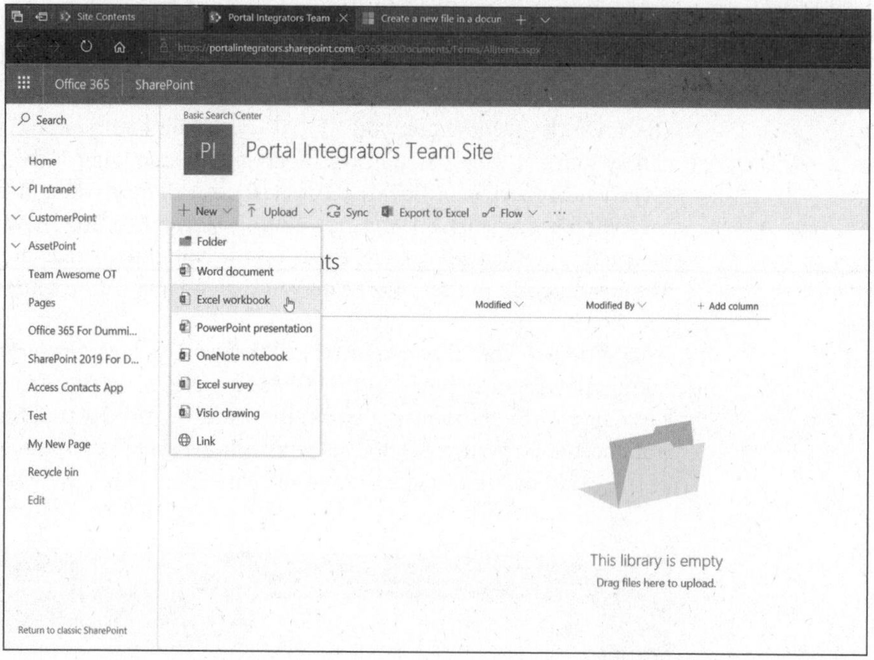

FIGURE 12-4:
Creating a new
Excel workbook
in SharePoint.

When you create a new workbook, SharePoint is smart enough to create the workbook and place you in Excel Online in Editing Mode. If you already have Microsoft Excel installed locally on your computer, you can switch to the Excel client by clicking the Edit in Excel button in the ribbon. This will open up the workbook in the full-featured application. If you don't have Excel installed locally, you can continue to work on the spreadsheet with your web browser and Excel Online.

After you have finished developing your spreadsheet, you can save it, which will automatically save it to the document library app in which you created it. You can then click on the workbook to view it and then edit it further by using either Excel Online or the local Excel application running on your computer.

Editing Mode and Reading View

There may be times when you do not need to edit a workbook. For example, you might want to just view the latest spreadsheet report or show a colleague a set of data. Excel Online contains two different modes. When you are editing the workbook you are using Editing Mode. When you want to read the workbook, you can simply click it in SharePoint to open it and view it. This is called Reading View, which looks very similar to a workbook that is printed on paper. A workbook in Reading View is shown in Figure 12-5.

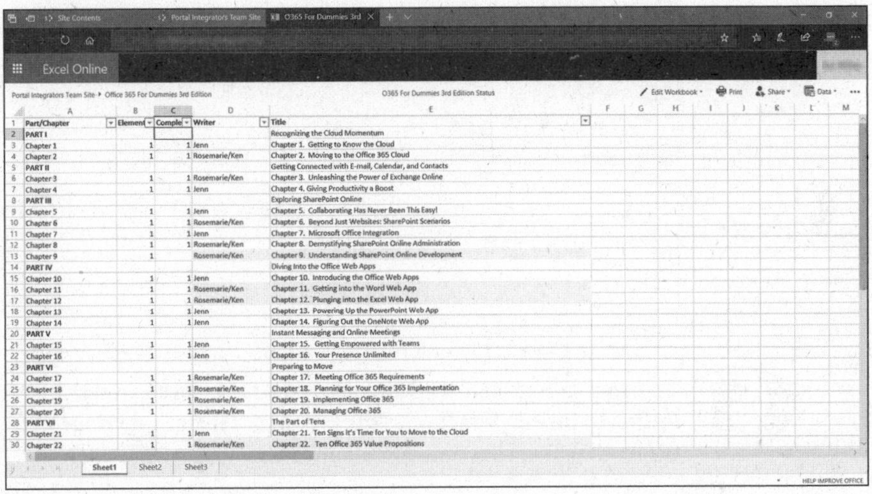

FIGURE 12-5:
An Excel workbook in Reading View in Excel Online.

Using Advanced Features

In addition to the basic features that you will use in Excel Online, there are also some advanced features. In particular, you can work with formulas and functions, manipulate data, and even coauthor spreadsheets in real time in the cloud.

Adding functions

One of the primary reasons for the popularity of Excel as a data analysis tool is the seemingly endless supply of functions. A *function* is a bit of logic that performs some calculation or manipulates data in a certain way. For example, you may want a cell to display the addition of two other cells. You can use a simple plus (+) sign to accomplish this addition. Going farther, however, you might want a cell to display the current time. You can use a function, such as Now ( ), which would display the current time. The power of this function lies in the fact that Excel updates the time each time it recalculates the spreadsheet.

To enter a function in a cell, enter the equal (=) sign followed by the function. For example, to enter the Now( ) function, you type **=Now()**, as shown in Figure 12-6.

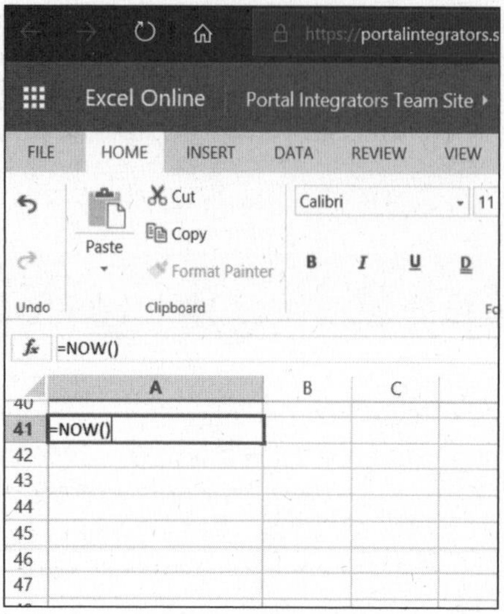

FIGURE 12-6:
Using the
Now( ) function
in Excel Online.

TIP

To insert a function you can also use the Insert tab and then click the Function button to insert a function. This provides a list of functions in case you don't know off hand which function you want to use.

After you finish entering the function and press Enter, you will see the current time rather than the =Now( ) function in the cell. This simple yet powerful functionality is what lets users create very valuable and complex spreadsheets with minimal training.

TIP

If you are following along, notice that as you begin to type the function, Excel Online automatically starts to show you all the functions and narrows in on the list of possible functions as you continue typing. This feature is useful when you cannot remember the exact name of the function but remember it starts with a specific letter.

An excellent list of the available Excel Online functions listed alphabetically or by category is available on the Microsoft Office website. To find the functions, open your browser and navigate to http://support.office.com. Then search for "excel functions" in the search tool. There are many different functions and spending some time looking through them can save you a lot of time in the future when you are crunching data.

Manipulating data

The ability to manipulate data is a staple of Excel and continues in Excel Online. You can manipulate data by using functions or by creating your own formulas. Excel includes functions for manipulating numeric data and also text data. You can dynamically link the contents of a cell to other cells. For example, you might have a column for sales and a column for costs and then a third column that denotes profit by subtracting the costs column from the sales column. Using formulas and mathematical functions, with nothing more than your web browser, you can quickly whip data into shape by using Excel Online.

Coauthoring workbooks in the cloud

One of the exciting features found in Excel Online is the ability to coauthor spreadsheets with others in real time and at the same time. For example, imagine that you are in Seattle and your colleague is in Manila. You can edit the same workbook in real time by using the browser. When your colleague enters text or numeric data, you see it appear on your screen. Coauthoring allows for a much more productive experience because you are both editing the same workbook, which maintains a single version of the truth.

With a spreadsheet open in Excel Online, you can see the other users who are currently editing the workbook in the lower-right hand corner of the screen. For example, if two people are editing, you will see text that says "2 People Editing." If you click on this text, you will see the two users who are currently editing the spreadsheet.

When one of the users makes change to the workbook, everyone who is currently viewing the workbook will see the changes take place in their view as well. This turns out to be an extremely useful feature because the new changes do not have to be emailed to other people in order for them to see the most recent version of the spreadsheet. The spreadsheet only exists in one place, so there is only one version of the truth for this spreadsheet.

Building Reports with Power BI

Power BI (*BI* is short for *Business Intelligence*) is a service-based product that lives in the Microsoft cloud. It is part of what Microsoft calls its "Power Platform," which also includes Microsoft Flow and PowerApps. Microsoft Flow is a next generation workflow tool. (If you have used SharePoint Designer to build workflows in the past, then you will want to take a look at Microsoft Flow to build your next generation workflows.) PowerApps is a product for building apps for mobile devices — think iPhone and Android. Power BI is the data component of this group of products. All of these products work closely with other Office 365 products and are included in Office 365 depending on the subscription you have.

Think of Power BI as a website that lets you connect hundreds of data sources to it so you can build reports and integrate those reports in other products (like Office 365).

TIP

Power BI for Office 365 and Power BI are two separate products. Power BI for Office 365 has gone away and Power BI is the next evolution of it. Power BI comes with your Office 365 E5 subscription or you can purchase licensing for it separately at `https://powerbi.microsoft.com`. It even starts with a free trial.

To access Power BI, go to your Office 365 tenant and select it from the app menu on the left side of your screen as shown in Figure 12-7.

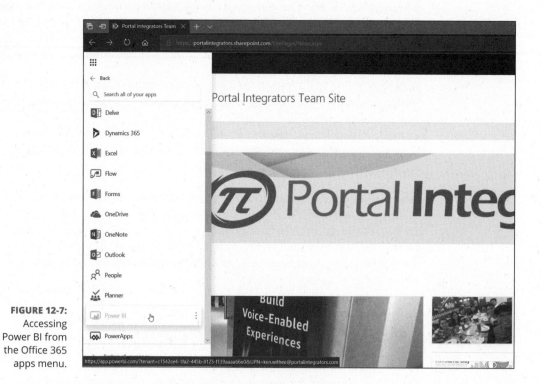

FIGURE 12-7:
Accessing Power BI from the Office 365 apps menu.

Pulling data into Power BI

When you first open Power BI you are prompted to add data. You can get data from a number of sources, but the easiest and quickest way to add data to Power BI is to pull data from the apps and services your organization already uses. For example, you can connect to everything from Google Analytics to GitHub to MailChimp and ZenDesk. And of course you can connect to other Office 365 apps as well!

To pull data into Power BI to analyze, click the Get button under Services from the initial landing page. You will then be presented with options for the services from which you can pull data, as shown in Figure 12-8.

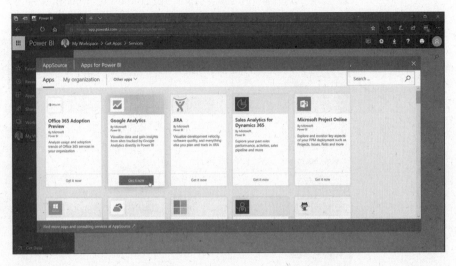

In this case, let's pull in some data from a local Excel file. Power BI uses a concept called *Workspaces* to keep things organized. By default, you have a workspace that is just for you. You can create organizational workspaces, but you will need something beyond the free plan to do so.

To pull Excel data into Power BI:

1. **Open your browser and navigate to the Power BI website.**

   You can find Power BI on the apps menu in Office 365 (refer back to Figure 12-7) or you can navigate to it directly at https://app.powerbi.com.

2. **On the welcome screen, click the Get button in the Files box under the Create New Content section as shown in Figure 12-9.**

   You can also get to this welcome screen by clicking on the Workspaces tab on the left and selecting your personal workspace.

3. **Choose the location of the Excel file you want to import.**

   If it is on your local computer, choose Local File. If it is in your OneDrive or SharePoint site, select those options. In this example we will use the Financial Sample data Microsoft provides. You can find this file at https://docs.microsoft.com/en-us/power-bi/sample-financial-download.

4. **Choose whether you want to connect Power BI to your Excel file or import the entire Excel file into Power BI.**

In our case we just want the data, so we will choose to Import Excel Data into Power BI. Once the process is complete, you will find the spreadsheet data in your Workspace under the Datasets tab as shown in Figure 12-10.

You are now ready to build reports and share them with others.

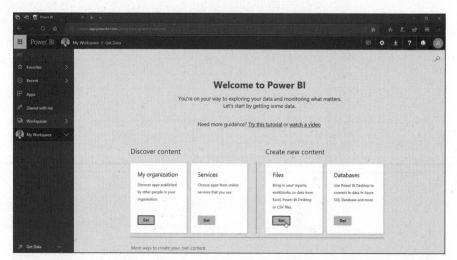

FIGURE 12-9:
Adding local data to Power BI.

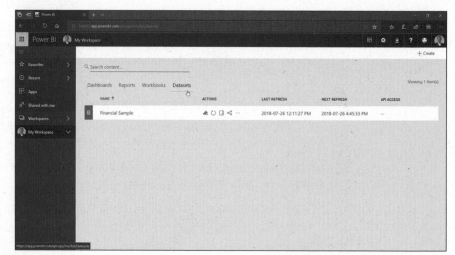

FIGURE 12-10:
An Excel files data imported into Power BI as a dataset.

Creating reports in Power BI

Once you have data connected to Power BI, you are ready to create a report. A report consists of elements such as bar charts and graphs. To begin creating a report:

1. **Click the Reports tab in your Workspace and then click the Create button in the upper-right corner.**

2. **Choose the dataset you just imported and click Create.**

In this case it is the Financial Sample from Microsoft. The report builder page appears and you can build your report by adding visuals such as charts, graphs, and filters. The report builder page can be overwhelming at first, but as you play around with it you will find it is rather like Excel.

In our case, we will add a simple line chart that shows sales per month.

3. **Click the line chart to add the control to the report and then select the data for Month Name and Sales as shown in Figure 12-11.**

4. **Click the Save button on the upper-right corner of the report builder and give the report a name.**

We named ours "Sales Report."

5. **Click on your Workspace again and select the Reports tab to see your shiny new report.**

You can view the report in your browser by clicking on it.

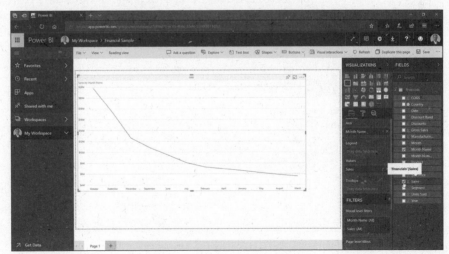

FIGURE 12-11:
A simple report showing sales by month.

Displaying reports in Office 365

You can always display your reports in a Workspace that others can navigate to through the Power BI interface. In our case, let's embed our report in a SharePoint site so that it becomes part of the intranet portal.

To add a Power BI report to a SharePoint page, follow these steps:

1. **Navigate to the SharePoint page where you want to add the report.**

    See Chapter 9 for more on how to add a SharePoint page.

2. **Click the plus icon and select Power BI as shown in Figure 12-12.**

3. **On the Power BI control that appears, click the Add Report button.**

4. **Paste in the URL of the report and press Enter.**

    This is the address from the web browser when you viewed the report earlier in the previous steps.

    The report is embeded in the page.

5. **Click the Publish button to publish your page to the SharePoint site.**

Adding reports has finally become straightforward, but this is just scratching the surface of what is possible. You can pull data from all types of services and build reports from them. You can then embed those reports in SharePoint or other apps so that people viewing them see real-time data.

When you are ready to take the next step, you can jump into PowerApps and Microsoft Flow for building mobile apps and creating workflows. These are beyond the scope of this book, but as you can see, the possibilities start to become limitless.

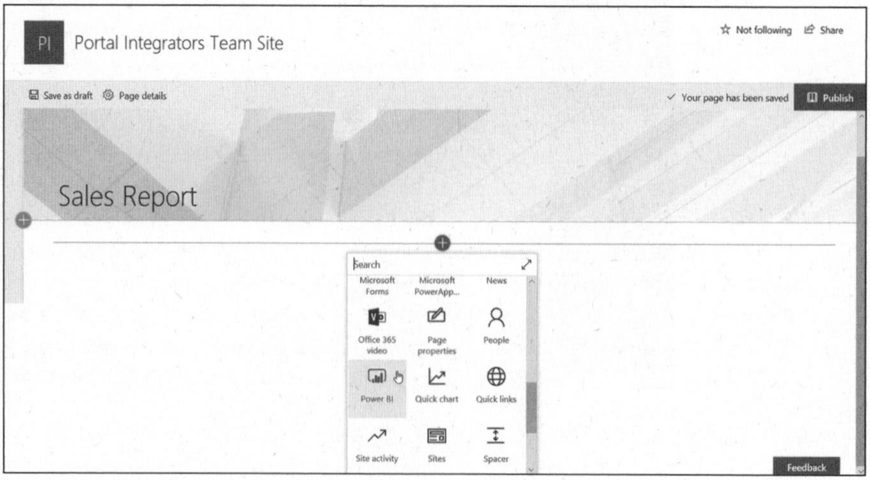

FIGURE 12-12:
Adding a Power BI report to a SharePoint page.

Chapter **13**

Presenting Like a Pro with PowerPoint Online

W hether you like or loathe Microsoft PowerPoint, there is no denying that it is here to stay. Since its launch 30 years ago, PowerPoint has grown to approximately 500 million users worldwide. And why not? With the recent updates and new feature sets, PowerPoint serves as a great visual aid for telling a story. Executives, businesspeople, educators, and students use PowerPoint to communicate their goals and persuade their audience to agree with their arguments. It has gotten so mainstream that you might have seen some comedies where a grade school kid uses a PowerPoint presentation to convince his parents where to go for summer vacation.

PowerPoint is one of the bundled applications in the Office ProPlus desktop application in Office 365. It is also available as a free online application (PowerPoint Online) as well as in the form of a mobile app (PowerPoint app). While the desktop application offers a robust set of features and functionalities, the "lightweight" online and app versions also offer the most used features needed to create beautiful, professional, and elegant presentations. We purposely put "lightweight" in quotes because PowerPoint Online comes loaded with advanced features for animating text and graphics, video editing, ink annotations, presence for real-time collaboration, morph effects, and even artificial intelligence–driven design ideas!

In this chapter, you explore the basics of PowerPoint Online. After you create a simple presentation, you step up to the next level by applying artificial intelligence to make your presentation pop.

Starting with Basic Tasks in PowerPoint Online

When you click on a PowerPoint file from SharePoint Online or OneDrive for Business, PowerPoint Online displays your presentation in Editing Mode by default. In this mode, the online document stays faithful to what you would see in the desktop and mobile app versions. If you toggle the switch to view the classic ribbon interface (see Figure 13-1), you'll see the most common menus and commands to power up a great looking presentation: Home, Insert, Design, Transitions, Animations, Review, and View.

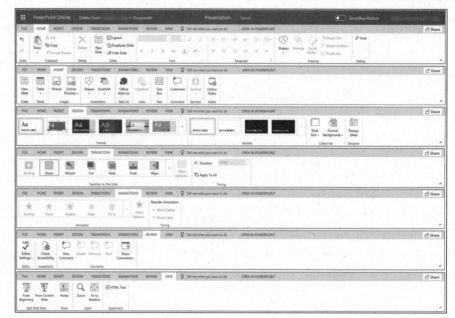

FIGURE 13-1:
The PowerPoint Online classic ribbon menu.

Similar to the rest of the Office Online apps, coauthoring a PowerPoint Online presentation is done by sharing the document with others. To share a presentation:

1. **Click Share from the menu bar.**

2. **From the Share windows that pops up, enter the name or email address whom you want to share the document with.**

3. **Add an option message.**

4. **Click the Send button.**

As you work on your document, your changes are automatically saved. As a result, you'll notice there is no Save button in PowerPoint Online. You can, however, save the current document as a new file by selecting File → Save a Copy.

When you finish your edits, you can close the document by navigating back to your document library (either in SharePoint Online or OneDrive for Business) from the hyperlinked breadcrumb next to "PowerPoint Online" on the Office 365 navigation bar.

Getting started with PowerPoint Online

With an Internet-connected device, you can create professional-looking presentations without installing any software. To get started, navigate to `https://office.com` and log in with your Office 365 credentials. From the landing page, click PowerPoint to launch the online application. The intuitive PowerPoint Online Welcome page (see Figure 13-2) displays several options to choose from. You can create a new blank presentation, start with a template, or continue working on a recent file.

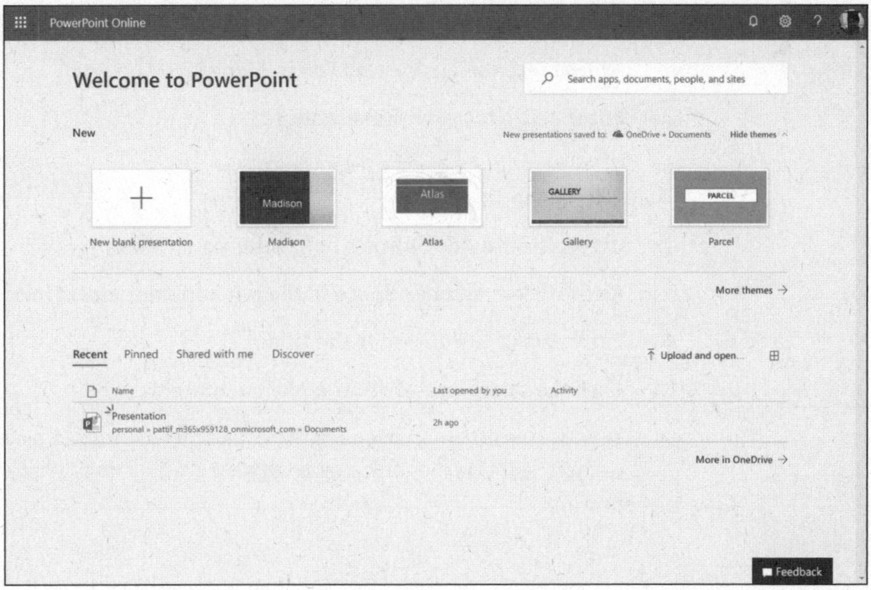

FIGURE 13-2:
The PowerPoint Online Welcome page.

Below the selection of themes in the Welcome page are several tabs:

>> The Recent tab displays a list of documents you were working on

>> The Pinned tab displays the documents you've pinned for easy access later. You can pin a document from the Recent tab by hovering over the file and clicking the *Add to pinned* icon (looks like a push pin)

>> The Shared With Me tab displays documents others have shared with you.

>> The Discover tab is powered by Office Delve, a service in Office 365 that uses machine-learning technology to serve up content that's relevant to you based on your interactions with documents and people in Office 365. It's important to note that what is displayed in the Discover tab varies from one user to another.

Creating a blank presentation

The fastest way to create a beautiful presentation to tell your story is to pick a theme from the Welcome page and customize it to fit your needs. If you click More Themes from the welcome page, you'll find a host of templates to choose from. If none of the templates suits your fancy, don't worry. You can start from a new blank presentation and let the built-in artificial intelligence and machine learning capabilities in Office 365 guide you through to a professional-looking presentation.

To create a new presentation:

1. **Click New blank presentation from the themes list.**

    A new presentation opens in Editing Mode in the browser.

2. **Enter a title for your presentation.**

    In this example, we enter "Fostering a Diverse and Inclusive Workplace" in the Click to Add Title box.

3. **In the Click to Add Subtitle box, enter your name.**

4. **Right-click in an open space in the left pan and select New Slide.**

5. **Enter** Facts and Figures **for the title.**

6. **Click the text box and enter a few bullet items.**

    Your work is automatically saved when using PowerPoint Online. Keep it open; we will use this presentation again a little bit later in this chapter.

Taking Your Presentation to the Next Level with AI

From Siri to Cortana to driverless cars, we are entering an era of artificial intelligence (AI) interwoven in our daily lives. And while this technology is still in its infancy today, there are already numerous ways AI can be applied in the workplace to drive productivity.

Microsoft understands the value of AI and has infused the technology in Office 365. In PowerPoint Online, AI enables users with minimal to no design skills to create professional-looking presentations. AI also helps foster a culture of inclusion in the workplace by incorporating features to make documents accessible to everyone.

Designing a beautiful presentation with a few clicks

Now that you have a simple presentation from the previous exercise, let's use the AI built into PowerPoint Designer to make it beautiful with a few clicks.

1. **From the ribbon, click the Design tab and then click the Design Ideas command, as shown in Figure 13-3.**

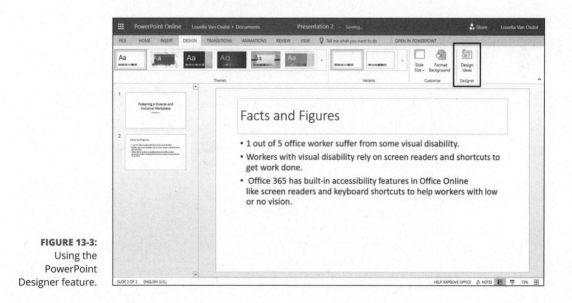

FIGURE 13-3:
Using the PowerPoint Designer feature.

2. **From the suggested Design Ideas in the right pane, select one that suits your needs.**

   The design will be applied to your slide, as shown in Figure 13-4).

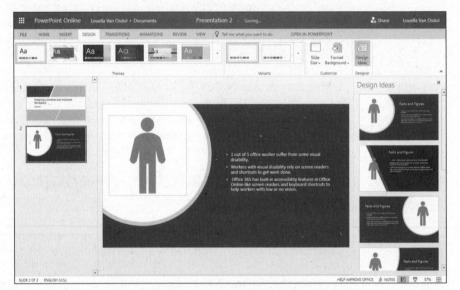

FIGURE 13-4:
Design idea
applied to a slide.

3. **Right-click in the left pane then select New Slide.**

4. **Enter a title for the slide and create a numbered list.**

5. **From the Design tab, click the Design Ideas command.**

   PowerPoint Designer will send the information to the AI service in the cloud, which will detect the type of content on the slide. AI will then give you a set of suggested layouts that include steps in the SmartArt feature of PowerPoint Online (see Figure 13-5).

6. **Select one of the suggested SmartArt design ideas to apply the design on the slide.**

With a few clicks, you now have a professional-looking presentation. Before artificial intelligence, this effort would have a required some design skills and some time adjusting colors, graphics, and fonts.

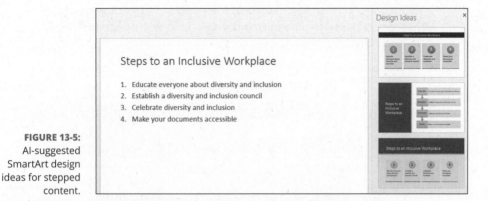

FIGURE 13-5:
AI-suggested
SmartArt design
ideas for stepped
content.

Adding an image and making your file accessible

They say a picture is worth a thousand words. This is especially true when you're telling a story using a PowerPoint presentation. Let's add an image to the presentation created in the previous section.

1. **Right-click in the left pane of the presentation and select New Slide.**

2. **From the ribbon, click the Insert tab.**

3. **Click Online Pictures and then select Picture from Bing.**

Notice that PowerPoint Online and the rest of the applications in Office Online now includes high-quality Creative Commons licensed pictures.

4. **In the search box, enter "workplace diversity" and press Enter on your keyboard.**

Several suggested images are presented, as shown in Figure 13-6. For this tutorial, we selected an image with a group of people and then clicked the Insert button.

Notice that when the image is inserted in the presentation, an Alt Text is automatically generated (see Figure 13-7). This new feature is powered by AI, so when you insert an image from either your hard drive or from a source online, the AI service automatically recognizes the image and adds a text description that can be read by screen readers to help those who have visual disabilities. Without any effort on your part, you just made your document accessible. Isn't that neat?

5. **Select a Design Idea from the right pane and then add a title to your slide.**

As you continue to edit your presentation, your work is automatically saved. When you're done, you can simply log out or navigate back to the PowerPoint Online Welcome page.

FIGURE 13-6:
Inserting a Bing
image.

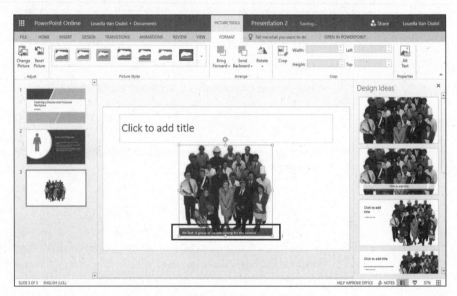

FIGURE 13-7:
Artificial
Intelligence
makes your
document
accessible.

Note that if you select several pictures and insert all of them into one slide, Designer will suggest various ways to create a photo collage. What's happening in the background is that the AI will recognize the content you are putting on your slide and will help you lay the content out in a more effective way.

Chapter **14**

Staying on Top of Things with OneNote Online

M icrosoft OneNote is a digital notebook perfect for gathering and storing all your notes, scribbles, email, digital handwriting, audio and video recordings, research materials, links, and other types of digital information. You can share your OneNote notebook so in a shared environment, other members of your team can see your notes, add to them, and even make changes or additions to collaborate.

OneNote Online is Microsoft OneNote's cloud version that comes bundled with Office Online in Office 365. Like Word, Excel, and PowerPoint, OneNote Online allows you to create, view, and edit notebooks from a web browser. It is deeply integrated with other services in Office 365 including OneDrive, SharePoint, Teams, Outlook, and more.

In this chapter, you find out about the basics of OneNote Online, get a walk-through of the user interface, and step through instructions for advanced features like restoring a previous version of a page. The topics covered in this chapter do not cover the entire breadth of features and functionalities available in the service, but with the knowledge you gain here, we think you will find using OneNote Online to be fairly intuitive.

Exploring Basic Functions

Microsoft OneNote is a beefed-up word processing program. You can enter text and graphics to gather, organize, search, and share literally anything you can think of, such as meeting notes, ideas, references, instructions, and brainstorms. Unlike word processors, however, OneNote lets you input free-form sketches, add unbound text, insert screen captures, and record audio and video directly into any section of the application's page. It's a great way for storing digital sticky notes so you can have a clutter-free desktop.

Introduction to Microsoft OneNote

Think back to a time when you had a spiral-bound notebook. It had sections, and the sections had pages. You organized your stuff by writing on a page that belonged to a particular section. OneNote is like that, but much better, handier, and smarter. If you put information on a page in OneNote, and decide later that the information belongs in a different section, you don't have to start from scratch and rewrite anything. A few mouse clicks do the trick.

Try adding audio and video in your spiral bound notebook. You can't. With OneNote, you can. Now, ask three people to take notes together with you on the same page at the same with your spiral-bound notebook. You can't. With OneNote, it's no problem. You can even see each other's edits in real time.

In OneNote, you also have sections and pages (see Figure 14-1). In Office 365, you can have more than one OneNote notebook.

A great example of how to use OneNote at work is for tracking projects. With a project notebook, you can have a single document to capture project information, such as background, meeting notes, team contacts, and task lists.

TIP

One of our favorite features in OneNote is the search capability. Using the search box, you can quickly find content based on keywords, jump to a page based on text within the pictures, and even find your handwritten notes!

Recently it has become apparent, however, that OneNote is a very valuable tool in the education sector in helping deliver best learning outcomes. In fact, Microsoft reported in January of 2018 that 15 million notebooks have been created since the beginning of the school year since the launch of OneNote Class Notebook, an app that helps teachers set up OneNote for their classes.

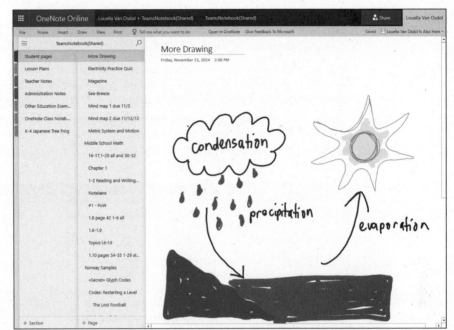

FIGURE 14-1:
Elements in
OneNote Online.

Using the OneNote Online interface

As a browser-based experience, OneNote Online is a pared-down version of the OneNote desktop version. Accessing more commands and features from the rich desktop application is as easy as clicking the Open in OneNote button on the top navigation bar or from the File tab.

The six tabs on the ribbon give you access to the most commonly used features in OneNote (see Figure 14-2). Note that there is no Save button — your notebook is automatically saved every time you make a change.

FIGURE 14-2:
The OneNote
Online ribbon
commands.

Although most of the commands and functionalities are common in the online and desktop versions, the user interface between the two is slightly different:

» Sections in the online app are displayed in the left navigation pane; on the desktop version, they're displayed as tabs in the middle pane (see Figure 14-3).

» Pages in the online app are displayed in the middle pane next to the sections; on the desktop, they're displayed in the right pane.

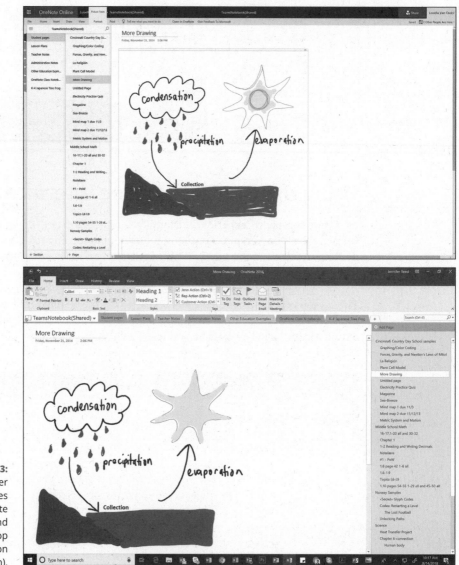

FIGURE 14-3:
The user interfaces for OneNote Online (top) and OneNote desktop application (bottom).

Working with notebooks

Creating a new notebook in OneNote Online can be done from a document library in SharePoint Online or OneDrive for Business. Click New, then select OneNote notebook, as shown in see Figure 14-4.

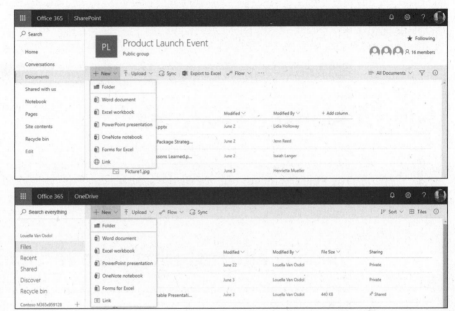

FIGURE 14-4:
Create a new OneNote notebook from SharePoint Online (top) or OneDrive for Business (bottom).

REMEMBER OneNote Online opens a notebook in Editing Mode by default. You can immediately make changes to your notebook; as you type, your changes are saved automatically. If another user opens the same notebook in either the online or the desktop application, simultaneous coauthoring automatically begins. Changes made by each of the authors are synchronized almost instantly.

To close the notebook, navigate away from the page by clicking the breadcrumb on the Office 365 navigation bar.

TIP A quick way to access all your notebooks in one spot is by navigating to `https://office.com` and logging in with your Office 365 credentials. On the Welcome page, click the OneNote icon to launch the OneNote page. One the landing page, you will see all the recent notebooks you've been working on in the Recent tab (see Figure 14-5). The My Notebooks tab displays all the notebooks you have created or have access to.

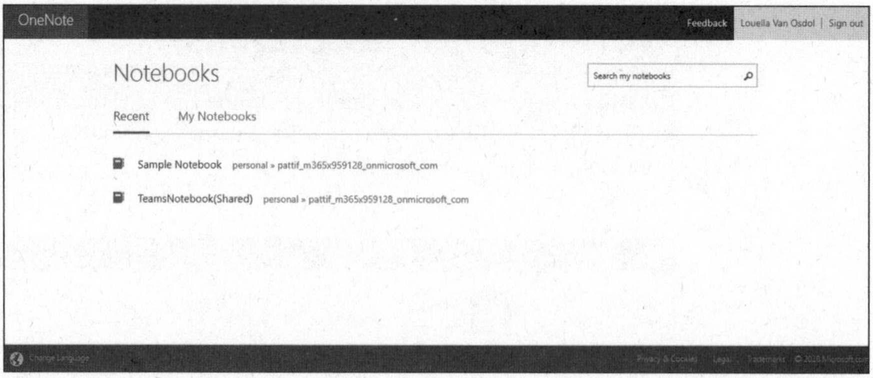

FIGURE 14-5: The OneNote Online landing page.

Using Advanced Features

Even if you've never used OneNote before, getting started with the app is easy. The intuitive ribbon commands are similar across all Office apps, so they don't require a lot of training. There are some handy features, however, that may not be apparent. Here's the story.

Viewing and restoring page versions

Sometimes coauthoring notebooks with other users can create undesirable results. For example, say a coworker overwrote your carefully worded instructions in your onboarding notebook for new employees. Not to worry. A page version is saved every time someone edits a shared notebook. OneNote Online allows you to view, restore, or delete previous versions of the page. To do this, follow these steps:

1. **Go to the View tab and click the Page Versions icon.**

   You see a list of all the page versions listed under the page name on the left pane with a date stamp and the author's name.

2. **Click any of the versions to view it.**

3. **After you determine the right version to restore, right-click the version to display the option to hide, restore, or delete it.**

   When you click on a previous version, you see a notification bar at the top of the page indicating that the version is read-only (see Figure 14-6).

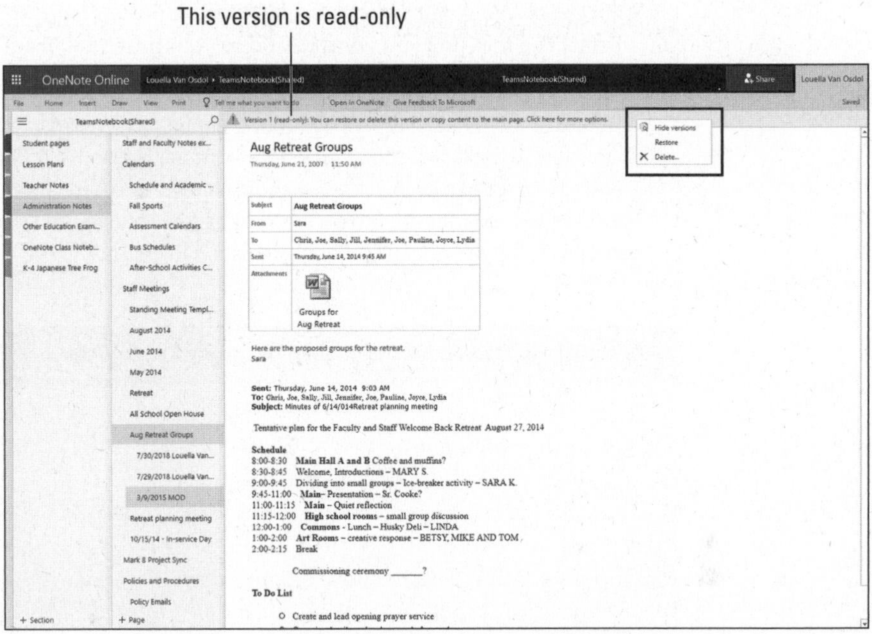

This version is read-only

FIGURE 14-6:
Viewing and
restoring
previous
versions.

Keeping up with your meetings

The Meetings feature in OneNote Online highlights the deep integration of the services in Office 365 resulting in greater productivity and enhancing collaboration. This feature allows you to pull details from your meeting in Outlook calendar, so you can add notes and keep a complete record of what transpired during the meeting. When you pull a meeting into OneNote, the date, location, agenda, topic, and attendees of the meeting are automatically captured in OneNote Online.

Follow these steps to add a meeting to OneNote:

1. **From the Home tab, click the Meeting Details command, as shown in Figure 14-7.**

You may be prompted to log in to your Office 365 account. If you do, select *work or school account.*

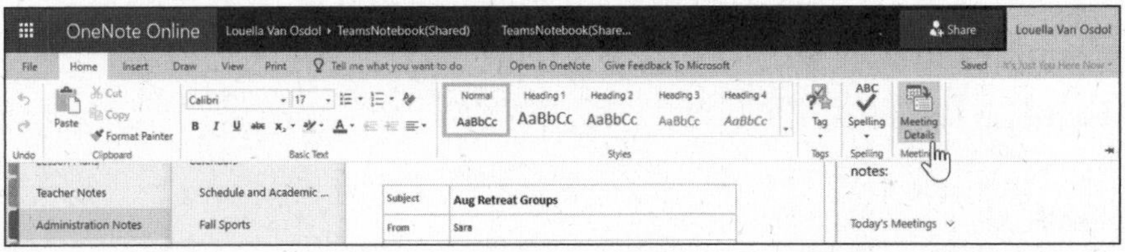

FIGURE 14-7:
Accessing the
Meetings feature
in OneNote
Online.

2. **Select the meeting you want to add to your notebook from the Add Meeting Details pane on the right, as shown in Figure 14-8.**

Details of the meeting in your Outlook calendar are copied to a new page in OneNote in the last section you worked on (see Figure 14-9). The details are added to the page as text. You can add, change, or delete anything on the page just like you can do with other OneNote pages. Changes you make on the page will not affect the original meeting invitation in Outlook.

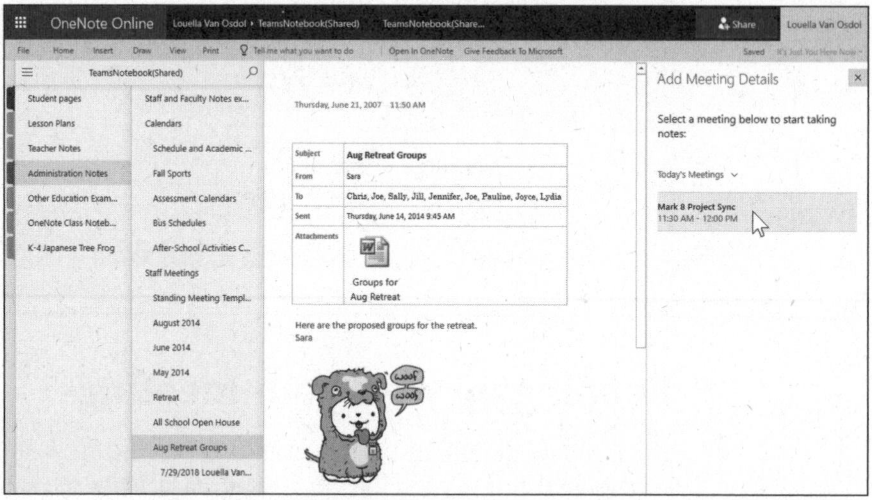

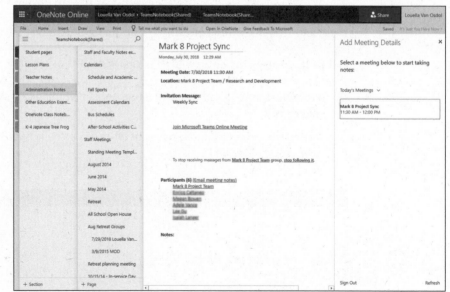

FIGURE 14-8: Selecting the meeting to track in OneNote Online.

FIGURE 14-9: Viewing the details of a meeting added to OneNote Online.

Making your notebook fun and social

Taking a cue from requests submitted by users in the education sector, Microsoft added the popular Stickers feature to OneNote Online. If you love memes and Office Drama stickers, you've got them in OneNote (see Figure 14-10).

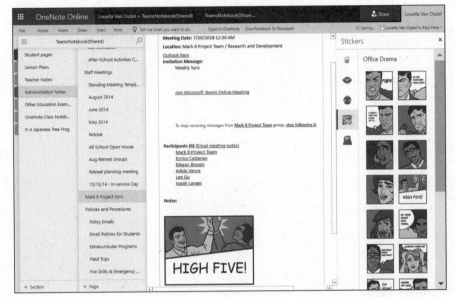

FIGURE 14-10:
Stickers fun in OneNote Online.

To add Stickers to your pages, go to the Insert tab and then click Stickers to display what's available in your Office 365 environment. Do note that the stickers may vary depending on your license. For example, the education licenses have stickers teachers would typically use. As of this writing, the stickers available in an Office 365 E3 license include Cats in Suits, Monkey, Octocorn, Office Drama, and Teamsquatch.

5

Using the Right Tool for the Right Purpose

Chapter **15**

Supercharging Your Team with Microsoft Teams

The way we run business today is very different from how it was done 20 years ago. The global availability of the Internet, the proliferation of mobile devices, and the explosion of cloud computing has forced the evolution of our workforce and our work styles.

To be successful as a business and as a workforce today requires more collaboration, real-time communication, and immediate access to critical information all the while ensuring online safety. Teamwork is no longer a buzzword for big corporations and sports teams — it is now the language for getting work done in small businesses and even solo entrepreneurs. Consequently, the amount of time a typical employee spends "collaborating" has greatly increased. From responding to email, attending meetings, answering phone calls, reporting on task status — employees are getting deluged with heightened expectations to collaborate better, effectively.

To make matters worse, teamwork no longer means working with team members in the same location, in the same time zone, for the same company. You may find that your team members live in various parts of the world and have vastly different working styles. When it is midnight for some members, it may be late morning for others. Getting everyone on the same page — even with the latest cloud technologies — can be challenging to say the least. The good news is that Office 365 now has a new feature designed to respond to the collaboration and communication needs of today's modern workplace: Microsoft Teams or *Teams* for short.

Teams is a digital hub for teamwork. It is a persistent chat-based workspace that incorporates all the bells and whistles of modern collaboration: chats, meetings, audio conferencing, web conferencing, file sharing, social media–like interactions, third-party tool integration, and even the addition of a robot to help you get work done!

In this chapter, you learn how to supercharge your team by providing your team members with the tools they need to work together effectively using the features of Teams as well as other Office 365 services integrated with the tool.

Benefitting from Teams

Microsoft Teams is available to users who have licenses with following Office 365 corporate subscriptions: E1, E3, E5, Business Premium, and Business Essentials. In the education plans, it is available in the A1, A1 Plus, A5, and A3 subscriptions. As of this writing, plans are in place to roll out Teams in the government cloud.

Teams can be accessed from the web browser, a desktop application, or a mobile app. The maximum number of users who can access the full functionality of Teams is based on the number of licensed users in the organization. Guest access is allowed, which means that users from other Office 365 tenants can be invited to an organization's Teams hub without the need for additional licenses.

With Teams, you can conduct one-on-one or group audio and video calls. You can share screens during web conferencing, schedule meetings, and record meetings. In addition, each user has up to 1TB of storage space.

From an administrator's standpoint, Teams offers tools for managing users and third-party applications. There are reports to glean usage and settings that can be configured with policies specific to the organization. For peace of mind, Microsoft offers a 99.9 percent financially-backed service-level agreement (SLA) uptime for Teams.

Touring the user interface

Tabs, bot, @mentions, and red bangs is just part of the new lingo you're going need to add to your vocabulary to use Teams. That's assuming you're already a savvy social media user who knows what emoji, Stickers, and Giphys are all about.

WHAT'S HAPPENING TO SKYPE FOR BUSINESS?

In the fall of 2017, Microsoft announced that Teams was going to replace Skype for Business as the tool for communication and collaboration. While support the non-cloud version of Skype for Business (in other words, on-premises or server version) will continue, Microsoft announced in July 2018 that Teams is "feature parity" with Skype for Business Online. What this means is that all the engineering work required to bring the features sets in Skype for Business Online to Teams is now complete and will soon be rolled out to Office 365 customers. Organizations who are still using Skype for Business will continue to be supported but any future enhancements will be focused on Teams.

To get us grounded, let's take a tour of the Teams user interface. When you run the desktop application, the first screen you see after you log in is shown in Figure 15-1.

>> **App bar:** Here you can navigate to the various sections in Teams. From the top, you'll see the following icons:

- *Activity* is where you'll find mentions, replies, and other notifications.

- *Chat* is where you'll see your recent one-on-one or group chats and your Contacts list.

- *Teams* displays all the Teams you are a member of.

- *Meetings* is synched with your Outlook calendar and displays all your upcoming meetings.

- *Files* aggregates all the files from all the Teams you are a member of. It is also where you access your personal OneDrive for Business storage.

- *[. . .]* includes links to apps that are tied to Teams and the channels within Teams.

- *Store* takes you to apps and services that can be integrated into Teams.

- *Feedback* takes you to the Microsoft Teams user voice page where you can leave feedback about the service.

>> **Teams section:** In Figure 15-1, the Teams icon is selected in the App bar, so the list of the teams we are members of are displayed here.

>> **Channel:** A dedicated section within a Team to organize conversations and tasks into specific topics or projects.

>> **Join or Create a Team button:** Clicking this button takes you through the process of creating or joining a team. This button is only visible when the Teams icon is selected in the App bar.

App bar

Channel

Teams section

New Chat button

Tabs

Command bar

Channel Conversations

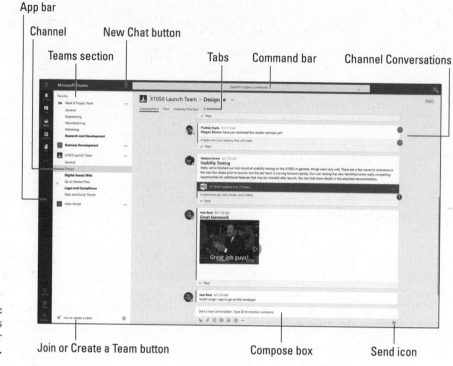

FIGURE 15-1:
The Teams
desktop user
interface.

Join or Create a Team button

Compose box

Send icon

>> **New Chat button:** Clicking this button selects the Chat icon in the App bar and allows you to start a new chat with an individual or a group.

>> **Command bar:** This bar at the top is used to query apps or perform a search in Teams.

>> **Tabs:** Switch between different Teams pages with these tabs. Conversations and Files are automatically included; the + sign tab allows you to add short-cuts to content in Teams.

>> **Channel Conversations:** This section displays all the conversations in the selected channel. Chats in Channel Conversations are persistent, so if you've been away, it's easy to scroll through to get caught up when you get back. Chats can include visual indicators such as the @mention, which indicates that the chat specifically mentions a user, or a red bang to indicate high importance. Take note that chats are open by design so everyone in the team has visibility to the conversation to help speed up the decision-making process when needed.

>> **Compose box:** This is where you can type a message to start a conversation. You can send a quick chat or expand the Compose box to access rich format-ting tools.

>> **Send icon:** When you're ready to share your chat, click the Send icon to post your chat to the team.

Getting help from the Command bar

Teams is intuitive to use, but you if you need quick assistance, the Command bar is your one-stop destination for help. You can do a search across conversations, users, files, and apps. For example, if you enter the word "launch" in the command bar, the left pane will display the search results grouped by Messages, People, and Files, as shown in Figure 15-2.

FIGURE 15-2:
Command bar
search results.

You can also run a command right from the Command bar by entering a slash (/). This action will display the available commands or shortcuts (see Figure 15-3). Select the appropriate command from the list to initiate the command.

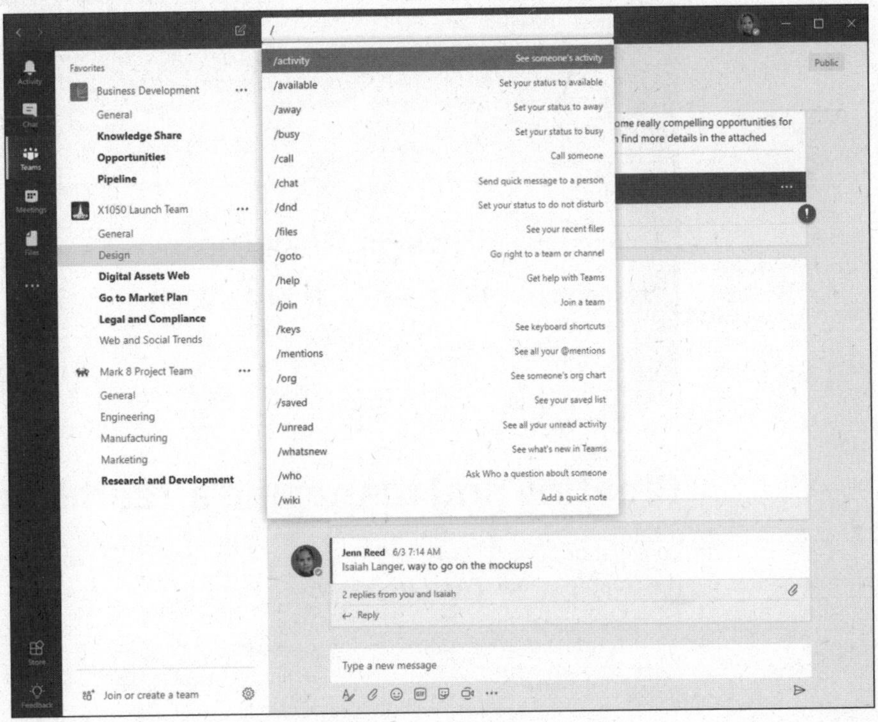

TIP

FIGURE 15-3:
Slash command
shortcuts.

Collaborating in the Teams Hub

We used to think that the "email tree" phenomenon was isolated to big enterprise environments, but it often rears its ugly head in small organizations, too. Imagine the following scenario: Someone sends an email to three people asking for their input on something. Two of the recipients immediately respond. Recipient #3 replies to Recipient #2 but forgets to reply to all. Now Recipient #2 has information the others don't have. Recipient #1 then forwards the email to yet another person (Recipient #4) who replies to all with his feedback, which doesn't account for what's already been discussed prior to him being involved. Pretty soon, everyone's mailbox explodes with replies to replies and replies to all that the sender finally throws her hands up in frustration because now the conversation has gotten out of hand and she's spending too much time getting everyone up to speed. On top of that, she now must consolidate all the feedback manually.

Teams makes email trees go away. In Teams, the sender can avoid the previous scenario by uploading the file into the Teams channel, @mention the people she needs feedback from, and start a conversation right from the document in Teams (see Figure 15-4). This way, everyone sees everyone's comments and edits. A new person joining the conversation can just scroll up to get up to speed and everyone is happy.

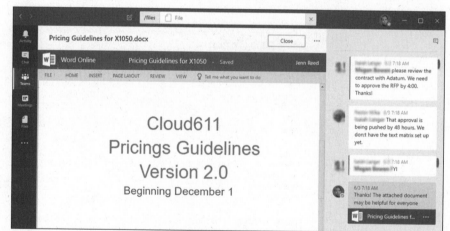

FIGURE 15-4: Starting a conversation about a document in Teams.

Creating and managing a Teams hub

To collaborate in Teams, you first need to be either a member of a Teams hub or the creator of one. To create a Team:

1. **Click Teams from the App bar.**

2. **Click the Join or Create a Team link that appears at the bottom of the App bar.**

3. **Click the Create a Team card.**

4. **Enter the name and description of the Team.**

5. **Choose the privacy settings for your Team (Private or Public).**

   A *Private* Team means only team owners can add members, while a *Public* Team means anyone in your organization can join the Team.

6. **Click Next.**

7. **Add members to your team by adding either a name, email address, a distribution list, or a mail-enabled security group in the Add box.**

   A Team can have a maximum of 2,500 members from either your organization or external users through secure guest access.

8. **Optionally, you can choose the role of the Team member (Owner or Member) by clicking the drop-down arrow next to Member.**

   If you forget to do this, you can update the membership type later.

9. **Click Close.**

   Team management features are accessed by clicking the ellipses next to your Team name in the App bar. The following management options are available:

   - *Manage Team* launches the Members tab where you can add or remove members, change the role of a member, or search for a member (see Figure 15-5).

   - *Add a channel* launches a dialog box where you can enter a channel name and the description for the channel.

   - *Add members* launches a dialog box where you can enter the names of people, distribution lists, or mail-enabled security groups to add to your Team.

   - *Leave the team* launches a validation window that asks you to confirm your intent to leave the Team.

   - *Edit team* launches a dialog box where you can change the Team name, the team description, and privacy settings.

   - *Get link to team* launches a dialog box where you can copy the URL for the Team to share with others.

   - *Delete the team* launches a validation window that asks you to confirm your intent to delete the Team.

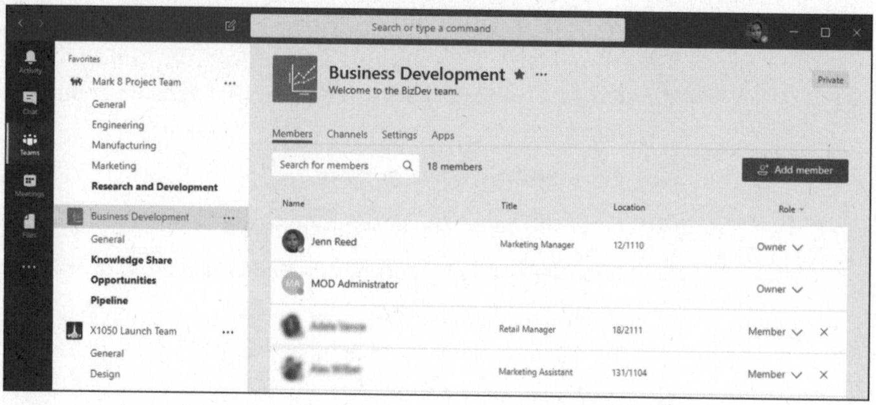

FIGURE 15-5:
Managing
members of
the Team.

Chatting in Teams

When a new member is added to a Team, that member automatically gets access to all previous conversations, files, and other types of information shared in the Team's hub. This is especially helpful for onboarding a new team member to a project. There is no need to think about what files to forward to get the new member up to speed, since he or she can self-serve from the content available in the hub or simply ask for help from others through chat.

To start a chat, click on the Compose Box and start typing your message while in either the Activity, Chat, or Teams sections. When you're done, click the Send icon to post your message. Depending on the culture of your team, you can spice up your chats with emojis, Giphys, or stickers. You'll find a variety of options when you click these icons below the Compose Box.

TIP

Sometimes conversations in a Team can become noisy when there are many members talking about different topics. To help with that, take advantage of the *threaded messages* feature in Teams by replying directly to a specific message so the reply in in context with the original message.

Sharing files in Teams

When you create a Teams hub, a SharePoint site is automatically created in the backend, which in turn, creates a document library for each channel. Files uploaded in a Teams channel show up the Files tab and are stored in a SharePoint document library. In fact, you can click the ellipses next to the file name and then choose to open the file from its location in SharePoint, as shown in Figure 15-6.

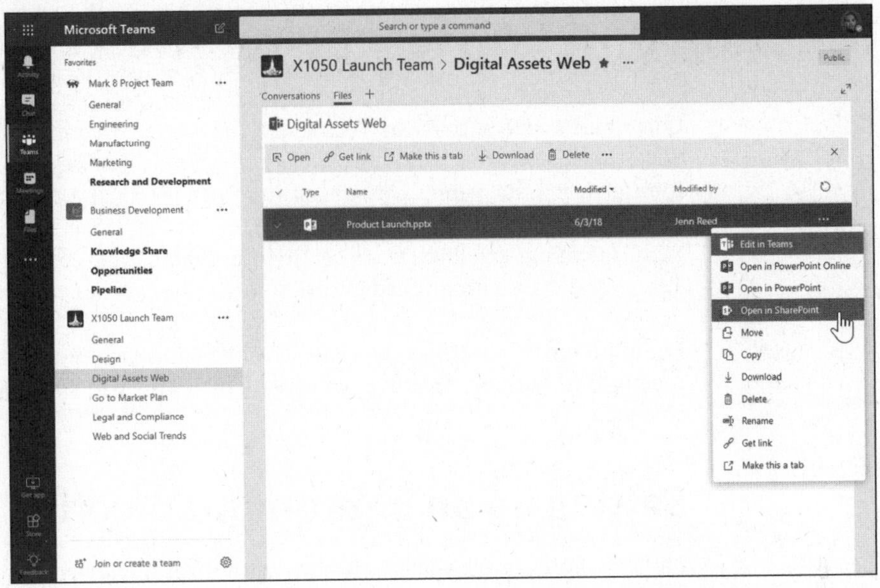

FIGURE 15-6:
Opening a file
in SharePoint
from Teams.

To share a file in Teams:

1. **Select Teams from the App bar.**

2. **Compose a message in the Compose box from a channel.**

3. **Click the Attach icon (it looks like a paperclip) below the Compose box and select the source for the attachment you want to share.**

4. **Select the file from the source and upload it.**

   The file you uploaded will now be embedded in the message.

5. **Click the Send icon (it looks like an airplane) to post your message.**

   The file you shared will also show up in the Files tab.

Alternatively, you can go directly to the Files tab and click the Upload button to upload a file. Once the file is uploaded, click the name of the file to open it. Once opened, you can start a conversation with others regarding the document.

Meeting and Conferencing the Teams Way

Chats and conversations in Teams are fun ways to communicate with others. Sometimes, however, it's more efficient to get on a quick call with team members to resolve an issue versus going back and forth in a chat. Fortunately, Teams provides a complete meeting solution with support for audio and video conferencing. Because calling capabilities are built into Teams, you don't need to log out of Teams and start a separate application to start an ad-hoc meeting.

For more formal meetings, you can schedule a meeting much like how you set up meetings in Outlook. Meetings you create in Teams will show up in your Outlook calendar.

Setting up an impromptu meeting

Let's say for example you are chatting with three members of your team about an issue. After a lengthy back and forth and waiting times in between, you decided it's much faster to just get on a call and talk about the issue. To start an impromptu meeting:

1. **Reply to the conversation thread and click the Video icon that appears at the bottom of the Compose box.**

2. **From the video window that pops up, enter a subject for your call.**

3. **Toggle the video camera on or off to choose between sharing your video or just audio.**

4. **Click Meet Now to start the conference.**

   A conference window will open with a pane on the right where you can invite others to join the meeting (Figure 15-7).

5. **When you're done with the meeting, click the red phone icon to end the call and leave the meeting.**

MAKE YOUR MEETINGS ENGAGING!

Drive engagement during meetings by using the rich meeting capabilities available in Teams. The Meeting Notes icon, which appears above the Invite someone or dial a number box allows team members to contribute to the meeting notes in real time. Next to the Meeting Notes icon is the Show Conversation icon, which allows team members to continue to chat and add attachments during the meeting to capture relevant information.

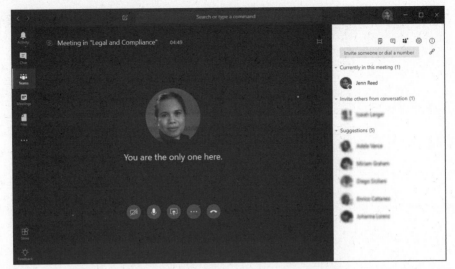

FIGURE 15-7:
Starting an
impromptu
meeting.

TIP

After the meeting, notes and conversations are posted to the channel so others who couldn't make it to the meeting can quickly catch up on what they've missed.

Scheduling a Teams meeting

You can set up a formal meeting ahead of time and give the invited participants enough notice about a meeting. Like Outlook, formal meeting requests in Teams include a Meeting Title (the equivalent of Subject in Outlook), Location, Start and End Date or Time, Details, and a list of participants. In Teams, you can select a channel to meet in. When a channel is selected, artifacts from the meeting are posted in the channel.

To schedule a meeting:

1. **Click Meetings from the Apps bar.**

2. **Click the Schedule a Meeting button that appears at the bottom of the left pane (see Figure 15-8).**

3. **From the New meeting window, enter the Title, Location, Start and End Date/Time, Details, Channel, and the names of the people you want to invite to the meeting.**

   Optionally, you can add a channel for the meeting.

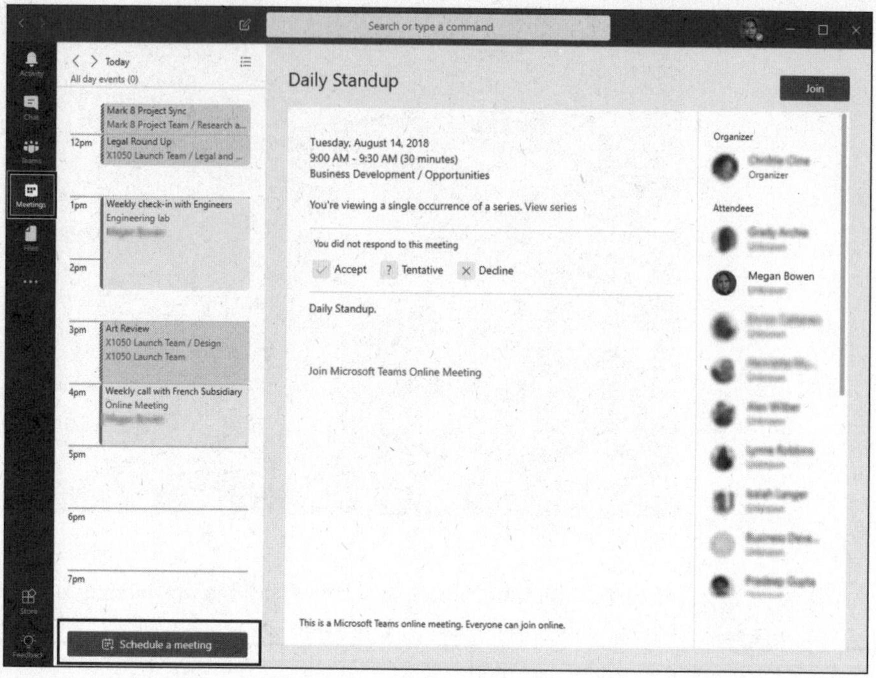

FIGURE 15-8:
Scheduling a
Teams meeting.

4. **If you want to check people's availability, click Schedule Assistant above the Details section to display your participants' availability based on their Outlook calendars.**

5. **Click the Schedule a Meeting button.**

    The meeting is now scheduled and will appear in the Meetings section in Teams as well as in your Outlook calendar.

Chapter **16**

Choosing the Right Collaboration Tool

The advantage of a software as a service (SaaS) solution like Office 365 is that you get new features and updates to functionalities on a regular basis. This means that your productivity tools are always current and in keeping with the current cloud-computing environment. The disadvantage with this model, however, is that you have so many choices that it can become confusing and frustrating.

Collaboration in Office 365 comes in many flavors: email, Teams, Yammer, Groups, Outlook, SharePoint, OneDrive, and so on. While these services integrate with each other, the sheer number of options for collaboration could pose a challenge if team members are not clear on what tool to use for what type of communication.

It's not unusual to find startup and retail companies with Gen Z employees: young, tech-savvy, and heavily reliant on social media for their communication needs. Their managers, on the other hand, may be the traditional corporate Baby Boomers who have been in the industry for some time and relies on email for communication and SharePoint for collaboration.

Try to visualize a typical interaction between a Baby Boomer and a Gen Z working on a project. Baby Boomer manager asks the Gen Z project manager to share the outcome of a meeting with another Gen Z developer who couldn't make it to the meeting. Gen Z project manager says, "sure." An hour went by and Baby Boomer manager keeps checking Outlook for an email to our team distribution list and sees nothing. Worried that Gen Z developer may not have the latest information before he starts coding, Baby Boomer manager finally asks the project manager if the meeting notes had gone out to the developer. Gen Z project manager says: "They sure did. I Snapped him."

If you're wondering, yes, this story did happen in real life. After Baby Boomer manager recovered from the initial shock, she later realized that "Snapped" meant the message was delivered via Snapchat, a popular app that obliterates everything you share with others within a few seconds.

The moral of this story is that for effective collaboration to happen, there has to be an agreement on the method and the tools to use. In Office 365, you could potentially end up in a situation where you're waiting for a response to a chat in Teams only to realize that your coworker was looking for your message in Yammer. Or you could be waiting for someone's input on a file shared from SharePoint only to realize your coworker was waiting for the file to come via email. And yes, these are true stories from a different time, different company.

In this chapter, we explore the various communication and collaboration options in Office 365 and gain enough understanding to determine which tool or tools can be used best for a particular purpose.

Exploring the New Era of Teamwork

The global availability of the Internet and the corresponding rise of interconnected devices have brought us to a new frontier where working together as a team no longer means being in the same building from 9 a.m. to 5 p.m. and working off of a single device tethered to a desk.

Today, teamwork can mean working closely on a project with someone whom you may not have met — and never will meet — in person. It can also mean working closely with people outside of your organization, sharing information with them while ensuring the data stays controlled by the organization. In many situations, teamwork means collaborating with a diverse workforce with different preferences and varying areas of expertise.

This is a new era of teamwork we live in and it's a challenge we'll address with collaboration solutions in Office 365.

Trends in today's modern workplace

In a Harvard Business Review article entitled "Collaborative Overload" (https://hbr.org/2016/01/collaborative-overload), managers and employees are reporting that the time they spend in collaborative activities has increased by 50 percent or more. That should be good news were it not for the fact that on average, employees spend 80 percent of their time in meetings, on the phone, and responding to email. This means that for most of us, we have very little time left to do focused, critical work of our own.

According to a study from Intuit (https://money.cnn.com/2017/05/24/news/economy/gig-economy-intuit/index.html), 40 percent of the workforce in 2020 will be freelancers and consultants. The Internet has given rise to a gig economy where the barrier for entry in the consulting gig is low. Sites like Upwork and Freelancer are filled with workers from all part of the globe offering a wide variety of services: designers, developers, writers, accountants, and so on.

Today's business casual is a far cry from what is was ten years ago. The modern office today is more fluid and flexible. If you're looking for proof on our assertions, check your Instagram freed for ads on yoga pants for the workplace.

Collaboration questions to ask yourself

To determine which tool in Office 365 should be used for collaboration, you need to first understand how you collaborate. Here are some considerations:

>> Who are the people you collaborate very closely with on a daily basis? These could be people within or outside your organization with whom you share information that's not ready for general consumption. You work with these people regularly to produce an output to serve the organization. This is your *inner circle*.

>> Who are the people you collaborate with generally and communicate with more openly? Again, these could be people within or outside your organization from whom you don't necessarily need to get input to produce a product, but may be important as a source of input for ideas and recommendations. These could also be customers you provide support for. This is your *outer circle*.

>> What toolsets do the people you collaborate with use? In our experience, we've found that developers tend to prefer team chats while executives prefer email.

The answers to the questions are a good starting point for determining which tool (or a combination of tools) to use in Office 365.

Tools for Teamwork in Office 365

The tools in Office 365 are built from a combination of more than 40 years of industry experience and insights from customers on business productivity. To illustrate the point, Microsoft Outlook is the undisputed leader in email and calendar; there are 190 million end users on SharePoint; and 85 percent of Fortune 500 companies use Yammer. Let's take a closer look at each of the key collaboration solutions in Office 365.

Office 365 Groups

Office 365 was designed to meet the needs of diverse teams whether the teams are in your inner or outer circles. From SharePoint to Outlook to Teams to Yammer, these collaboration solutions work well independently but are better when used together. What's important to understand, however, is that these collaboration solutions are built on a shared foundation of intelligent services: Office 365 Groups or simply *Groups.* Groups is the service that enables users to use a single identity across these different solutions. Powered by machine learning and artificial intelligence (AI), Groups maps the connection between the people and the content you interact with in Office 365. This AI then feeds into all the experiences in Office 365 to help you discover relevant content and save you time by making efficient connections.

When you create an Office 365 Group, resources are created to help you share and collaborate with the members of your group. The resources include a shared Outlook inbox, a shared calendar, and a shared document library for storing files.

You can create a Group in Outlook if your team is organized around email and calendar. If your group is designed for your outer circle, then you should create Groups in Yammer. For a chat-based collaboration, Groups can be created in Teams.

A Group can be public (visible to everyone in the organization) or private (visible to members only). To create a group in Outlook:

1. In Outlook, click New Group from the Home tab, as shown in Figure 16-1.

2. From the Create Group window, enter the required information: Name, Description, Classification, and Privacy.

3. Click Create.

4. Add members to the group and then click the Add button.

   You can skip this step and add members later by clicking Not Now.

   A new Office 365 Group will be created and you will be taken to the Group's default page.

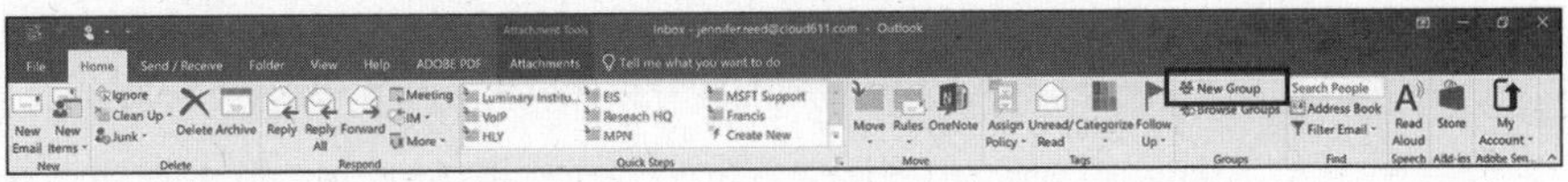

FIGURE 16-1:
Create a new
Office 365 Group
in Outlook.

Outlook/email

Outlook continues to the be undisputed leader for email and calendar. Today's version of Outlook, however, comes with a feature called Focused Inbox that automatically sorts your email, creates @mentions to catch someone's attention, and uses built-in AI.

When you create an Office 365 Group, the shared mailbox and calendar for the group are visible in Outlook. This makes it easy for members to see the latest conversations, files, and other content without leaving the Outlook interface.

Teams

We cover Teams in great detail in Chapter 15, but as a summary, Teams is a digital hub for teamwork. It is a chat-based environment designed to foster easy connections and conversations to help build relationships. Teams is also built on top of Office 365 Groups.

Yammer

Yammer is your social network for the enterprise. It is your Facebook at work — but better. It's what you use for open team discussions and can be used to crowd source ideas and collect knowledge. You can get a pulse for your organization via polls, praise, and follows. Actionable updates and alerts help drive engagement. When integrated with Office 365 Groups, Yammer gets the added benefit of Groups experiences such as a shared notebook, a SharePoint team site, a document library, and more.

SharePoint

SharePoint is still your go-to solution for content management and collaboration with the benefit of custom workflows and advanced permissions. You can design beautiful sites with zero coding skills, and it integrates seamlessly across all of the collaboration solutions in Office 365. See Part 3 for more on using SharePoint.

Picking your tool set

There is a good chance that you may end up using all the collaboration solutions we cover in this chapter. If that's the case, then you are in a good spot. Knowing all the toolsets gives you a competitive advantage. If you're still unsure, Figure 16-2 summarizes the use cases and the integration of the possible solutions.

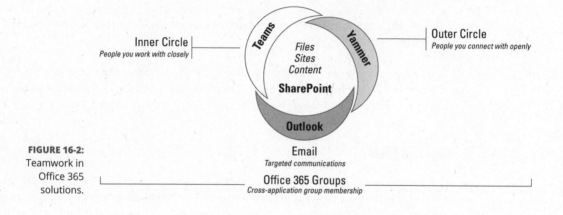

FIGURE 16-2: Teamwork in Office 365 solutions.

6

Preparing to Move

Chapter **17**

Meeting Office 365 Requirements

You can think of Office 365 under two broad umbrellas. The first covers consumers, and the second covers businesses, non-profits, schools, governments, and other large organizations.

If you're part of a large organization, then moving from a nice and cozy on-site data center (or storage closet) to the cloud is a big change. You won't be able to walk through the server room and see all the computers with the lights flashing, disks whizzing, and screens glowing. You have a connection to the Internet, and the software and data live *out there* somewhere. To access your software, you begin by using it. You won't need to go through a lengthy installation and deployment process. It can take some time to get used to, but the change can be well worth the effort.

For consumers, the same process holds true. You only need a device (such as a smart phone, tablet, laptop, or desktop computer) and a connection to the Internet, and your data lives *out there*. Of course, you can save your data on your local device, but you run the risk of losing your data if you lose your device or if your device crashes. Also, you can't pick up another device and keep working. You'll be stuck using the device where your data lives. In our new world of mobile phones and tablets, the cloud is a very convenient place to store your data.

This chapter covers some of the pros and cons of moving to the cloud for organizations and personal use. We also cover some of the specific requirements of the Microsoft Office 365 offering.

Office 365 constantly is being updated, upgraded, and developed. The user interface on any individual product can change frequently. The concepts are the same, but if you see something a little bit different than what is shown in a screenshot or described in this book, then Microsoft has made some changes.

Cloud Attraction

One of the biggest pain points in the corporate world is the interaction between business users and tech people. The business users couldn't care less about technology and just want the ability to do their job easier and more efficiently. The tech folks want to provide the best solution possible for the business users but get bogged down with time-intensive technical tasks. This concept is illustrated in Figure 17-1.

FIGURE 17-1:
When infrastructure is on premise, IT spends time keeping the lights blinking green, and the business users spend time pestering the IT team for help.

The cloud attempts to alleviate this tension by offloading the infrastructure to someone else — Microsoft in the case of Office 365. This frees up the tech people and lets them spend time optimizing the software for their business users instead of keeping the lights blinking green. Business users are happy because they get a better solution and IT people are happy because their valuable time isn't wasted searching the Internet for instructions on installing and configuring the latest software patch to fix a particular problem. This new paradigm is illustrated in Figure 17-2.

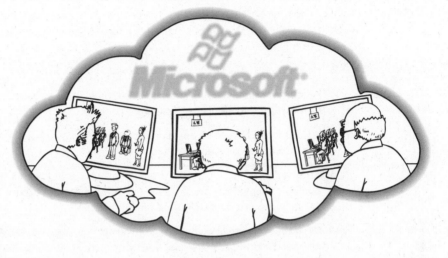

TIP

Offloading the work it takes to manage and maintain infrastructure allows you to repurpose resources to more valuable tasks, such as providing solutions that use software, including SharePoint to help sales.

On the consumer side, the world has moved on from the tagline *a computer on every desktop.* Today, everyone has a computer in a pocket, a tablet computer on the bedside, a laptop for work on weekends, a desktop at work, and maybe another phone or tablet or Mac for good measure. In short, if you're the average person, you have a lot of devices now. Oh, and you're always on the move. You don't sit still, and you expect to take your work with you.

To accommodate our active and mobile lives where we use lots of devices, Office 365 saves our data in the cloud. The apps you use to work on data can be installed on multiple devices, but the actual data itself is stored only once, up in the cloud. You can work, regardless of where you are or which device you happen to be using at the time.

Looking at the Pros and Cons of the Cloud

As with any decision in life, there are generally pros and cons; moving to the cloud is no exception. Depending on whom you're talking with, the cloud is either the greatest thing since the invention of the wheel or a devilish ploy by big companies to wrestle away control of your data. The truth is that many people find that the benefits of the cloud greatly outweigh the detriments.

Some of the benefits of moving to the Microsoft cloud include the following:

>> Outsourcing the hassle of installing, managing, patching, and upgrading extremely complex software systems.

>> Having predictable and known costs associated with adoption.

>> Keeping the lights blinking green and the software up-to-date and secure falls on Microsoft and is backed by service guarantee.

>> Reducing cost is not only an immediate monetary value but also has efficiency and resource reallocation benefits.

>> Backing up and securing your data. After all, Microsoft may not be perfect, but its teams of engineers are extremely specialized and are experts at hosting the software that their colleagues have developed.

>> Using the software over the Internet — simply sign up and you're ready to go. Without the cloud, a SharePoint deployment could take months.

>> Forgetting where your data is located and working on whatever device you happen to have in front of you.

Some of the cons that come along with adopting a cloud solution in general include the following:

>> Relying on network and bandwidth. If your Internet provider goes down, then you haven't any access to your enterprise software and data. Microsoft doesn't control how you access the Internet and, therefore, cannot account for any failures. If you live in a location with slow Internet or no cellular Internet coverage, then having your data on a local device might be your only option.

>> Having data controlled by someone else. Your data is hosted in Microsoft's data center. That can be both a benefit and a detriment. If you feel uncomfortable with your data *out there* somewhere, then you can either research the Microsoft data centers further or keep your data and applications locally in your own controlled data center or on your local device. In addition, when you sign up for enterprise licensing of Office 365, you also gain licensing rights to On Premise deployments. This capability makes it possible to store extremely sensitive data or user portals on site. For example, you may want your executive, accounting, and human resources portals on site but the rest of your SharePoint implementation in the cloud. Microsoft lets you mix and match this way to fit your comfort level, and terms it a *hybrid* approach to the cloud.

TIP

Microsoft has invested billions of dollars in its state-of-the-art data centers and has gone to great lengths to calm the concern of not knowing where your data is located. For a great video on the Microsoft data centers, check out the video on YouTube by the MSGFSTeam titled "Microsoft GFS Datacenter Tour." You can find this video by searching for "Microsoft GFS Datacenter Tour" on YouTube and then looking for the specific video. Want to take a peek into the future of data centers? Do a quick YouTube search for "Microsoft's underwater datacenter: Project Natick." Microsoft is researching putting computers underwater and using ocean tides for green power. Who would believe the "cloud" might actually be underwater in the future?

Overall Office 365 Requirements

Although by definition a cloud offering is available to anyone with an Internet connection, there are a few other requirements that must be observed should you choose to use Office 365. In particular, you must be located in a supported country and must have supported software and a high-speed Internet connection.

Geographic requirements

Microsoft has launched Office 365 in over 140 countries around the world, and allows a user license to be assigned to anyone in the world, with the exception of those who live in Cuba, Iran, Democratic People's Republic of Korea (North Korea), Sudan, and Syria.

Software requirements

To get the most out of Office 365, it is best to use Windows 10 with Office 2019 and the latest Edge web browser. Doing this gives you the fully integrated experience. Office 365 does, however, support just about every other popular device including Mac desktops and laptops, Android phones and tablets, and iPhones. In addition, Office Online apps can be run within a browser. If you use a device that doesn't have an app available, you can open your web browser and edit Office documents without even installing Office.

When you sign up for an Office 365 subscription, you pay for Office on a monthly basis. The upside is that Microsoft guarantees you the latest version of Office 365 products with automatic updates. Microsoft is quickly moving to a world where requirements won't really matter, because your devices will always have the latest and greatest software.

As with the rest of Office 365, Microsoft continually is updating requirements. The current version of Microsoft Office is 2019 and others will surely follow. To see whether your existing software will work with Office 365, jump over to your favorite search engine and type "Office 365 requirements." Look for a link to a page on either www.office.com or www.microsoft.com and check whether your existing software will work.

A key feature of Office 365 provides the ability for your business's Active Directory instance to sync with your Office 365 account. To achieve this integration, however, your Active Directory domain must be a single forest. What does this mean? It means you can use your existing username and password from work with Office 365. (After it's set up, of course.)

Device requirements

In the old days, you had to use Microsoft Windows if you wanted to use most Microsoft software. The old days are history. Today, Microsoft has Office 365 apps for Mac desktops and laptops, iPads, Android tablets, Android phones, iPhones, plus Windows devices. Microsoft is constantly adding and upgrading Office 365 apps, so be sure to stay up to date on available Office 365 apps for your particular device.

Internet access requirements

Because the Office 365 software lives in a Microsoft data center and is accessed over the Internet, having high-speed Internet access available on a regular basis is important. For some of the components of Office 365, such as the Outlook Web App (OWA), high-speed Internet access isn't required, but as a general rule, you want to make sure that you have a pleasant experience and that equals a high-speed Internet connection when dealing with the cloud.

In addition, because Office 365 is a subscription-based product, you will constantly get a stream of updates. This is great because your software is always up to date and you don't have to worry about requirements. However, if you have a slow Internet connection, updates might be more of a problem than a benefit.

Because Office 365 can be accessed from any computer anywhere in the world with an Internet connection, you have no control over the network connectivity. Most people understand that the speed of their Internet connection directly relates to the speed of a software update or download and will not blame the Office 365 service — that doesn't mean the experience is less painful on a slow Internet connection.

Identifying browser requirements

There are many points of contact with Office 365. Depending on which computer you're using to access the cloud services, you need to make sure that your web browser is supported.

Microsoft guarantees that Office 365 will work with the latest versions of Safari, Chrome, and Firefox, in addition to Microsoft's Edge browser. Although Office 365 will work with the older Microsoft browser, Internet Explorer, it's clear that Edge is the future and it's unclear how long Internet Explorer will be supported.

You can find the latest specifics around supported browsers by cracking open your favorite search engine and typing "Office 365 requirements." Look for a link to a page on either www.office.com or www.microsoft.com and check for specifics around older browsers.

TIP

When you find yourself using or borrowing a computer that doesn't meet the minimum requirements for the full-featured version of the Outlook Web App, you can use a light version of the Outlook Web App instead. The light version also loads much faster, and is useful if you're temporarily using a very slow Internet connection. Even though the light version isn't as feature rich as the full version, it accomplishes the basic tasks of email very well.

Microsoft Teams requirements

As we cover in Part 5, Microsoft Teams is a powerful communication platform that is used for online meetings and instant communication. Teams installs as a client on your device, and is then used in conjunction with other Office 365 apps (such as Microsoft Word, Excel, PowerPoint, and Outlook) or as its own communications app.

If you're familiar with communications tools such as Slack, Google Hangouts, or Skype, then you're already familiar with Teams. Teams is a next-generation communication tool that was built to integrate with Office 365. What does that mean? Think of interacting with SharePoint without ever leaving Teams and think of a shared chat that multiple people can communicate in (a team) on their own terms. All of a sudden Outlook can go back to being for email and not for chatting among teammates.

REMEMBER

Microsoft Teams is replacing Skype for Business, which itself used to be called Lync.

Real-time communications apps, like Teams, use a high amount of bandwidth for voice, video, and screen sharing. For these reasons, you should plan on a fairly fast Internet connection to ensure a good experience. We use Teams on our iPhones with regular 4G cellular service all the time and don't have any problems. If you're on a slow connection, your mileage may vary.

UNDERSTANDING BANDWIDTH

It definitely takes some time to get your mind wrapped around bandwidth. What exactly is *bandwidth* anyway? Trying to understand bandwidth can be like trying to understand warp speed in *Star Trek*. Nobody really understood what it was, but we knew that it made the Enterprise ship go very fast. Punch it, Scotty! Because bandwidth is such a fuzzy topic, it is best to use an analogy in order to understand it.

In a nutshell, bandwidth is the amount of data that can pass over a network at any given time. The best analogy for this is water moving through a hose or pipe. You can think of your data as a pool full of water. If you have a lot of data, such as those massive PDF documents, or 300-page PowerPoint presentations, then you have a lot of water. Say the amount of an Olympic-size swimming pool. If you have just a little, such as a two-page Notepad document, then you just have a small cereal bowl-size of water.

Now, to get that water from Point A to Point B, you need to pipe it through plumbing. If you have a massive 3-foot diameter pipe, then your water will move very quickly. If you have a garden hose, your water will move very slowly. This concept is illustrated in the following figure.

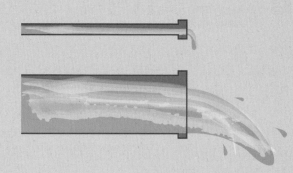

The rate at which you can move water through the plumbing and data through the network is called bandwidth. The 3-foot diameter pipe provides high bandwidth and the garden hose provides a small amount of bandwidth. The trick with bandwidth is to remember that the least common denominator always wins. For example, in the water analogy, you might be moving that swimming pool full of water across town, but if the pump siphoning the water out of the pool is only a small hose that attaches to a 3-foot diameter pipe, then guess what — the water will only move as fast as the small hose can move it. The 3-foot pipe will just trickle the water along as it comes out of the small hose. On the other hand, if you have a 3-foot pump to go along with that 3-foot hose, then the water will fly through the pipe at a rapid rate.

It is the same with data over the network. If you have a very slow wireless router in your house, then it doesn't matter how fast the Internet speed is coming in and out of your house.

Chapter **18**

Planning for Your Office 365 Implementation

R eading this book is the first step of preparing for your Office 365 journey. Throughout the book, we explain how Office 365 can benefit your organization. Now that you're up to speed on the product, you can plan how to get started with Office 365.

Microsoft divides Office 365 into business plans and consumer plans:

» If you're a business or organization, you need to put some thought into Office 365 and think of it as an implementation.

» If you're just looking for Office 365 for your family or personal needs, the process is much easier.

In this chapter, you find information to get started with Office 365. Because setting up a business or organization requires much more work than a personal subscription, most of the chapter is geared around planning an Office 365 implementation for your business or organization. You walk through preparing and then planning for deploying Office 365, including such tasks as choosing a subscription plan, cataloging your internal resources, and finding a partner.

Choosing an Office 365 Plan

Office 365 has blossomed over the years. It isn't a one-size-fits-all product. Microsoft recognized this and broke up the product into specific plans to fit the needs of individuals, families, small business, and all the way up to multinational enterprises and educators.

When you're first getting your head wrapped around Office 365, you can think of it as two different products under the same marketing umbrella:

>> If you're a consumer, and you would initially think of buying software at a store like Best Buy, then you're likely looking for one of the Home plans.

>> If you're looking for Office 365 for your business or organization, then you're likely looking for one of the Business plans.

When you land on the Office 365 page, this choice is neatly set in front of you with a For Home button and a For Business button, as shown in Figure 18-1.

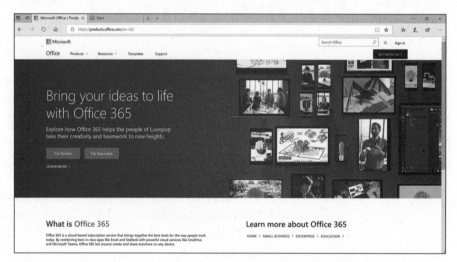

Bring your ideas to life with Office 365

FIGURE 18-1:
The Office 365 landing page.

TIP

You can find the Office 365 plans for educators by clicking the Products drop-down menu at the top of the Office home page (`https://products.office.com`). There are plans for schools, teachers, and students.

If you're looking for a personal plan and you click the For Home button, the process of purchasing and installing Office 365 is relatively straightforward. Microsoft is constantly changing the terminology so we're hesitant to name the plans. As of this writing, they're offering two plans with the following primary differences:

>> With a Home plan, you have five users that can each install Office products on five devices.

>> With a Personal plan, you have only one user that can install Office products on five devices.

Both of these plans are on a subscription basis and you're constantly guaranteed to have the most up-to-date software. When a new version of the products comes out you instantly get to install and use it. If you don't like the subscription model, there's a one-time purchase option, but you don't get the updated products as they come out.

The For Home plans are shown in Figure 18-2.

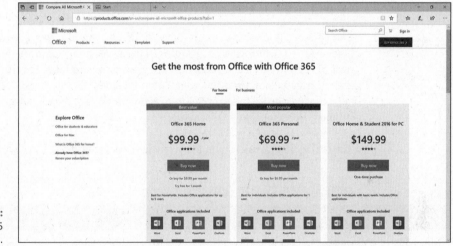

FIGURE 18-2:
The Office 365
For Home plans.

When you're looking for a business or organization plan, the options require much more thought and planning. Again, Microsoft is constantly jiggering the plans to try to segment the offerings in the smartest way for each type of organization. As of 2018, the business plans range from $5 per user per month (the Business Essentials plan) to $35 per user per month (the Enterprise E5 plan). These can be charged annually.

TIP

If you also use Windows 10, you can save money by bundling Office 365 with other Microsoft products. Microsoft labels these bundled packages as Microsoft 365. Check it out with a quick Google search.

The For Business plans are shown in Figure 18-3.

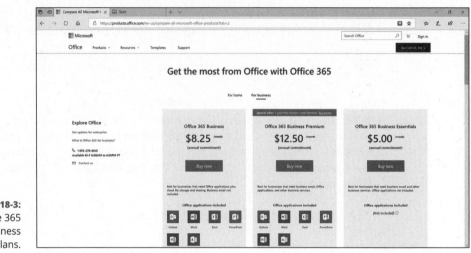

FIGURE 18-3:
The Office 365
For Business
plans.

The Office 365 business plans have changed over the years and Microsoft has landed on a fairly intuitive grouping. There are small- and medium-sized business plans and there are plans that are geared toward large enterprises. One of the main things to look for is whether a plan includes the Microsoft Office productivity apps that can be installed on your local device (Word, Excel, PowerPoint, OneNote, Outlook, Publisher, and OneDrive).

The Office 365 business plans are outlined in Table 18-1.

TABLE 18-1 ## Office 365 For Business Plans

Plan	Description	Price / User / Mo.*
Office 365 Business Essentials	Online versions of Office. Comes with 50GB mailbox (Exchange), 1TB file storage, and video conferencing. The max number of users is 300.	$5.00
Office 365 Business	Doesn't include email (Exchange) but includes the full versions of Microsoft Office that you can install on your local device. The max number of users is 300.	$8.25
Office 365 Business Premium	Includes both email (Exchange) and the full versions of Microsoft Office. The max number of users is 300.	$12.50
Office 365 Pro Plus	Includes the full version of Microsoft Office and adds Microsoft Access. The Office apps can be installed on up to 5 devices per user. Think of this offering as just Microsoft Office, because it doesn't include email or conferencing. Includes 1TB of online file storage. The max number of users is unlimited.	$12.00

Plan	Description	Price / User / Mo.*
Office 365 Enterprise E1	The entry level enterprise plan that includes features such as business class email, calendar, and contacts (Exchange) with 50GB of space, online meetings (Teams and Skype for Business), and a content management system and intranet (SharePoint). Also includes 1TB of file storage. This initial offering doesn't include the full versions of Microsoft Office however.	$8.00
Office 365 Enterprise E3	Similar to the E1 plan but this plan includes the full versions of Microsoft Office that can be installed on your local device and an unlimited email box.	$20.00
Office 365 Enterprise E5	Similar to the E3 plan but this plan adds some additional security and analytics features and the biggest addition is Public Switched Telephone Network (PSTN) calling and Cloud PBX for cloud-based call management.	$35.00

Prices as of this writing. They have been known to change. You can also add various options, which affects the price, too.

WARNING

Rather than try to get into the specifics of each plan in this book, we recommend you carefully research each plan option based on what is available at the time you're looking to implement Office 365 for your business or organization. Microsoft is constantly adding new features and shifting things around. Be sure to check the specific plans before basing your decision on Table 18-1.

In addition to the plans outlined for business there are also Office 365 offerings for educational institutions, government institutions, and non-profit organizations. Some of these Office 365 plans are even *free* for qualifying institutions and organizations.

Laying the Groundwork

You should keep in mind that the size and complexity of your organization, as well as the Office 365 plan you choose, will directly affect your implementation. If you're a one-person consultant or small business using a business plan, then your implementation will be very straightforward. If your organization contains thousands of employees with offices around the world, your implementation will be much more in depth and will require extensive planning.

Regardless of your organization's size and the plan you choose, your implementation follows three primary steps — plan, prepare, and migrate, as outlined in this section and illustrated in Figure 18-4. The migration phase is covered in Chapter 19.

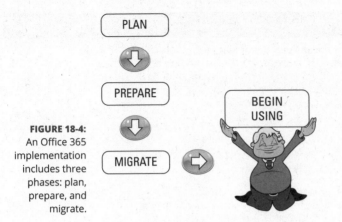

FIGURE 18-4:
An Office 365
implementation
includes three
phases: plan,
prepare, and
migrate.

The best implementation processes follow an iterative cycle in that you continually plan, prepare, and migrate. You need to start somewhere, however, and you always start with a plan. When you get your plan in order, you then move onto preparing to migrate. As you're preparing, you realize some additional things that you didn't include in your plan. As a result, you continually update your plan. Perhaps a better representation of the process is shown in Figure 18-5, even though this might not sit well with organizations that have extensive gating requirements for every project undertaken.

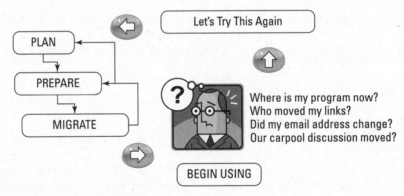

FIGURE 18-5:
The Office 365
implementation
phases in an
iterative diagram.

Planning phase

The planning phase of an Office 365 implementation greatly depends on many factors, including whether you're using one of the business plans or enterprise plans. Regardless of which plan you're using, you want to get a handle on the resources and roles that you will need for the implementation as well as such tasks as:

>> Meeting synchronization

>> Issue tracking

>> Strategies around email, such as mailbox size and emailed integration with SharePoint

>> Account provisioning and licensing

>> Internet bandwidth consideration

>> Software and hardware inventories

>> Administrator and end-user training

>> Communication planning

Getting a handle on resources you will need

The in-house, human-based resources you need for an Office 365 business or enterprise implementation are outlined in Table 18-2. Note that if you're implementing one of the business plans, then a single person or hired contractor might play all these roles with a negligible amount of work required for each role. If you're a large organization implementing the enterprise plan, then you may contract out these roles to a partner or have a team of in-house staff assigned to specific roles.

TABLE 18-2   **Human-Based Resources**

Resource	Description
Project Manager	The Project Manager is responsible for making sure that each resource is on the same page as the Office 365 implementation proceeds.
Office 365 Administrator	Responsibilities include managing the Office 365 interface with such technical tasks as domains, security groups, users, and licenses.
SharePoint Administrator	Responsible for administering the SharePoint Online platform, including creating sites, installing solutions, and activating features.
Exchange Administrator	Responsible for maintaining the settings for user mailboxes and email, including the settings required for connectivity with Outlook.
Communications Administrator	The Communications Administrator is responsible for all configuration with the Teams and Skype for Business program and helping users move from using Skype for Business to using Teams.
Network Administrator	Responsible for maintaining the Internet connection for the organization. Because Office 365 is in the cloud and accessed over the Internet, the connection is critical.
Trainer	Takes on the role of learning how the software works and then teaching others the best practices as they relate to your organization.

The enterprise plan includes a number of additional roles that can be used to create a very granular distribution of duties. Chapter 8 outlines the administrative roles in further detail. In addition, SharePoint administrators can control the SharePoint Online environment for the site as well as at the individual lists and library levels. For example, you may have an accounting department that has very sensitive data. The SharePoint administrator for that accounting site can add or remove user rights for different parts of the site. All this SharePoint administration is done within SharePoint and isn't part of the Office 365 administrative interface.

Synchronization meetings

With any Enterprise software adoption, maintaining open lines of communication is important. If everyone is on the same page, then it is easier to navigate issues as they arise rather than at the end of the project. Pulling a page from Scrum methodology, it is a good idea to have daily stand-ups where the teams stand in a circle and quickly announce what they're working on and which obstacles are blocking them from continuing with their tasks.

The software development methodology known as Scrum is a process for completing complicated software development cycles. The term comes from the Australian sport of rugby where the entire team moves down the field as one unit rather than as individual players. If you aren't familiar with Scrum, then we highly recommend you check out the Scrum Alliance website at www.scrumalliance.org and Jeff Sutherland's site, the father and co-founder of Scrum, at www.scruminc.com.

Issue tracking

Tracking issues as they arise is critical, and you need a process in place. SharePoint is ideal at issue tracking, so you may want to use a pilot implementation of Office 365 that includes SharePoint Online to track your issues for your Office 365 implementation. Isn't that tactic a mind bender?

Email strategies

Email plays a very important role in nearly every organization. When moving to Office 365, you will be moving your email system. Email can be widely spread and integrated into many different nooks and crannies of your infrastructure. You want to make sure that you do a thorough audit to find out which systems and applications are using email, and which you want to move to Office 365. In addition, you need to be aware of the size of users' email boxes and the amount of email that will be migrated to Exchange Online (which is the email portion of Office 365). In particular, take note of how you're using SharePoint and how

SharePoint is using email. If you're new to SharePoint, then you're in for a treat because you gain an understanding of how the product integrates with email. For more on SharePoint, check out Part 3.

Account provisioning and licensing

The good news is that Office 365 is very flexible in licensing, user provisioning, and administration. With that said, however, you want to plan out the number of users and the licensing requirements you need for your organization. You may choose to adopt Office 365 all at once or as a phased approach by moving a single group over to Office 365 as a pilot. In either case, you need to understand your licensing requirements so that you can plan resources and costs accordingly. The plus side of a subscription-based model is that you can add licenses as you need them or remove them when you don't. Before subscription-based pricing, you had to spend a lot of money for licensing whether you used it or not. Those days are gone.

Internet bandwidth consideration

Because Office 365 lives in the cloud and is accessed over the Internet, your connection must be top-notch. Your network administrator or IT consultant can use a number of different network bandwidth testing tools so that you have firsthand reports on how much bandwidth you're currently using in your organization and how moving to the cloud will affect the users.

Software and hardware inventories

Undertaking an audit of your current software and hardware resources is important. Fortunately, Microsoft has a tool available for just such a task. It is called the Microsoft Assessment and Planning (MAP) toolkit, it is updated frequently, and it can be downloaded by searching for it in the Microsoft Download Center located at www.microsoft.com/download.

TIP

After you have a handle on the software and hardware in your organization, you need to reference the requirements for Office 365 to determine if you need to make changes. Refer to Chapter 17 for Office 365 software and hardware requirements.

Administrator and end-user training

As with any new system, training is a required element. Office 365 has been designed with intuitive user interfaces for both administration and end users, but without a training plan, you're rolling the dice. A popular and successful approach to training when it comes to intuitive designs is called "train the trainer." The idea being that you invest in formal training for a power user and then that user trains the rest of the company. This strategy is very effective even for large organizations because the training scales exponentially. As people are trained, they then train other people.

Communication planning

The best communication is clear, transparent, and all-inclusive. Everyone in the organization has ideas and an opinion. By garnering as many thoughts and as much brainpower (crowd sourcing) as possible, the organization will accomplish two clear objectives.

The first is that you will shed light on problems, issues, and risks early and often and can adjust early in the process rather than down the road when it is too late. The second big win an organization achieves involves ownership and engagement. In order for a project to be successful, you need for the users to be engaged and take ownership of the solution.

Microsoft has taken great effort to make the adoption of Office 365 as painless as possible but, in the end, it will still be a change. It can be argued that it is a change for the better in moving to Office 365 and taking advantage of all the cloud has to offer, but any change at all involves discomfort, apprehension, and stress. Having a good communication plan keeps everyone in the loop and feeling a part of the process. When you effect change at a grassroots level and let the wave of adoption swell up from great user experiences, then the organization as a whole wins.

Migration needs

One of the biggest aspects of moving to Office 365 will be migration of content, including mailboxes and other content. The ideal situation is that your organization has been living under a rock and has no document management system in place or custom portal functionality. In this scenario, you simply start using SharePoint in all of its glory and bathe in the efficiency and productivity gains of a modern portal environment.

The chances are, however, that you already have a number of systems in place. These systems might be SharePoint, or they might be a custom developed solution. In any case, you need to plan to migrate the content and functionality of these systems into Office 365. The good news is that Office 365 is definitely a product worth spending the time, effort, and resources in adopting.

Preparing phase

After you have a good handle on what you plan to do, you need to prepare to do it. Keep in mind that because every organization is different, you should only use these steps as a guide. If you're a small organization, then moving to Office 365 might be as easy as a walk in the park. If you're part of a thousand-person multinational organization with offices around the world, then the process will be much more involved.

TIP

As you begin preparing, you will inevitably realize some deficiencies in your plan. Think of these steps as iterative. When you know more about what you should include in your plan, go back and update your plan. As you walk through the preparation phase, you will know more than you did during the planning phase. This is why an iterative process is so very important. You don't know what you don't know, and to think that you could plan everything without being all-knowing is a ridiculous thought.

DNS

The Domain Name System (DNS) is a standard used to let computers communicate over the Internet. For example, Microsoft manages the domain microsoft.com. All the Microsoft computers that are accessed over the Internet are part of this domain, and each is assigned a specific number, known as an Internet Protocol (IP) address. When you send an email to someone at Microsoft, your computer asks the microsoft.com DNS server which computer handles email.

When you move to Office 365, you must make changes in DNS so that network traffic understands where it should be routed. In essence, what happens is that when the DNS is changed, anyone sending you an email will have that email routed to your Office 365 implementation rather than to the current location.

Mailboxes

As you just discovered in the preceding section on DNS, there are specific computers responsible for hosting your email. If you keep your email on your local computer, then you won't have any email data to migrate. However, if you leave your email on the server, then all that data will need to be migrated to the Office 365 mailboxes. This migration can be one of the most technically difficult parts of moving email systems, but with guidance from a partner, it can be pain free.

Portals

A web portal, also known as an *Intranet site,* can be as simple as a static web page, or as complex as a fully integrated solution. SharePoint provides a tremendous amount of functionality, and it has seen massive adoption in the last decade. Office 365 includes SharePoint Online, which is nothing more than SharePoint hosted by Microsoft. During the migration phase of an implementation, you need to decide which content you want to move to SharePoint and which you can leave where it is currently located. In addition, you need to decide which functionality you want to integrate into your portal and which systems are better left in place.

Logins and licensing

If you're a part of a very large organization, then your IT team probably manages your users with a Microsoft technology called Active Directory. For large organizations, you can sync this on-site management of users with the Office 365 users, which results in a single login and simplified access to the cloud environment. If you're part of a small organization, then you might manage all your users in Office 365 directly. In either case, you need to come up with a list of the people who need to have access to Office 365 and the associated licensing.

Training

Even the best software is useless unless people know about it and know how to use it. Microsoft has created a wealth of documentation and user training that can be had for little or no cost. In addition, any partner you decide to work with will have training plans available and can conduct training for Office 365.

Support

After users start adopting Office 365, they're bound to have questions. You need to have a support system in place in order to accommodate even the simplest questions. The support system should include power users as a first point of content and then a formal support system that escalates all the way up to Microsoft supporting Office 365.

Office 365 Online Documentation

This chapter alone isn't intended as a complete guide for implementing Office 365. Your primary source of information about all things Office 365 can be found at `http://support.office.com`.

On the Office Support site, you will find navigation at the top of the page for Apps, Setup, Training, and Admin, as shown in Figure 18-6.

These links are your key to learning about Office 365. Spend time going through this content. If you're implementing Office 365 for a business as we discuss in this chapter, then you will find the Admin → Office 365 For Business is a great place to dive into right away.

In addition, Microsoft has released a number of downloadable guides for Office 365. Search the Microsoft Download Center for Office 365 at `www.microsoft.com/download`.

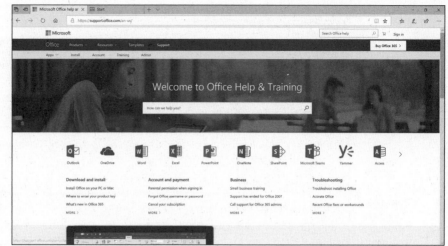

FIGURE 18-6:
The main landing page of the Office Support site.

Choosing a Partner

Throughout the chapter, we cover planning and preparing for an Office 365 implementation. As noted, the process isn't linear but is iterative. For example, you don't plan and then stop planning and move into preparing, and then stop preparing and move into migration. Instead, it is an iterative process in that you know what you know at the time and you will know more later on down the road. Luckily, if you use a partner, that partner will have been through this iterative cycle many times with other customers and can make the process much easier than undertaking the process on your own.

Microsoft provides the ability to find a partner on their Office 365 product page. Simply navigate to `https://partner.microsoft.com`, then type *Office 365* into the search link about halfway down the page. The results will show you information about the partners and reviews for each partner, as shown in Figure 18-7.

TIP

Reading the reviews and doing your homework can pay huge dividends when it comes time to implementing Office 365. An experienced partner can make the process seem like a dream, whereas an inexperienced partner can taint your view of the Office 365 product forever.

TIP

You can save money by bundling Office 365 with other products such as Windows 10 licensing. Microsoft calls this Microsoft 365. If you use a partner, or even if you don't, make sure you look into Microsoft 365.

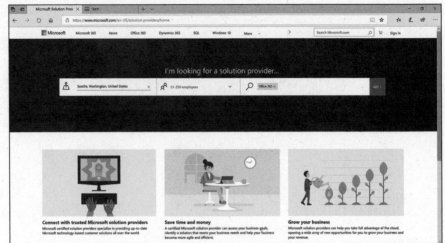

FIGURE 18-7:
Finding a
Microsoft
partner.

Chapter **19**

Implementing Office 365

I n Chapter 18, we detail how to prepare and plan for an Office 365 implementation. In this chapter, you get to throw the switch and make the move to the Microsoft cloud.

Office 365 is designed for nearly every type of organization — ranging from a one-person mom-and-pop shop, to a stay-at-home dad tracking chores, to a student, and all the way up to a multinational enterprise. Because of this massively different audience, every implementation is different, both in complexity and in time.

This chapter covers the general process and gives you some pointers on where to go for more information. If you're planning to use one of the Office 365 For Home plans, you're in for a treat. Its implementation is simple and straightforward. The challenge with Office 365 can be when you're implementing it for an organization. If you're a small organization, then some of the steps in this chapter may be overkill. If you're a very large enterprise, then you will surely want to work with a partner, such as an IT services firm specializing in Office 365, that can guide you through the process.

This chapter provides a high-level overview of the steps required to implement Office 365, including preparing users through training, activating licensing, providing a support mechanism, and migrating data and custom portal functionality. It also provides a quick section on getting started with the For Home plans. Microsoft has gone out of its way to keep the consumer plans simple; with Windows 10, the process is a snap. For this reason, this chapter focuses mostly on implementing the For Business plans.

Getting Started with Office 365 For Home Plans

If you're choosing an Office 365 For Home plan, the process is very straightforward. You just buy it and start using it. If you purchased a plan with the full version of Office, you also install those apps. The process is simple and straightforward.

To get started with Office 365 For Home, follow these steps:

1. **Open your favorite web browser and navigate to** `https://products.office.com`.

2. **Click the For Home button to see the consumer-based Office 365 plans.**

3. **Decide which plan fits your needs and click the Buy Now button.**

    The main choices (which may change) are the Home plan and the Personal plan:

    - The Home plan allows you to install Microsoft Office on up to five PC/Mac computers and up to five tablet or phone devices.

    - The Personal plan allows only a single PC/Mac and a single tablet and phone device.

4. **Follow the purchasing wizard to complete your purchase.**

5. **Open your Office 365 consumer portal at** `https://products.office.com`.

6. **Click the sign-in link in the upper-right corner, then select For Home to sign in with your Microsoft account.**

    After you sign in, the portal is displayed, as shown in Figure 19-1.

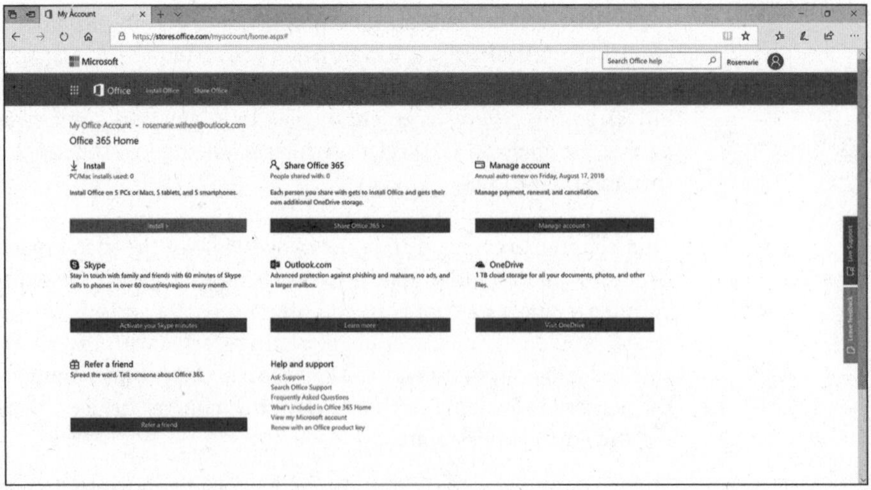

FIGURE 19-1: The Office 365 portal after signing up for a consumer plan.

After you purchase Office 365 For Home, you can begin using it. Your main landing page is always `https://portal.office.com`, which you can open in any browser. For help, open `https://support.office.com` in your browser and check out the excellent documentation for the apps and the products contained within your Office 365 subscription.

Getting Started with Office 365 For Business Plans

The initial process for purchasing a For Business plan is very similar to the process for purchasing a For Home plan. However, the similarities end there; many of the For Business plans contain advanced software that you will need to plan for and administer. This is such software as SharePoint, Exchange, and Teams.

To purchase a For Business plan, follow these steps:

1. **Open your favorite web browser and navigate to** `https://products.office.com`.

2. **Click the For Business button to see the business-based Office 365 plans.**

3. **Decide which plan fits your needs and click the Buy Now button.**

   Within the business plans, a major choice you will need to make is whether to go with the small and medium business plans or the enterprise plans. For more information on these plans, see Chapter 18.

4. **Follow the purchasing wizard to complete your purchase.**

5. **Head over to your Office 365 portal at** `https://portal.office.com` **and sign in with your Microsoft account as shown in Figure 19-2.**

   Here, you can read about your Office 365 subscription and get things set up.

Purchasing an initial Office 365 For Business plan is just the beginning. Because you're managing a business, you will need to add users, add licensing, configure the services you're planning to use, migrate data, add your organization's domain, build out your intranet portal, train people, and generally get everything set up and ready to go. You do all of this from your main Office 365 portal at `https://portal.office.com`.

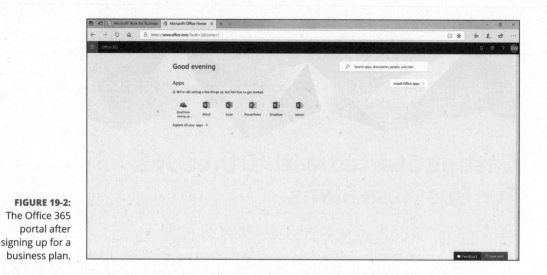

Getting Users Ready for Office 365

Microsoft Office 365 is easy to use and has very intuitive interfaces. However, that doesn't mean that you can just turn it on and tell everyone to "go wild." Although you may be familiar with the Microsoft Office products, understanding how these same products integrate and the value that results from that integration is critical in increasing productivity and boosting efficiency. To get users ready for the plunge, you need to start with training and follow up with a support system so that everyone knows where to go when they need help.

Training

We recommend using a simple formula known as the *tell, show, do* method. Here's what you do:

1. **Tell people how Office 365 works.**
2. **Show everyone how it works with a live demo.**
3. **Let people get their hands dirty and do it on their own.**

    This strategy works great for all types of technology training.

TIP

The Office 365 product is made up of a basket of products. These products include the Microsoft Office productivity suite, SharePoint Online, Exchange Online, and Teams. The different plans that make up Office 365 include various permutations of product features. For example, in order to get Microsoft Office with your plan, you need to purchase one of the plans that includes licensing to install it on local devices. For more information about the features that make up the different plans, refer to Chapter 18.

Attempting training for such a broad product as Office 365 can be challenging. For example, providing training on just the Microsoft Office piece can consume a great deal of effort because the product is made up of a number of applications, including Word, Excel, PowerPoint, Outlook, OneNote, Publisher, Access, and Teams. Rather than focus on training for each of these components, a better strategy might be to focus on how to achieve specific business functionality without going into the details of each product. For example, for email you use Outlook, for the company intranet you use a web browser and navigate to it (SharePoint is the technology behind it, but you don't need to worry so much about that), and for instant communication and meetings you use Teams.

TIP

Microsoft has a number of partners that provide training for Office 365. You can search Pinpoint for the word "training" to find a list of training companies. Access Pinpoint by using the following URL in your browser: `https://pinpoint.microsoft.com`.

Support

Even the most experienced and seasoned mountain climbers have a support system, and your organization shouldn't be any different. Establishing a support system doesn't mean spending a lot of money. A support system can be as simple as a go-to power user on the team or as complex as a full-fledged call center. Depending on the size of your organization, your support system can take many different forms. A good strategy, however, is to take a tiered approach by starting with communal support through some of the collaborative features of Office 365, such as SharePoint and Teams. Besides, isn't it poetic to use Office 365 to support Office 365? You can find out more by checking out Part 3 (SharePoint) and Part 5 (Teams).

The community can provide base-level support and work together to figure out the technology. When the community cannot help, then you can call in the big guns by requesting support from your partner or even from Microsoft itself.

TIP

By creating a vibrant community that collaborates and supports each other, your organization will have a much better Office 365 experience. The cultural changes that come about from an integrated and connected workforce can add a tremendous return on investment to the organization. With Office 365, you have the tools, but every employee must use them to make the transition effective.

When you need to enter a service request with Microsoft, you can do so from within the Office 365 Admin Center, as shown in Figure 19-3. The Admin Center is accessed by logging into `https://portal.office.com` and then clicking the waffle in the upper left corner and choosing Admin.

FIGURE 19-3:
The Service
Request section
of the Office 365
Admin Center.

Migrating to Office 365

The nice thing about Office 365 is that it lives in the cloud and is very flexible. You can migrate small test runs of data to a trial Office 365 subscription and figure out what might go wrong when you migrate the entire organization. In fact, we highly recommend that you sign up for an Office 365 trial right now. The trial is absolutely free, and you can be up and exploring the product in a matter of minutes.

TIP

In the past, it was difficult to gain access to enterprise software, such as Share-Point, because it took an astute tech person to set up the environment. The tech person had to find hardware capable of running the software and then install the operating system, all supporting software, and finally SharePoint. Even if everything went as planned, the process took at least a week and possibly a lot longer. With Office 365, you, as a business user, can go straight to the Office 365 website, sign up for a trial, and start exploring SharePoint in a matter of minutes!

Activating licensing

The process for assigning and activating licensing has dramatically improved over the last year. In the past, the process was often described as painful. The new process is streamlined and lets you add and remove users and licenses based on your immediate needs.

To add licensing, you need to add users to the plan by clicking on the Users tab, and then selecting Active Users as shown in Figure 19-4.

242   PART 6 **Preparing to Move**

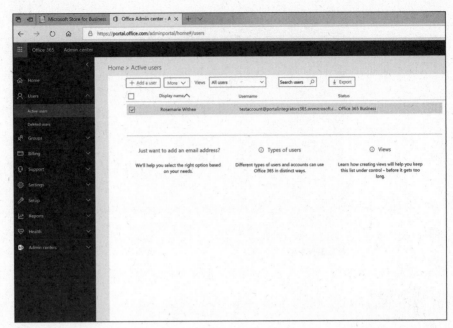

FIGURE 19-4:
The Active
Users screen in
the Office 365
Admin Center.

You begin the process of adding a user by clicking the plus symbol from the Ribbon of the Active Users screen. As you walk through the wizard, you're asked to enter information, such as the user's first and last name and administrative rights the user should be assigned. In addition, you have the opportunity to assign specific licensing to the user, as shown in Figure 19-5.

Migrating mailbox data (Exchange)

One of the most visible aspects of an Office 365 implementation is the migration of email data into the Exchange Online system. To begin a migration, you use the Email Migration page. You can access this page by clicking the Manage link under the Exchange Online section on the main Office 365 Admin Center and then clicking the Recipients link in the left navigation pane. Then, click the Migration tab as shown in Figure 19-6.

To begin a new migration, click the plus symbol, then click Migrate to Exchange Online to begin walking through the Migration wizard, as shown in Figure 19-7. The Migration wizard will let you migrate your Exchange settings. If you're migrating from Exchange 2007 or later, the wizard will use Autodiscover to auto detect settings. If you're migrating from Exchange 2003 or IMAP, then you need to enter the settings manually. After completion of a migration, user email will be available in the Office 365 system.

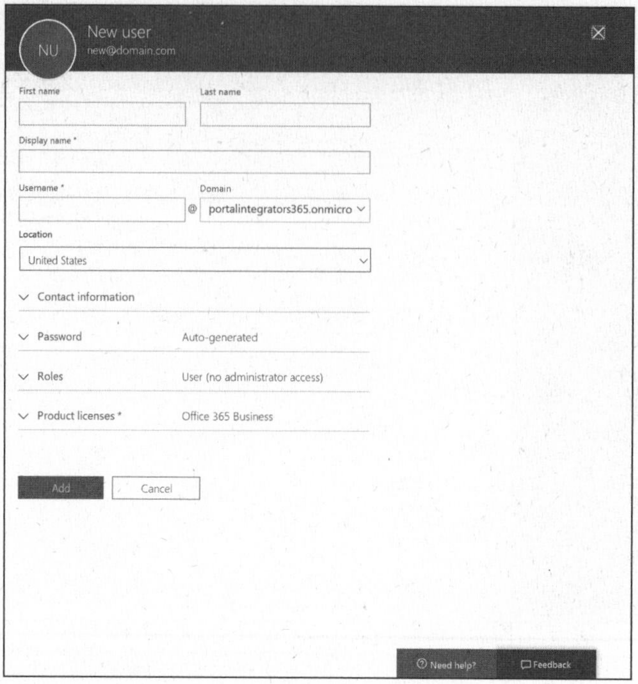

FIGURE 19-5:
Assigning
Office 365
licensing to
a new user.

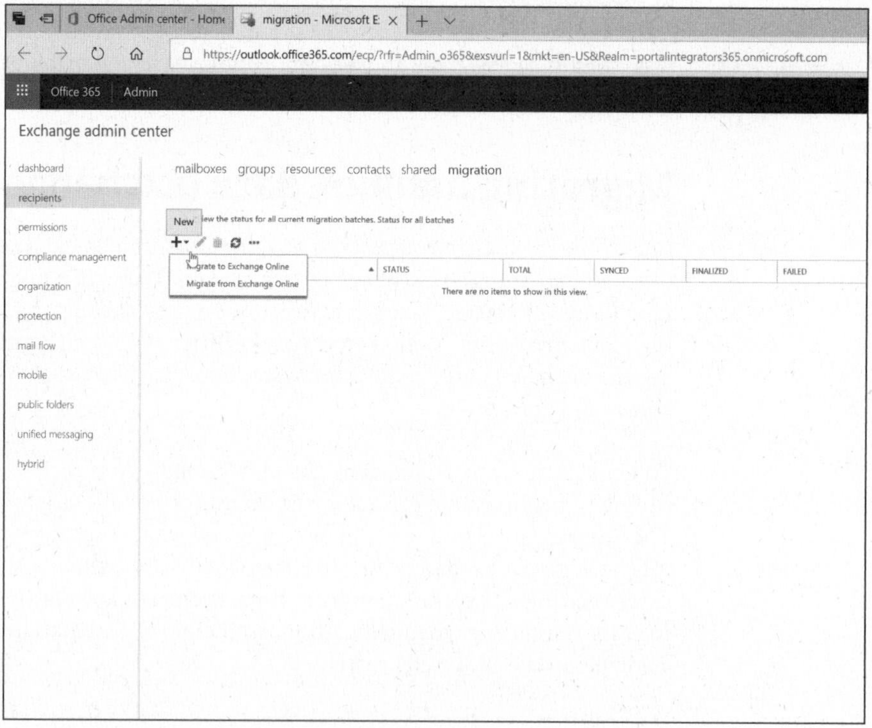

FIGURE 19-6:
Migrating mailbox
data on the
Exchange Online
Admin Center.

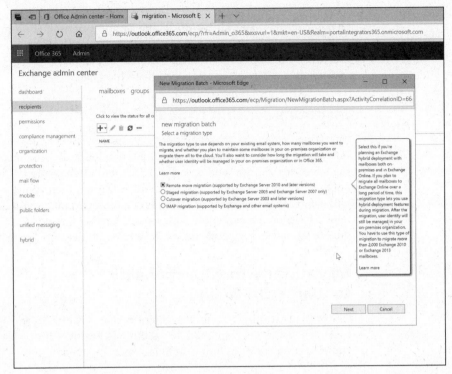

<figure>
<caption>

FIGURE 19-7:
Beginning a new email migration in Office 365.
</caption>
</figure>

TIP

A number of other tools and partners are available to assist in email migration. Find these resources in Pinpoint located at `https://pinpoint.microsoft.com`.

Migrating portal content and functionality (SharePoint)

The SharePoint platform has become one of the most successful products in Microsoft's history. As SharePoint experts, we have spent countless hours working with clients in every industry on SharePoint projects. SharePoint is a platform and as a result, it tends to get complicated, which often leads to an organization employing the help of consultants. Much of the complexity of SharePoint lies in the infrastructure of the platform. A SharePoint implementation requires a number of different engineers all working in unison to make the platform available to users. The good news with Office 365 is that Microsoft takes over this complexity of building and maintaining the platform, and you, as a user, can focus on just using the product.

Migrating to SharePoint Online (which is part of Office 365) requires you to migrate any content or custom functionality that you may currently be using in your portal environment. As you begin to delve farther into SharePoint, you find that one of the major attractions is the ability to consolidate the functionality of multiple disparate systems into the SharePoint platform. This consolidation creates a one-stop shop for business tasks as compared to logging into multiple systems that rarely communicate with each other.

Migrating content to SharePoint Online

Migrating content to SharePoint can be as easy as uploading the documents you have saved on your local computer or as complex as moving massive amounts of digital content from one Enterprise Content Management (ECM) system to another. If you're a small or medium organization, then you can gain familiarity with content management in SharePoint and in particular with document library apps. SharePoint document libraries are covered in Chapter 6. You can also check out *SharePoint 2019 For Dummies* by Rosemarie Withee and Ken Withee.

Migrating custom functionality to SharePoint Online

One of the best things about SharePoint is that it is a platform and not a specific tool. As a result, you can build just about any business functionality you need to run your business right into your SharePoint implementation.

With so much power at your disposal in SharePoint, you need to think about what you have developed. If you're one of the rare few who has never used SharePoint, then you can simply start using SharePoint Online. If, however, you have already used SharePoint either on premise or through another hosting provider and are moving into SharePoint Online, then you will need to move your custom functionality into your new portal. Migrating functionality that you have developed can be a challenge. One of the best ways to tackle this challenge, however, is to carefully document your current environment and then determine if it is better to try to migrate the functionality or to re-create it in the new environment.

If the functionality you have developed is a simple list or library app, then you can go into the List Settings page and save the list as a template with content. This creates a file that you download to your computer and then upload to SharePoint Online. After you install the template into SharePoint Online, you can then re-create the list or library app by using the template. The result is that your list or library app is transported into SharePoint Online with only a few clicks of a mouse.

TIP

For more advanced functionality, you can either redevelop it in the new environment or hire a consultant to undertake the project under your guidance.

Throwing the switch

After you have migrated both email and portal data, you're ready to throw the switch and direct all traffic to the new Office 365 environment. Throwing the switch is accomplished by updating your Domain Name System (DNS) records in your domain registrar. The results of this simple procedure are enormous. After you update DNS, every user of your current system is directed to the Office 365 system.

A DNS record is a translator from human readable computer names to computer readable computer names. For example, if you type www.microsoft.com into your web browser, the Microsoft home page appears. How does this happen? Your computer sees microsoft.com and knows it is a text entry. Computers talk to other computers by using numbers known as Internet Protocol (IP) addresses. Your computer needs to find out the IP address of the computer running the microsoft.com website. It does this by querying a DNS server. The DNS server looks up the text-based address (known as a domain name) and sends back the IP address. Your computer can now use the IP address to contact the Microsoft computer.

When you update the DNS records for the email, for example, you're telling the DNS lookup system that when someone wants to send you an email, their computer should use the IP address of Office 365 rather than the one you were using before. In essence, after you update DNS you have thrown the switch and are using Office 365 rather than the old system.

Configuring mobile phones

The cloud offers the advantage of being fully connected at all times to your important data and communications. There is no better way to access your Office 365 environment on the go than with your mobile phone. Mobile apps are available for both iOS and Android, which allows you to connect with your SharePoint and Office documents as well.

Microsoft has taken the approach that they will make Office 365 available to people regardless of the device they use. Gone are the days when you needed a Windows device to use Microsoft products. Today you can get Office 365 apps for your iPhone, iPad, Android Phone, and Android Tablet. You can even get Office for your Mac.

Microsoft has worked hard to make Windows 10 a seamlessly integrated experience with Microsoft Office, but that doesn't mean you have to choose Windows 10. Microsoft is taking the approach that they want you to choose Windows 10 because it's a better and more integrated experience. However, if you don't choose it, they're still spending billions of dollars to make Office 365 apps available on Apple and Android phones.

You can find more information about setting up your mobile phone with Office 365 by navigating to https://support.office.com.

For example, for Outlook, you can navigate to the Apps → Outlook support page. You can then browse support for the Outlook app on such topics as getting started, scheduling meetings, working with tasks, and Outlook on mobile and tablet devices. The Outlook help page is shown in Figure 19-8.

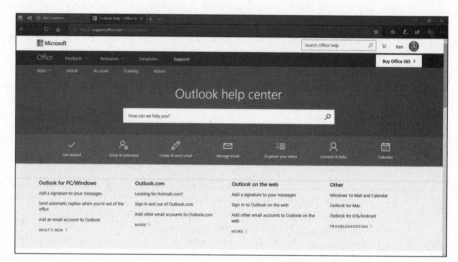

FIGURE 19-8:
The Outlook
Help Center.

Chapter **20**

Administering Office 365

A s you find out throughout the book, the Office 365 product is actually a suite of products consisting of SharePoint Online for portals, Exchange Online for email, Teams for instant and ad-hoc communication, and Microsoft Office for productivity. When it comes time to manage these components, Microsoft has created a web-based interface that is intuitive and easy to use.

In this chapter, you explore the management interfaces for Office 365. You can gain an understanding of the general Office 365 management pages and then move into exploring the specific management pages for each of the individual services.

Going Over Office 365 Management

Microsoft has taken a great deal of time and put a tremendous amount of resources into developing the management interface for Office 365, and it continues to do so.

TIP

The Office 365 interfaces continually change and are updated based on improvements from customer feedback. It is not uncommon that what we talk about today might be different tomorrow. However, the concepts are still the same.

Microsoft designed this interface for everyday users with the idea being that it doesn't take an IT expert to manage the Office 365 product. The main Office 365 management interface is actually a website you navigate to with your favorite web browser.

TIP

A web interface for managing an online product is nothing new. If you have ever used Facebook or LinkedIn, then you are familiar with using your web browser to manage an online product. The Office 365 management interface is no different; it is just the interface designed by Microsoft to manage their business cloud product.

The Office 365 management page can be accessed by navigating to the following URL in your web browser: `https://www.office.com`.

You sign in by using the credentials you used to sign up for the Office 365 product. After you have signed in, click the waffle in the upper-left corner of the screen, then select Admin. The Office 365 management website appears, as shown in Figure 20-1.

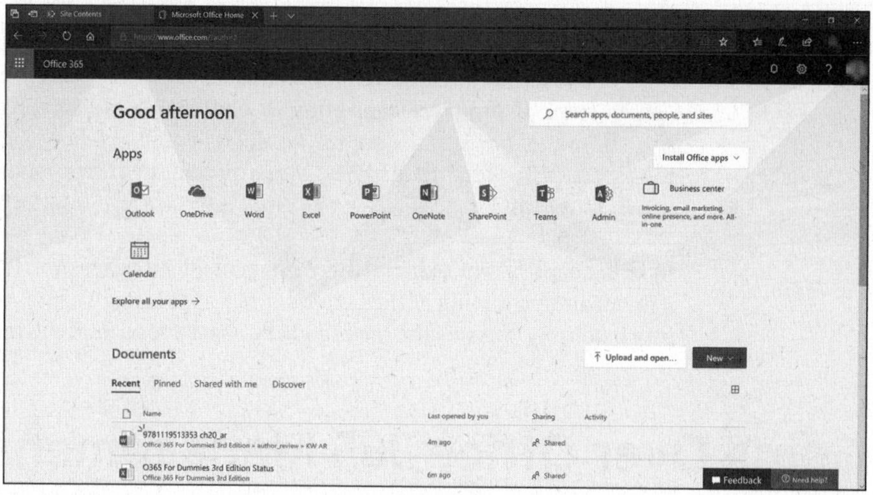

FIGURE 20-1:
The Office 365 management website.

TIP

The management interface discussed in this chapter focuses on the Office 365 Business Premium plan. If you are using one of the Enterprise plans, you will have more management options. For example, the new voice and phone options are only available in the Enterprise E5 plan. Depending on your plan, the options for that plan are available in the management interface.

The management website includes the following sections down the left navigation pane: Home, Users, Groups, Resources, Billing, Support, Settings, Setup, Reports, Health, and Admin Centers. Wow, that is a lot of options! It can be a bit overwhelming at first but Microsoft is trying hard to make it as organized and intuitive as possible. Keep in mind that Microsoft is constantly changing this interface, so the options you see may be different. The concept for achieving a task is the same, but you may have to hunt around the management interface to find the exact option you want at the time you're looking for it.

In addition, whenever you are logged in to Office 365, you have access to the affectionately named *waffle menu.* The waffle menu is in the upper-left corner of the screen and looks like, well, a waffle. When you click this menu, it expands to show you all of the Office 365 apps you have for your account. For example, if you want to check your email, you can click the waffle menu, then click Outlook. Remember what we said about things changing? This Outlook icon used to say "Mail" and it was recently changed to say "Outlook." Both the old and new icon take you to the same place, though. Your browser then opens the Outlook Web App. Likewise, if you select SharePoint (which used to say "Sites"), you see the SharePoint sites.

The waffle is always there when you are logged into Office 365; if you want to go back to the management interface, click the waffle again, then choose Admin.

The waffle only shows apps for which the user account has access. If a regular user is logged into Office 365, he or she can't see the Admin option in the waffle (unless they have admin access, of course).

Table 20-1 outlines the functionality of the left-hand navigational groups and links.

When you land on the administration screen, you are on the Home Dashboard. The Dashboard can be customized to fit your specific needs. You can add Cards to the page so that you only see what you want to see for your specific use case. Check out our Portal Integrators dashboard as shown in Figure 20-2.

Microsoft is constantly adding new services and expanding the Office 365 product. The dashboard is your quick launch place so you can tailor your work as you administer Office 365.

TABLE 20-1   ## Office 365 Administration Links

Link	Description
Home	The main landing page where you can see the health of the Office 365 services.
Users	Add users and manage partner relationships here.
Groups	Manage groups. You can also do this in the Exchange Admin Center, but it's a common task, so it's also available here.
Resources	Manage rooms and equipment that show up in Outlook. SharePoint sites that are accessed by external users and also guidance on setting up a website through Go Daddy or Wix.
Billing	Manage billing-related tasks, such as your subscriptions, bills, licenses, and billing-related notifications.
Support	If you get stuck, you can open a service request with Microsoft. This section provides information on known issues, documentation, and a way to open a new support ticket.
Settings	Settings for specific services, such as for mail, sites, and communications. Most settings also are available in the specific Admin Centers (such as for Exchange, SharePoint, and Teams), but some settings are used often, so they're available here, too.
Setup	Set up the licensing for your products, manage domains, and migrate data.
Reports	All the reports you could ever imagine about what is happening in Office 365. There are reports for usage, mail, SharePoint, Teams, and auditing, among others.
Health	The current and historical health of the services that make up Office 365, and any upcoming maintenance, are outlined in this section.
Admin Centers	The Admin Centers section has a link for the main administrative pages for each particular service, among some additional admin links. The service admin links include Exchange, Teams, and SharePoint. We explore these management pages later in the chapter.

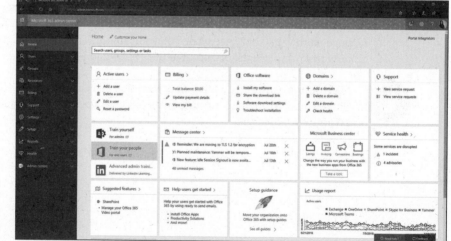

FIGURE 20-2:
The Office 365
Dashboard page
for Portal
Integrators.

Managing Exchange

The management section for Exchange can be accessed by expanding the Admin link in the lower-left of the main Office 365 administration page and then clicking the Exchange link. When you click the Exchange link, you are presented with the Exchange Admin Center, as shown in Figure 20-3.

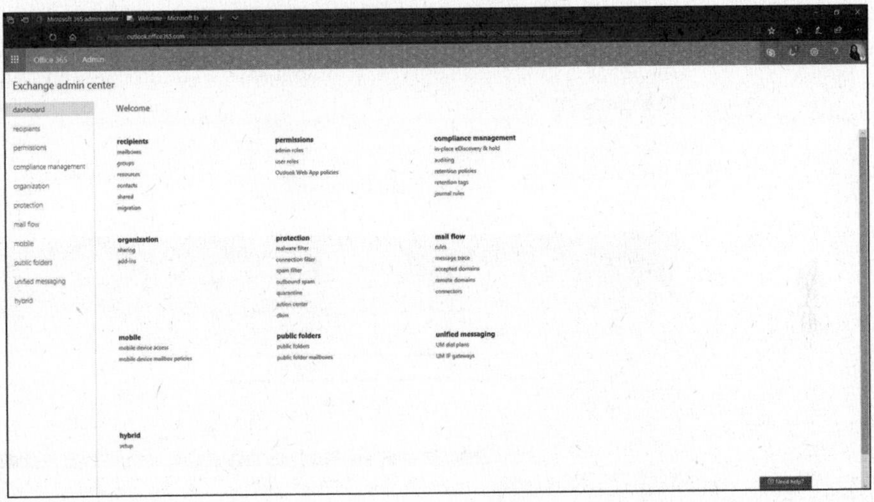

FIGURE 20-3:
The Exchange
Admin Center.

The Exchange Admin Center follows the same theme as the Office 365 Admin Center with navigational links down the left side. The links include Dashboard, Recipients, Permissions, Compliance Management, Organization, Protection, Mail Flow, Mobile, Public Folders, and Unified Messaging.

When you are administering Exchange, there are tasks you will find yourself constantly doing. Navigating through a long set of clicks can be a hassle. For this reason, the Dashboard has links to admin pages you find you use frequently. The Dashboard provides a quick place to perform common tasks, such as working with recipients of email, setting permissions, working with compliance and security, and handling mail flow.

The Exchange Online management pages contain a tremendous number of configuration settings that could only fully be covered with a dedicated book on the topic. The following sections provide an overview to managing Exchange for yourself or your organization.

REMEMBER

The standard Office 365 disclaimer also applies to Exchange. Microsoft is constantly updating, changing, and improving the product. You may not find the menus and options exactly as we outline in the book. If things look different, Microsoft has made an update. The concepts remain the same, but you may have to look around to find exactly what you're looking for.

Managing recipients

The management pages for managing recipients include pages for managing user mailboxes, groups, resources, contacts, shared mailboxes, and migration (as shown in Figure 20-4).

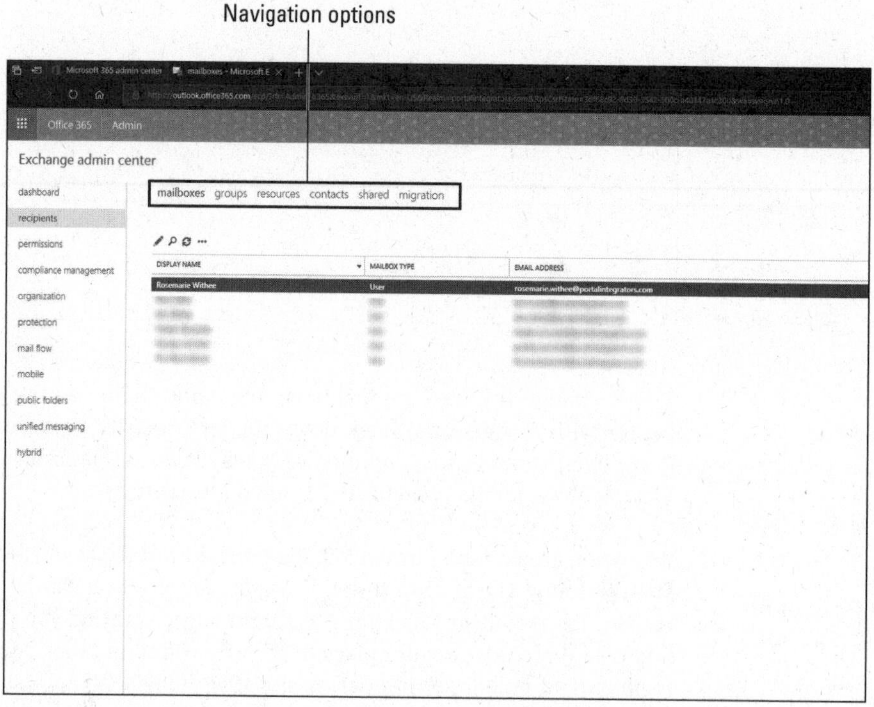

Navigation options

FIGURE 20-4:
The management landing page for recipients.

Mailboxes

The main landing page when you open the recipients link is for managing mailboxes. This is where you will spend most of your time, so it makes sense that this is the landing page. On this page, you can edit user mailboxes, and also enable or disable features, place holds, configure archiving, and even turn on or off email connectivity for a mailbox. You can click the navigation bar across the top to change to other related management pages for recipients, such as groups, resources, and contacts (as shown in Figure 20-4).

Exchange even lets users connect external accounts so they can view email from other systems.

Groups

The Groups page provides configuration options for managing users in groups. You can create groups for distribution and security:

>> A *distribution group* is a collection of mailboxes that all receive a message when an email is sent to the group.

>> A *security group* is a collection of security settings that are applied to everyone within the group.

Resources

The Resources page lets you create a room mailbox or an equipment mailbox:

>> A *room mailbox* is used for a fixed location, such as a meeting or conference room.

>> An *equipment mailbox* is for items that are not in a fixed location, such as a truck or another piece of equipment.

Contacts

The Contacts page is where you can add contacts that everyone in your organization can find when sending an email. For example, you might need to add a contact for your contact at a law firm or a lawn service.

Shared

The Shared page lets you create shared mailboxes. A shared mailbox is an email address that multiple people can access. A common use of a shared mailbox is for support. You may have multiple people, on different shifts, monitoring and responding to email. As long as everyone has access to the shared mailbox, they can check it and reply to messages.

Migration

The Migration page is where you can either migrate email into Exchange, or migrate email from Exchange to another email system.

Managing permissions

You can manage permissions for Exchange by clicking the Permissions link in the left navigation pane. Once on the permissions page, you can create various admin and user roles:

>> An *admin role* assigns permissions to a user to manage a certain portion of Exchange, such as a help desk or records.

>> A *user role* lets you assign certain user behavior to people, such as allowing them to manage their own distribution groups or associated apps.

The Permissions page also is where you find the Outlook Web App (OWA) policies. OWA policies provide you with the ability to customize the behavior of the browser-based OWA email app. You can enable or disable such features as instant messaging, text messaging, LinkedIn contacts sync, and Facebook contacts sync (see Figure 20-5).

Enabled features

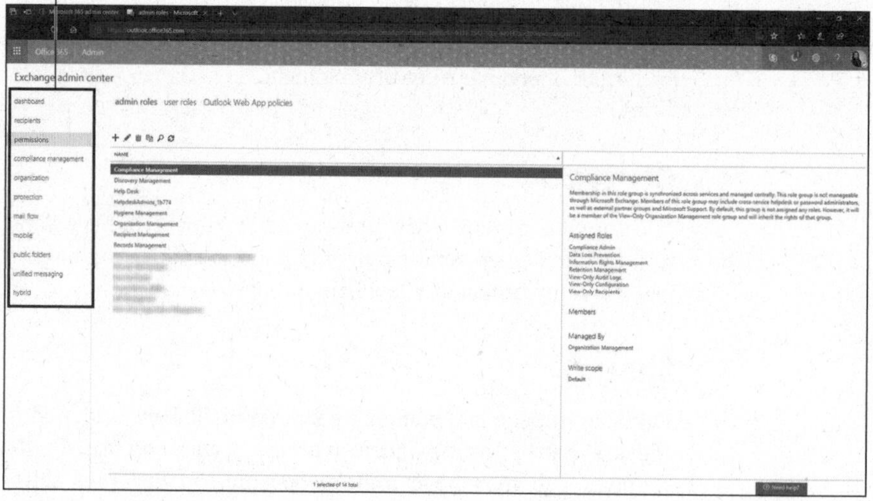

FIGURE 20-5:
The OWA policies
admin page.

More Exchange management

In addition to managing recipients and permissions, you can also manage such features as how mail flows through the Exchange system, compliance require-ments, mobile connections, and public folders. Each of these features has a cor-responding navigational link.

TIP

The possibilities for managing Exchange are nearly endless. Whole books are dedicated to the subject. Take some time to explore the Exchange Admin Center. Exchange is an administrative area that requires a person with dedicated time to conquer.

The Mail Flow page provides the ability to create rules, configure domains, journaling, and reports of email delivery.

Rules let you control the flow of email within your organization. For example, if an email is sent to a mailbox (such as info@portalintegrators.com), then you can have a rule that forwards the email to everyone on the support team.

You can also configure domains and journaling:

>> Configuring *domains* allows you to accept email for specific domains, such as portalintegrators.com.

>> Configuring *journaling* allows you to record email communications in support of email retention or archiving policies. This functionality is critical for highly regulated industries, such as banking.

Delivery reports let you search for specifics on email communication, such as messages with certain keywords or from a specific person. This can be very handy when you need to dig into your email system and understand what is going on.

Managing Teams and Skype for Business

Teams is the new one-stop-shop for all communications. If you have used, or heard of, a product called Slack then you are already familiar with Teams. Microsoft created Teams as a direct competitor to Slack and then incorporated a close integration with the rest of the Office 365 products in order to try to add value and differentiate Teams from Slack.

TIP

Teams is fully replacing Skype for Business. If you are using Skype for Business then plan to "upgrade" to Teams. (Microsoft is calling it an *upgrade* because Skype for Business is not getting any more investment, and all of the love at Microsoft is going into Teams.) If you are just starting out, we suggest you start using Teams to save yourself the headache of trying to move from Skype for Business to Teams in the future.

You can manage Teams by clicking the Teams & Skype link in the Admin Center drop-down menu. Your browser will open a new tab and you will be presented with the Dashboard for Teams and Skype for Business. The Dashboard is the main landing page when you open the Teams & Skype for Business Admin Center. The Dashboard includes key user statistics and organizational information, as shown in Figure 20-6.

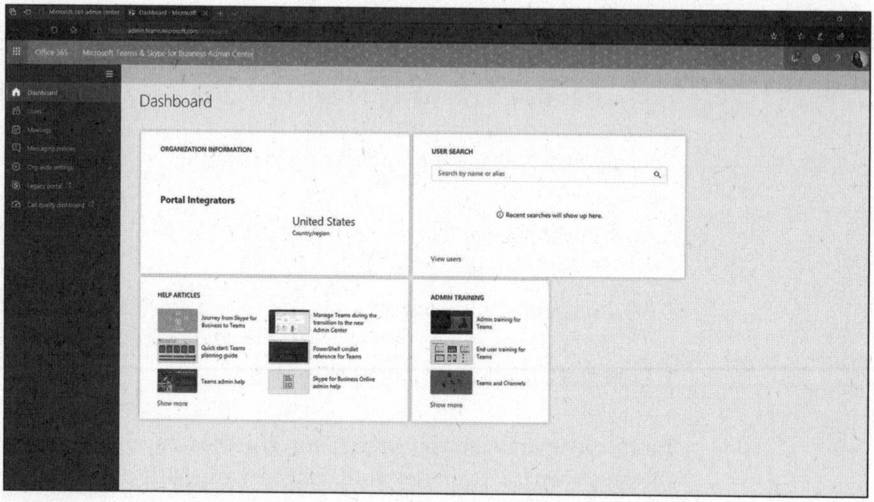

FIGURE 20-6: The Teams & Skype for Business Admin Center.

Managing Teams

On the Teams and Skype for Business Admin Center Dashboard you will find links to manage users, meetings, messaging policies, organizational-wide settings such as external users and guests, a link to the legacy dashboard, and a call quality dashboard.

The Users screen is where you manage Teams and Skype users. You can set the location of the users and configure whether they can use specific features, such as being able to communicate with people outside of the organization. You can also set features such as external communication, at the organizational level so that it affects everyone.

Managing legacy Skype for Business

If you have become used to the legacy management interfaces, you can click the Legacy Portal link and go to the older portal for managing Skype for Business.

Using Skype for Business at the same time as using Teams can be confusing for users. We recommend you get your users onto Teams as quickly as possible so that they are not caught in a split personality–type of situation where some users are on Teams and some are on Skype for Business. In a split situation like this some messages will go to Teams and some to Skype depending on which client the users are sending their messages from. Get all of your users to Teams and it will make everyone's life much easier.

Managing SharePoint

You can manage SharePoint by clicking the SharePoint link nested under the Admin Center link on the main Office 365 Admin Center. Refer to Figure 20-2 to view the link.

After you click the link, you land on the SharePoint Admin Center page where you manage site collections, user profiles, the Term Store, and apps, among other things. The SharePoint Admin Center is shown in Figure 20-7.

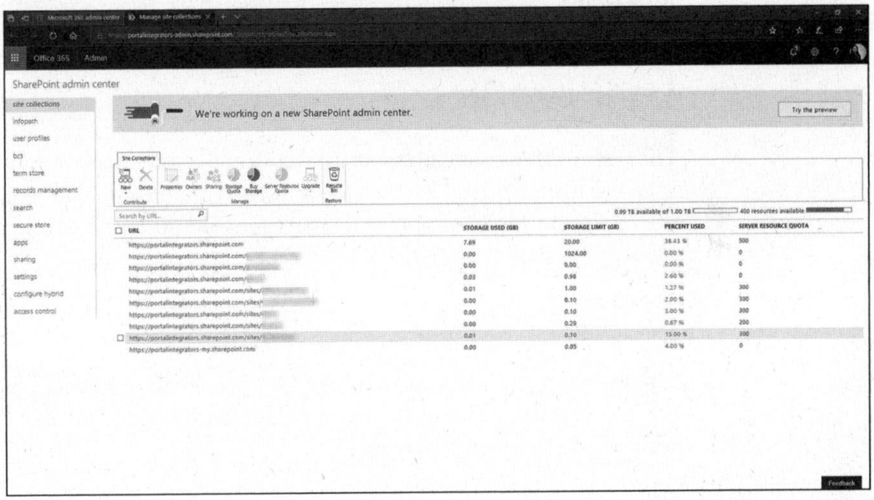

FIGURE 20-7: The SharePoint Admin Center.

The SharePoint Admin Center is unique to certain business plans in Office 365. If you are using a plan that doesn't have SharePoint included, you won't see the management link for the SharePoint Admin Center.

Managing site collections

When you first land on the SharePoint Admin Center page, you are presented with the management screen for site collections. Everything that is user facing in SharePoint is contained within a site collection, so this is a logical landing spot for the SharePoint Admin Center. In other words, site collections are always front and center in your mind as the SharePoint admin for Office 365.

TIP

A site collection is a unique instance of SharePoint so you can create a site collection for sensitive areas of the organization (such as Accounting or Human Resources), then create a separate site collection for the rest of the organization. Think of a site collection as a logical collection of SharePoint websites. A site collection isolates SharePoint components, such as user permissions, navigational components, and content types.

The site collection management screen lets you create and configure site collections. In particular, you can perform tasks, such as assigning site collection administrators, allocating resources, and setting resource and domain information.

Managing SharePoint site collections is nearly a book unto itself. We talk a little about it in Part 3 but we recommend finding a book dedicated to SharePoint to go deeper.

User profiles

The User Profiles page provides the ability to manage SharePoint components that relate to user profiles, such as the ability to manage people, the organization, and the configuration settings for the personal SharePoint site functionality known as My Site, as shown in Figure 20-8.

People

The People section lets you manage user properties and user profiles. You can create new profiles and edit existing profiles. In addition, you can manage audiences, user permissions, and policies.

TIP

An audience is a grouping of users that match specific criteria. For example, you might create a policy for everyone with the department property of their profile set to Executive. You could then target specific SharePoint functionality for only this audience. A policy provides specific functionality for users, such as the ability to add colleagues to their profiles themselves.

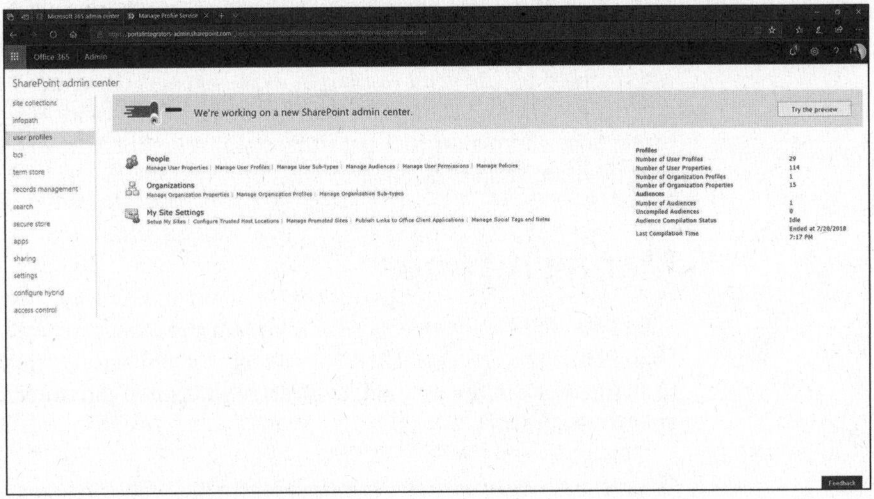

FIGURE 20-8:
The User Profiles
configuration
page in the
SharePoint
Admin Center.

Organizations

The Organizations section of the User Profiles screen lets you manage the properties and profiles of the organization. For example, one of the properties of the organization might be the company logo, and another property might be the physical address or web address. By using this screen, you can create new properties or edit existing properties. The Profiles section lets you manage a separate profile for different departments within the organization.

TIP

An easy way to think of properties and profiles throughout SharePoint is that properties define the fields used in the profiles. For example, a property might be First Name, and the profile would use this property but would associate Rosemarie with the property in the profile.

My Site settings

A SharePoint My Site is a personal site for every single user. A My Site allows users to create their own SharePoint space without worrying about having the right administrative access to a shared site. The My Site section provides the ability to set up and configure the My Site functionality for SharePoint Online.

SharePoint Term Store

The Term Store is a global directory of common terms that might be used in your organization. The idea behind the Term Store is that you want to create consistency in the way data is entered and managed throughout your SharePoint environment. For example, you might have a Human Resources Department. You don't want people to enter data, such as "HR," "HR Dept.," "Human Resources Dept.," and "Human Resources Department."

These are all actually the same thing, but because people enter names in different ways, it becomes difficult to maintain consistency. Using the Term Store, you can enter the term as "Human Resources Department" and know that every place throughout SharePoint that uses this field will enter it in a consistent way when referring to that specific department.

Managing apps

SharePoint apps are widgets of packaged features that can be added to SharePoint. SharePoint apps are also called SharePoint *add-ins*, because they add functionality to SharePoint. SharePoint includes a store where you can find and install apps into your environment.

Using the SharePoint apps management page, you can manage the purchasing and licensing of apps and configure SharePoint store settings such as turning off the ability of end users to purchase apps in the store. You can also monitor apps that you have installed, and set permissions on apps so that you have full control on who is allowed to use which particular apps.

The SharePoint apps management page is shown in Figure 20-9.

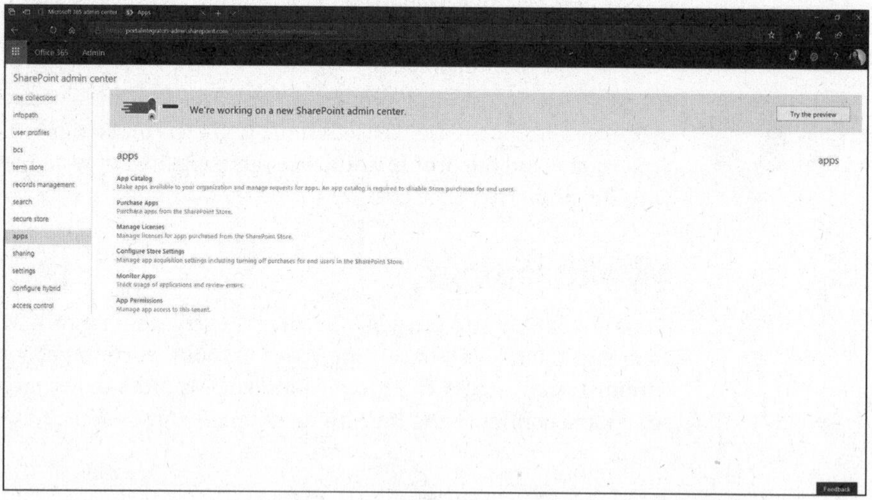

FIGURE 20-9:
The SharePoint apps management page.

TIP

In addition to the configuration information discussed in this section regarding Office 365, you also have full access to configuring the site collection within SharePoint. SharePoint is deserving of a book unto itself. A good place to start is *SharePoint 2019 For Dummies* by Rosemarie Withee and Ken Withee.

7

The Part of Tens

IN THIS PART . . .

Uncover ten signs that it might be a good time to move to the Office 365 cloud.

Explore ten great value propositions of Office 365.

Nail down ten tips for increasing efficiency and boosting productivity with the components of Office 365.

Chapter **21**

Ten Signs It's Time for You to Move to Office 365

S ince its release in 2011, millions of organizations around the world have adopted Office 365 and realized the benefits of the service to drive productivity in the workplace. From Fortune 500 companies with hundreds and thousands of employees to midsize businesses to small companies and even a solo musician — Office 365 has afforded its users the tools to make them productive in an environment that enhances the organization's security posture.

If you're still holding back and hanging onto your in-house servers (dutifully patching and maintaining them) or using a "free" solution from another provider, let us give you some good reasons to let go. If you're still using a patchwork of services to stitch together a semblance of enterprise-class productivity solutions, let us break it down for you: that is so five years ago. It's time to move to Office 365. Here are the top ten reasons why.

Your Team Likes to Collaborate

Cloud and collaboration are a match made in heaven. Using collaboration tools hosted in the cloud allows you and your colleagues to make edits simultaneously to a document online.

In Office 365, coauthoring is a given for documents saved in OneDrive for Business and SharePoint Online. There's something magical about working on a document with team members and automatically seeing their edits appear on your screen in real time. No more of this emailing back and forth to get people's updates, compiling them manually, and creating several versions. In the new world of Office 365 collaboration, the document you're working on is the latest version. You can even get clarification from your coauthor when you see what he or she is typing simply by starting an instant message conversation right from the document itself.

Version history is enabled by default in SharePoint Online, so if you ever need to restore an older version of a document, all it takes is a few mouse clicks. You can also set up your document library in such a way that only one person at a time can edit the document without blocking others from viewing a read-only copy of the file.

Your Employees Are Facebook Friends

The world has become a giant network. Now more than ever, cloud technologies have enabled all of us to connect with friends, relatives, acquaintances, and even strangers without stepping outside of our homes. We're used to checking our smartphones for updates from our network, getting advice from Facebook friends on what movies to watch, and reading reviews from Yelp about a hotel or restaurant.

If you learn that two or more of your employees are Facebook friends, then you know it's time to bring social networking to your organization. Empower your employees to use the social capabilities of Yammer or the chat-based collaboration hub in Teams to get information, share best practices, crowdsource ideas, have meaningful interactions, and stay connected with their colleagues — all within the confines of your company's secure virtual walls.

You Are the IT Department

Enterprise-size companies spend a lot of money buying, installing, configuring, maintaining, and upgrading their IT infrastructures. In addition, there are soft costs associated with justifying these IT infrastructure purchases such as:

- » Writing the business case

- » "Selling" the proposal to management

- » Sending out the request for proposal (RFP) to potential vendors

- » Reviewing and vetting the bids received

- » Selecting and contracting with the selected vendors

If you are running a small business, don't make the mistake of thinking that just because you don't do all the tasks that large companies do, your IT infrastructure cost will be negligible. You may not house a roomful of servers with technicians, but the time you spend maintaining even two servers — maintaining, patching, fixing, calling tech support, missing or forgetting an anniversary dinner in the process — all adds up to not just hard and soft costs but also productivity loss.

Office 365 saves you from all these troubles. Highly trained engineers are working and available 'round the clock to ensure your services are up and running so you don't have to worry about it.

So instead of doubling up as the IT guy, you can now relax and just focus on growing your business. And of course, have enough of a work/life balance so you won't forget your next anniversary.

Your Emails Got (Almost) Obliterated

Office 365 is the caretaker of your email data in Exchange Online. Regardless of whether your data is highly confidential or low priority, your data is stored, backed up, replicated, and protected in redundant remote data centers accessible anywhere there's an Internet connection. With a 99.9 percent uptime, financially backed service level agreement, you know that Microsoft is better positioned to help you avoid business disruptions due to a malfunctioning in-house email server than you or your IT team.

So don't wait until it happens again — move to Office 365 now before an email disaster causes work stoppage and customer dissatisfaction.

You Love Paying Only for What You Use

Most of us have enjoyed the benefits of "on demand" movies and TV shows from our cable and streaming companies. The model is simple. You sign up for a service and you get access to movies and TV shows that you can watch at your leisure.

Office 365 is your "on demand" cloud computing service provider. This means that you pay only for the capacity that you need at any given period. If you need 100 user accounts during the peak season of the business, then you pay for those 100 accounts. During the lean months when you only need 10 user accounts, you only need to pay for those 10. You don't have to own the infrastructure with capacity good for 100 users all the time. It's like paying for metered services just like you do for electricity and water.

So if you love saving money and paying only for what you use, you'll love Office 365.

You're a Tree Hugger (or Wannabe)

From recycling to composting to carpooling to driving hybrid cars, you've put in your share of effort to encourage a green workplace. Yet you still feel a yearning in your heart to do more. Listen to your heart because you're right; you can do more.

Logic dictates that shifting to the cloud will reduce IT carbon emissions footprint through data center efficiencies. And the good news? Microsoft's modular data centers consume 50 percent less energy than traditional data centers.

This means that if you subscribe to Office 365, you'll do the environment a favor through the reduction of your company's energy consumption from unneeded hardware, elimination of packaging peanuts and bubble wraps from packaged software, and doing away with paper printouts since your content can now be shared in full fidelity in the cloud.

You Don't Say "No" to Opportunities

We all want a work/life balance and would rather not do business while on vacation. But, if opportunity knocks in the form of a potential investor when you're on vacation and strolling on the beach, do you really want to ignore that knock?

Although it may be true that success is in large part due to luck, it's also true that the harder you work, the luckier you get. With Office 365, you don't have to work harder, just smarter!

For example, say you're vacationing in a remote village in Asia when, to your surprise, you meet someone interested in investing in your start-up company. You intentionally left your laptop at home, so you begin to panic at the thought of a lost opportunity. Then you remember that all your demos and presentations are saved in your OneDrive for Business account. You relax and walk over with your potential investor to the nearest Internet café and conduct an impromptu presentation. The pitch works, and you now have a new partner!

You Want to Web Conference Like the Boss

Web conferencing is not new to the enterprise — the technology has proven to be a real timesaver and cost reducer. Most of us probably have seen movies of high-powered board meetings with good-looking CEOs and senior management hooked up by live video conferencing to their operations folks in multiple locations across the globe. As a small-business owner or a professional, you've probably secretly coveted the sophistication of the people and the meeting by virtue of the technology they used.

Well, covet no more. Microsoft Teams brings you web conferencing tools so you don't need to invest in expensive equipment or hire an IT staff to conduct effective, high quality, high-definition web conferencing. The service is built in, it works, and it's great.

With Teams, you can start out with a chat with a co-worker, add voice to the session, invite more people to the conversation, convert the session into a web conference, share screens, whiteboard, and for good measure, record the web conference. The web conferencing solution allows for high-definition video capability using off-the-shelf webcams with a resolution display that adjusts to the waxing and waning of your Internet connection.

So put on a suit and a tie (or sweats), turn your webcam on, and start web conferencing like the boss from the comforts of your cubicle or your home office.

You Freaked Out Over a Lost Phone

Johnny, the tech-savvy new salesperson on the team, is leading the early adopters' pack by bringing in his own mobile devices to the workplace. He's got all his corporate email and other data synced to his smartphone and he's getting great results because he has access to information anytime, anywhere, and especially when he's with customers.

And then it happened. Somewhere between the huge industry conference with all your company's competitors and the big closing party, Johnny lost his phone. You freaked out, especially since you know Johnny's phone had all kinds of confidential, competitive data in it. Fortunately, some hotel personnel found the phone and Johnny got it back.

With mobile device management (MDM) in Office 365 and Intune, you never have to go through that stress again. With MDM, security policies are enforced on Bring Your Own Devices (BYODs) to ensure compliance with corporate policies. Your IT department can remotely wipe all the data on the device, lock it, and reset the password in the event of loss or theft.

You Don't Want to Be the Next Hacking Victim

The last several years have been banner years for hacking. Just as you start thinking this isn't going to happen to your organization, you read about a ransomware attack on a Los Angeles hospital whose administrators had to shell out $17,000 to restore their computer network. So now, you start to panic.

You can relax. You can protect your data with Office 365 with built-in, integrated security and compliance services across applications and devices. Multi-factor authentication, data loss prevention, anti-spam, anti-virus, advanced threat protection, and encryption are just the start of the story. Encryption in Office 365 comes in two layers: from the service level (Microsoft manages this) and from the part you, the customer, control.

On the service-level side, when your data is sitting or "at rest" in Office 365 data centers, they are encrypted so even in the unlikely event that a hacker gets access to the data, all the hacker sees will be garbled, unreadable text.

When your data is in transit, Office 365 applies a sophisticated data protection service to encrypt your file. You can specify the permissions for your email or documents to restrict what the recipients can do to the document. For example, you can apply a restriction that prevents a recipient from forwarding or printing an email. You can even revoke access to a document after it has left your mailbox.

There are a lot of Microsoft partners who can help you move your business to the cloud. Don't hesitate to reach out to them — they'd be more than happy to assist you in your cloud journey.

Chapter **22**

Ten Office 365 Value Propositions

I f you are relatively new to enterprise software, such as SharePoint, then moving to the Microsoft cloud is a straightforward decision. After all, you don't have an IT team in place and there is no chance of disrupting employees because they aren't currently using enterprise class software. In this situation, there is nothing but upside. If, on the other hand, you are a very technologically mature organization, then moving to the cloud can be a scary proposition. Anytime there is change at the enterprise level, there is a chance for things to go wrong. Even if the cloud assumes the risk of the technology causing problems, such as installation or patching, there is still the risk of user adoption, confusion, and push back for the new way of doing things.

In this chapter, you explore ten value propositions for Office 365. Although change can be scary, the cloud has a lot to offer regardless of the size of your organization. In particular, you explore some of the value that results from freeing up your technical folks and letting them focus on solving real-world business problems by using technology instead of keeping the lights blinking green. You also explore some of the productivity gains that come with moving to the cloud, such as the ability to connect anywhere you have Internet connectivity and the value added by using an integrated suite of products.

Offloaded Responsibility

You have probably heard the expression that "it takes an army" to do something. When it comes to Information Technology, this saying rings true. When you start thinking about all the people and resources responsible for enterprise-class software, the results can be mind-boggling. You need networking people, operating system administrators, email administrators, server administrators, domain administrators, DNS people, web developers, programmers, provisioning experts, backup engineers, infrastructure, maintenance, patches, backup generators, and the list goes on and on. It is no wonder that it used to take a very large company to adopt software, such as SharePoint.

The cloud is changing the paradigm behind enterprise class software by offloading the responsibility for the infrastructure to someone else. In the case of Office 365, that someone else is none other than Microsoft. Microsoft has invested heavily in building out data centers, installing computers, operating systems, backup systems, and maintenance plans. Microsoft takes care of it all. When you use Office 365, you simply sign up and start using the products over the Internet. The result is that you don't have to worry about the heavy lifting. You are free to focus on using the software instead of worrying about keeping the software running.

Reduced Infrastructure

The infrastructure required to run software grows exponentially as the organization adopts enterprise applications. Even a relatively modest set of servers needs a redundant power supply, multiple Internet connections, a backup plan, and a secure and fireproof location in which to reside. As an organization grows, the amount of infrastructure required grows quickly until an entire team is dedicated to keeping the servers running 24 hours a day.

The costs involved in purchasing, managing, and maintaining the infrastructure involved for enterprise class software can be downright daunting. When you move to Office 365, you are removing the need for onsite infrastructure. That is all taken care of by Microsoft. Without the need for all the servers and software required to run the software, you can focus on the more important issues affecting your business. In a nutshell, you are removing the burden of having on-site infrastructure but still achieve the competitive advantage that comes with using software, such as SharePoint, Teams, Office, and Exchange.

Predictable yet Flexible Costs

If you talk to a chief financial officer, accountant, or project manager and ask them the type of project they prefer, they will tell you the one that comes in on budget. Unfortunately, in the technology industry, a predictable budget can be a difficult goal to achieve. Technology, by its very nature, has a lot of uncertainty and gray areas. An analogy people like to use for custom software or a difficult implementation has to do with painting. Great technologists are often more artist than engineer. As a result, you might get an absolutely phenomenal product, or you might get a complete disaster that is five or ten times over budget and completely unusable.

The result of uncertainty is difficulty in planning and conflict. A CFO or project manager would rather have an accurate figure than a low figure that could triple. When you move to the cloud, you are taking all the uncertainty out of the cost of the infrastructure and implementation. With Office 365, Microsoft has already undertaken all the risky implementation projects that come along with enterprise software. That is not to say that Microsoft teams did not come in over budget or that Microsoft did not spend three or four times what they thought it would take to get Office 365 up and running. But that doesn't matter to you. You know exactly how much Office 365 will cost you, and you won't have to worry about overruns. Microsoft won't tell you that it is actually going to cost four times more per month because the software is complicated. In fact, Microsoft has a service guarantee so that if the software is not up and running per the agreement, then they are on the hook for it.

TIP

To raise the value proposition even further, you can add and remove licensing as you need it. When you have a hiring spree, you may need more licensing; in slower times, you may need to reduce your licensing. Office 365 provides this ability to scale up or down your licensing, and costs, depending on your organization's situation.

Reduced Complexity

You would think that after being a software consultant for years and years and years, that Rosemarie would know absolutely every possible thing you could or couldn't do with services-based software like Office 365. The secret that Rosemarie will tell you that no other consultant will tell you is that consultants and experts still learn something new every single day.

TIP

Just to clarify, Office 365 isn't the only game in town. Rosemarie consults organizations every day in other suites of tools such as Google Apps, Slack, Dropbox, and others. Those tools are not the focus of this book, but it is good to keep your options in mind when making a decision. Rosemarie focuses on the best tool for her clients and sometimes that is Office 365 and sometimes it isn't.

The Office 365 product includes Exchange, Teams, Office, and SharePoint, plus such newcomers as Power BI, PowerApps, Flow, Sway, and many, many others. There are probably a few souls out there who are absolute experts on all these technologies, but the fact is, to maintain such enterprise software, you need a fairly significant team.

TIP

To go deeper into the various apps that come with Office 365, check out "*Office 365 Apps For Dummies* by Rosemarie Withee".

Microsoft has made managing software systems easier by introducing products, such as Small Business Server, but the fact is that managing software is still a complicated endeavor. With Office 365, you remove that complexity by using a simple web interface to manage the various products. Need to create a new SharePoint site collection? You do it from within the Office 365 interface. Need to create retention rules for email? Again, the Office 365 management screens for Exchange are where you will find them. Microsoft engineers perform all the difficult responsibilities that go into keeping the lights blinking green on the servers. You just use the software in a way that best suits your business needs.

Anywhere Access

Office 365 lives in Microsoft's data centers and is accessed over the Internet. For this reason, you have connectivity to your enterprise software by using your desktop computer in your office, your laptop, or your mobile phone. In addition, all you need is an Internet connection rather than a special connection to your corporate network.

Having access to the software you use every day from anywhere provides a tremendous value and efficiency increase. When you have access, you can take advantage of unintended downtime. For example, you might be stuck waiting for someone and instead of just daydreaming away the time you could pull out your phone and respond to emails or tweak a Word or PowerPoint document. You will no longer feel that nagging urge that you need to get back to your desk to get work done. After all, other people might be waiting for you to respond so that they can do their job. In this way, you are not only maintaining your own efficiency during your downtime, but you are unblocking the people that require your input in order to maintain their efficiency and do their jobs. And, because Microsoft has embraced multiple operating systems, you can find your Office 365 apps on all your standard mobile devices such as iOS and Android.

Synchronized Data

A real inefficiency booster is having different versions of documents scattered all over the place. You might have one version of a document at work and another version on your home computer and yet another version on your laptop. Documents have a bad habit of multiplying as well. When you send a document to people in an email, they save it to their computer and then make changes. Very quickly, there are multiple documents, and it becomes nearly impossible to determine which version contains the needed information.

With Office 365 and SharePoint Online, you have a centralized home for all documents. You can access those documents from multiple computers (or even your mobile phone) and by multiple people. Regardless of how many people or devices are accessing the document, only a single version of the document exists on SharePoint. Because SharePoint is in the cloud and accessed over the Internet, you only need an Internet connection or cell reception in order to access your enterprise data.

In addition to documents, Office 365 lets you synchronize all your email, calendar, and contacts onto multiple devices. If you use Outlook at home, at the office, on your phone, and on your tablet, you don't have to worry about being on the wrong device when trying to find a contact at work. You don't have to worry about missing an appointment because all the devices you use synchronize with Exchange Online. You don't have to worry about forgetting a Word, Excel, or PowerPoint document, because it is on your phone or tablet and can be opened with Office. The result is that your appointments, email, contacts, and documents live in the cloud and are synchronized with all of your devices.

TIP
You can sync nearly any smartphone and any email app with Exchange Online as well so that you are never far from your appointments, contacts, and email. This feature is one of the most valuable. Not to mention that Outlook is one of the top-rated email apps for iPhones and Android phones.

Integrated Software

As we cover throughout the book, the Office 365 product is actually a suite of products that is hosted in the Microsoft data centers and accessed over the Internet. Microsoft has gone to great lengths to integrate the software as seamlessly as possible, which results in an increase in efficiency for users. For example, you might be performing a search for a document in your SharePoint portal. When you find the document, you can see the author and view his or her presence information based on the color of the icon next to their name in SharePoint. You can click the presence icon to launch Teams for instant chat, voice, or video communications, or Outlook to send an email.

Office 365 even integrates with your phone system so you can even call the author directly from the SharePoint environment. The integration between SharePoint, Exchange, Teams, and Office makes performing daily tasks as easy as possible. The end result is that the technology gets out of the way and lets you and those you work with do your jobs without fighting with technology.

Mobile Access to Enterprise Data

In the distant past (perhaps a handful of years ago in technology time), you most likely had to be at your desk in order to access your enterprise data. If you had an important Word document or needed a PowerPoint presentation, then you had to go into your office and copy it to a Flash drive or use a connection, such as virtual private network (VPN) in order to connect remotely.

Being tied to your desk in this manner created a lot of frustration and inefficiency. Companies, such as Go To My PC, flourished by providing remote access to the computer in your office from a remote computer. And then, all of a sudden, smartphones appeared. Everyone quickly became accustomed to having a small computer with them in their pocket at all times. Need some information from the Internet? Need to check movie times? Need to browse a website or catch up on the latest news? All you need to do is pull out your smartphone.

The only problem was that the corporate environment did not move as quickly as the consumer market, so a gap emerged. Yes, you had the Internet in your pocket, but you still couldn't connect to your corporate network or access your enterprise data. With Office 365, you can finally access your data from anywhere by using your smartphone. Microsoft is taking anywhere access a step farther by creating tools, such as PowerApps, that let you build your own mobile apps for your Office 365 data. You can then use these custom mobile apps on your phone in a familiar environment even though they are custom for your specific organization and workflow.

Now, for the first time, you can click a button on your phone and instantly browse your enterprise data in SharePoint, respond to corporate email, see your calendars, book appointments, and pretty much do almost everything you would do at your desk. Only now you can do it from anywhere you have cellphone reception and on almost any type of smartphone.

Increased IT Efficiency

Routine tasks have a way of creating snags that take hours or days to resolve. A small technical glitch has a way of cascading into an all-out war between the IT team and the software demons. What ends up happening is that the tech people spend all their time down in the weeds keeping the lights blinking green. The business folks become frustrated because they are not receiving the support they deserve, so the whole business and the culture suffer.

When you move to the cloud, you free up your IT resources to focus on working with your business users to solve problems that benefit the organization. Your business users receive the support they need, and the IT people receive the recognition they deserve.

Enter the Self-Service Software Revolution

The most exciting aspect of Office 365 for many organizations is the wealth of enterprise apps that have been added to Office 365. Yes, all the major enterprise products are there such as SharePoint, which provides a self-serve portal environment that can be developed to solve real-world business problems, but there are a ton of new apps and Microsoft keeps adding more all of the time. In fact, there are so many apps now that they warrant another book.

In the past, all of this software would have required an army of developers to tweak and manage for everyday users. The self-serve software revolution has taken hold and most of the Office 365 products can now be customized by the very users that use the software; developer not required.

Chapter **23**

Ten Tips for Increasing Productivity with Office 365

O ffice 365 as a cloud technology affords any organization the benefits of a sophisticated data center without the hassle and the cost of maintaining one. For the IT professional, Office 365 offers the best of both worlds: productivity and security. For end users, Office 365 means freedom from complete dependency on the IT team. The average end users are now able to perform advanced tasks using artificial intelligence (AI) with no coding skills!

In this chapter, you find "ready-to-apply" tips and tricks for increasing productivity and efficiency in your organization or your practice. The efficiency gains you realize from the service can be magnified to positively impact the productivity of everyone in the workplace including those with disabilities.

Self-Serve from the Service Health Dashboard

If you're the designated admin for your organization, you'll most likely receive inquiries about issues your users are experiencing in Office 365. Before you spend a lot of time troubleshooting an issue, check out the Service Health dashboard (see Figure 23-1) in the Microsoft 365 Admin Center to determine whether the issue is from your end. In this dashboard, you can manage your Office 365 tenant: manage users, create groups, update subscriptions, review billing, contact support, configure settings, run reports, and view the health of the service.

If any of the tracked services in the Service Health dashboard aren't green, click the item to view additional details like status, user impacts, and the message history.

Having insight into which service is up or down will save you a lot of time and even a phone call to support if you already know someone is working on it.

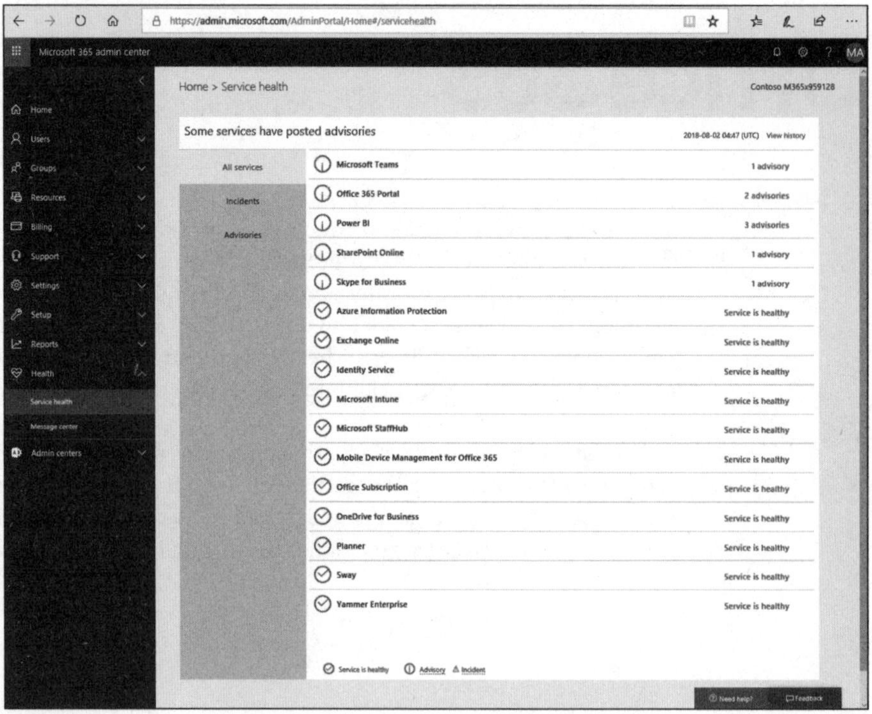

FIGURE 23-1:
The Microsoft 365 Admin Center Service Health dashboard.

The Microsoft 365 Admin Center is an update from the Office 365 Admin Center. The new Admin Center incorporates additional management capabilities for the new service offering from Microsoft called Microsoft 365. This service includes Office 365, Enterprise Mobility + Security, and Windows 10. If you're only using Office 365, then the management capabilities available to you will only be limited to Office 365. To learn more about Microsoft 365, please check out *Microsoft 365 Business for Admins For Dummies* by Jennifer Reed.

Act Like the IT Guy

At one point or another, we all secretly wish we had the awesome powers of the IT Guy. This is the person who can magically unlock your computer, reset your password, and give you access to privileged content in your organization.

So, what happens if you lose your phone with confidential data and the IT Guy isn't available? Well, you can act as the IT Guy. You can easily wipe data from your wireless device and even delete the device from your account to prevent a security and/or privacy breach.

Quickly wipe data or delete your device from your Exchange Online account by taking these steps:

1. Log into the Office 365 portal at https://portal.office.com.

2. From the app launcher or the landing page, click the Outlook icon.

3. To the right of the Office 365 navigation bar, click the Settings icon.

4. Click Mail from the Settings pane on the right.

5. Click General from the left pane.

6. Click Mobile devices, then select the mobile device that's synced to your account.

7. Click the Wipe device icon (see Figure 23-2).

   You may also want to remove the mobile device altogether from your account by clicking the Remove icon (looks like a minus sign).

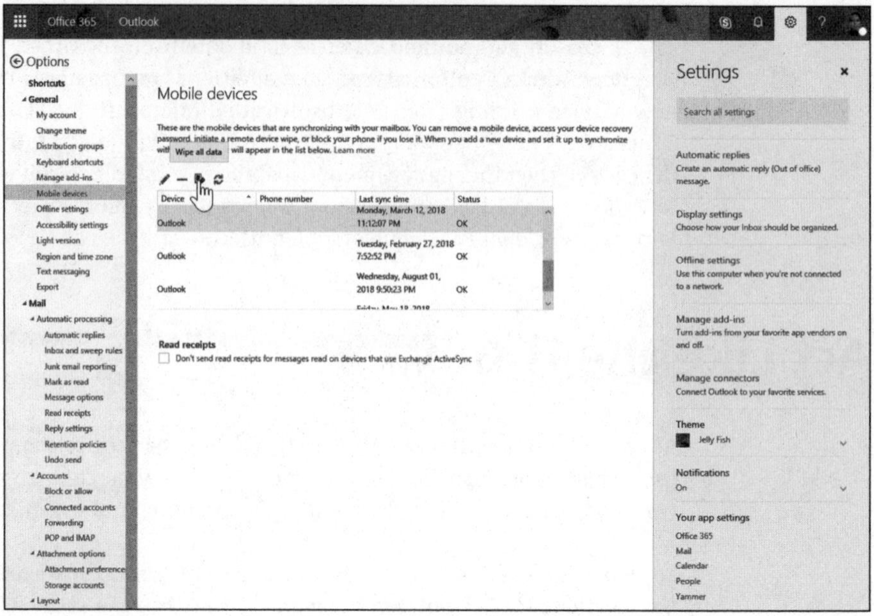

FIGURE 23-2:
Remotely wipe a device.

Use the Scheduling Assistant

There's nothing more maddening than trying to set up a meeting with a bunch of people and not knowing their availability. In Office 365, the free/busy information in Exchange Online saves the day. This functionality lets you know whether a person is free, busy, working elsewhere, out of the office, or has a tentative meeting on the calendar. It works not just for people but also for resources, such as conference rooms.

You see a person's free/busy information when you create a meeting and use the Scheduling Assistant. Here's how:

1. **From the Outlook calendar, click New Meeting from the ribbon.**

2. **Add the people you want to invite to the meeting in the To: line.**

3. **Add the Subject and the Location for the meeting.**

4. **Enter the Start time and End Time.**

5. **From the Ribbon, click Scheduling Assistant.**

    The attendees' availability will be displayed in Scheduling Assistant. Take note of the legend at the bottom of the window to determine a person's availability, for example, solid blue stands for Busy and solid purple means the person is out of office (see Figure 23-3).

6. If the time you picked looks blocked for any your invitees, find a time that works best for all, then click the Send button.

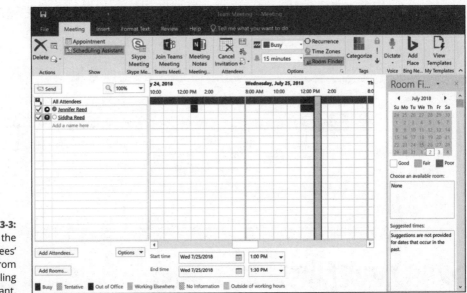

FIGURE 23-3:
Viewing the attendees' availability from the Scheduling Assistant.

Share Your Calendar

One cool feature of the Outlook Online is that the calendar is just as robust as the desktop application. You can apply colors to your appointments for an at-a-glance review of your day, week, or month, send a meeting request, set up alerts and notifications, and a whole lot more.

You can share your calendar to people outside your organization to make it easy for them to know your availability. You can choose to give them full details for your calendar, limited, or just show your availability.

To share your calendar from the Outlook Online, follow these steps:

1. Navigate to `https://portal.office.com` and log in with your Office 365 credentials.

2. Click the Outlook icon.

3. Click the Calendar icon.

4. Click Share from the top menu and enter the email address of the person you want to share your calendar with and choose the access level (see Figure 23-4).

5. Click the Share button and then click Done to close the window.

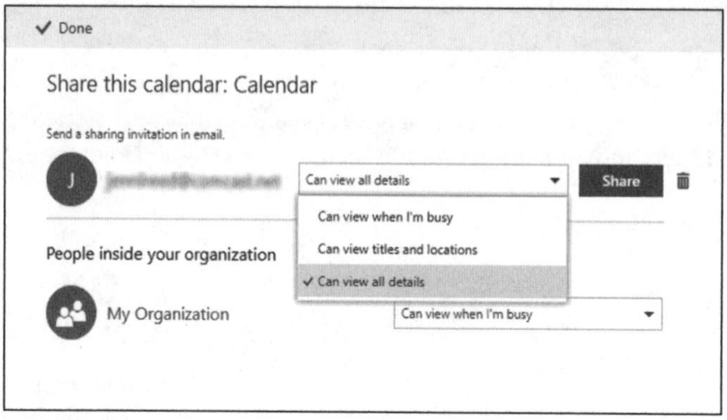

FIGURE 23-4:
Calendar
sharing in
Outlook
Online.

Sync Your Files

Regardless of how connected you are, you'll inevitably run into a situation where you don't have Internet access. Just because you're without access doesn't mean your efficiency has to suffer.

You can continue to work on your OneDrive for Business or SharePoint Online documents offline and sync them back to the server when you have an Internet connection. The OneDrive for Business app should be installed as part of Office Pro Plus. If you don't see it, click OneDrive from the app launcher in Office 365, click Sync from the top navigation bar, and then follow the prompts. The same Sync button is available in SharePoint Online document libraries. Once your files are synced to your hard drive, you can access them using File Explorer (the folder icon) from on your task bar on a Windows computer.

Kill the Email Tree with Teams

Here's the situation: You have a report due in three days and you need input from John, Jane, Mary, and Peter. You email all of them asking for input. John and Jane reply with their input. Mary didn't see your email. Peter replies and copies Beth.

Beth replies but bcc's David. David replies to all but forgets to include Beth. You finally have all the input and you're about to finalize the report but Mary, at the last minute, replies to all but doesn't look at the input from Beth and David. So now you have to add her feedback and resend the new version for everyone to review.

This story can go on and on until your hair turns gray, but there's a better way to do this: Kill the email tree. Use Microsoft Teams instead.

With Teams, everyone will see everyone's feedback. If someone new comes along, that person will see everyone's feedback. So there. No more email trees!

Stay Focused with Focused Inbox

Focused Inbox in the Outlook desktop or online version helps you prioritize your email so you can focus on important and critical work. When enabled, the functionality separates your email into two tabs: Focused and Other. Email that is important to you is in the Focused tab, while the rest is filed under the Other tab — out of the way but easily accessed.

If you wonder how the system determines what's important and what's not, it's really nothing but plain old AI and machine learning. Basically, the system considers the email you respond to, the contacts you interact with, and your activities and behaviors across the Office 365 ecosystem. Bulk email is automatically detected and dumped into the Other tab. So the more you use Office 365, the system becomes better in sorting your email so that it "feels right" to you.

Accessibility Features Make Everyone Productive

Did you know there are over 1 billion people with disabilities in the world? The U.S. Census Bureau reports that in the United States, nearly 1 in 5 people have a disability and 70 percent of disabilities are invisible. Whether it's visual, hearing, cognitive, speech, mobility, or neural, having a disability can be a blocker for success in the workplace. To address this issue, Microsoft has built accessibility features into Office 365 to ensure productivity can be enjoyed by everyone in the organization including those who have disabilities.

In Word, Excel, or PowerPoint, you can download templates designed to be accessible. Check them out by navigating to File ⇨ New and typing **accessible templates** in the Search for Online Templates box.

Once you have an accessible template applied to your file, test your accessible document by going to View ⇨ Read Mode. In Read Mode, navigate to View and then click Read Aloud (see Figure 23-5).

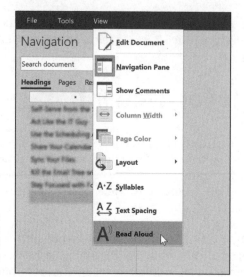

FIGURE 23-5:
Reading a document aloud with accessible templates.

Send Info to OneNote — Fast

The education community has discovered the value of using OneNote in the classroom to drive collaboration, participation, and productivity. It's high time we take a lesson from our teachers and apply it in our workplace. After all, we wouldn't be where we are in our careers were it not for those who have committed their lives to education.

OneNote integrates seamlessly with other Office products. In Outlook, you can send information from your calendar to OneNote so meeting notes include valuable information from the meeting such as the date, time, attendees, and the original message in the meeting invitation. Here's how to integrate OneNote into Outlook:

1. Open a calendar item from Outlook.

2. From the ribbon, click Meeting Notes (see Figure 23-6).

3. **From the Meeting Notes window, click Take Notes on Your Own.**

4. **Select the section in which you want to store the meeting notes.**

   The system automatically creates a new page in the section you selected and pulls the data that's in your calendar item.

Automatically Add Subtitles to Your Videos at Work

You may have noticed a feature in YouTube that allows you to watch videos with subtitles and closed captions. This is handy when you need to watch a video with no sound for one reason or another (say you don't have a headset and you don't want to bother the person next to you). If you have one of the following licenses in Office 365, you're in luck! These licenses come with *Stream*, a video service for the enterprise where you can upload, view, and share videos within the confines of your organization:

» Office 365 Education

» Office 365 Education Plus

» Office 365 Enterprise K

- » Office 365 Enterprise E1

- » Office 365 Enterprise E3

- » Office 365 Enterprise E5

You can also purchase Stream as a stand-alone plan for as low as $3 per user per month. The remarkable thing about Stream is that uploaded videos are automatically configured for subtitles and closed captions. You don't have to do any additional coding or transcription to add to the video. The subtitles are automatically generated using AI. To display the subtitles, click the Closed Caption icon ([CC]) while the video is playing (see Figure 23-7).

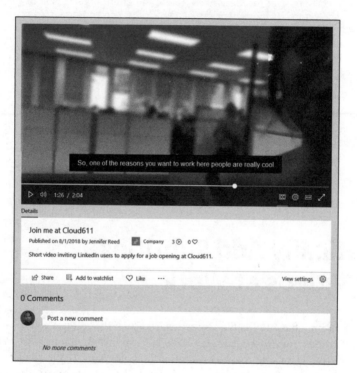

FIGURE 23-7:
Subtitles are automatically generated for videos in Stream.

Glossary

Blog: A Blog is a web log or online journal. A blog provides a forum for people to write communications that can be viewed across the entire organization or Internet. After a blog entry is posted, the content can be commented on and discussed on the blog entry page. Blogs are prevalent throughout modern society, and SharePoint provides the ability to get a blog up and running in a manner of minutes.

Cloud: A broad marketing term and buzzword that refers to accessing software over the Internet.

Discussion Board: A discussion board allows for online discussion throughout the organization. A discussion board provides a forum for people to post questions and replies that can be viewed throughout the organization.

Excel Services: Excel Services is a feature of SharePoint that allows Excel documents to be accessed through a SharePoint site and thus through a web browser.

Exchange: Exchange is Microsoft's email server designed to handle the heavy lifting of managing and routing email. In addition, Exchange handles functionality such as contacts, calendars, and tasks. Users generally use an email client such as Outlook to connect to Exchange.

Exchange Online: Exchange Online is the term for Microsoft's cloud version of Exchange. The Online portion refers to the fact that you access your Exchange instance over the Internet while you are online. Microsoft installs Exchange on servers running in their data centers, and you connect to it and use it over the Internet.

Extranet: An extranet is a computer network that is accessible by people outside your organization's network but is not accessible by the public at large.

InfoPath: An application designed to create nifty and useful forms that are used to collect data from people. InfoPath is being deprecated and isn't part of Office 2019.

Intranet: An intranet is a computer network that is private and only meant for your organization.

JavaScript: JavaScript is a scripting language that is designed for the web. You can use JavaScript to interact with a web page programmatically. Since JavaScript is run from the client web browser, you can create a rich interactive experience without the web browser having to communicate with the server, resulting in the page flickering and reloading with each interaction.

Master Page: A master page is a template that is responsible for the layout of the components that are found on every content page. For example, you wouldn't want to have to add navigational components to every single new page you create. If you did, and ever needed to make a change, you must change every single page. Keeping everything in sync would be a nightmare. Using a master page, you would only create the navigational components once and then all the other pages would reference this master page for the common components.

Microsoft Business Intelligence: Business Intelligence (BI) means many different things to many different people. The generally agreed upon definition of Business Intelligence involves using computer software to get a handle on the mountains of data that flow from modern business. The data is turned into information that is used to run a business in an intelligent fashion. Microsoft Business Intelligence refers to the Microsoft tools and technologies that fall into the Business Intelligence space.

Microsoft Flow: The next-generation of workflow for Microsoft products. Using Microsoft Flow, you can create workflow for Office 365 scenarios.

Microsoft .NET: The Microsoft .NET technology consists of programming languages and libraries designed to increase developer productivity and compatibility across Microsoft client and server computers.

Microsoft Office: Office is the nearly ubiquitous productivity suite used by information workers around the world. The Office product contains such applications as Word, Excel, PowerPoint, Outlook, OneNote, Publisher, Access, and Teams.

Microsoft Teams: The next-generation communications client. Microsoft Teams is a replacement for Skype for Business and lets you conduct online meetings by sharing your screen or presentations online with multiple users simultaneously, while communicating via voice, chat, and surveys. Teams is integrated with the other products in Office 365 in order to provide instant ability to communicate regardless of what software you are using.

Office 365: The Microsoft product that contains SharePoint, Exchange, and Teams (among others; Microsoft is adding more services all the time); all installed and managed in Microsoft's data centers and accessed over the Internet (also called over the cloud or in the cloud).

Outlook with Business Contact Manager: An application used for email, contacts, and calendaring, including scheduling meetings, meeting rooms, and other resources.

PowerApps: A tool for building mobile apps for iOS and Android. Think of PowerApps as a way to build mobile apps for Office 365 so people can interact with it from their phones.

Power BI: A tool for building reports and doing data analytics. You can pull data from many different sources, build reports in Power BI, and then display those reports in SharePoint or other apps.

PowerShell: PowerShell is a shell interface similar to DOS. Products such as SharePoint have PowerShell instructions, called cmdlets, which let you build scripts to interact with the product. For example, you might develop a series of PowerShell cmdlets that increases the specific configuration information of your SharePoint site.

Report: A report is nothing more than information describing the status of some topic. A report can be developed by using a number of technologies, such as Report Builder, Dashboard Designer, Excel, or even SharePoint web parts.

SharePoint: SharePoint is a term used to describe a technology from Microsoft. SharePoint has become the leader in communication, collaboration, and content management. SharePoint continues to evolve as functionality is folded into the product and additional features are developed. SharePoint 2019 is the most current release of the SharePoint product.

SharePoint Designer: SharePoint Designer is a software application that is used for Share-Point development. The content contained in a SharePoint application lives in a SQL Server database. SharePoint Designer provides a window into the SharePoint database that allows for customization and development. SharePoint Designer 2013 is the most recent version, and Microsoft doesn't seem to have plans to update it.

SharePoint Document Library: A Document Library is a mechanism to store content within SharePoint. A Document Library provides functionality for content management such as check-in and checkout, versioning, security, and workflow. An instance of a Document Library is called an app.

SharePoint List: A SharePoint List is simply a list of data. Much like you have a grocery list, a SharePoint List stores data in columns and rows. An instance of a SharePoint List is called an app.

SharePoint My Sites: The My Sites functionality of SharePoint offers every user her own SharePoint site.

SharePoint Online: SharePoint Online is the term for Microsoft's cloud version of SharePoint. The Online portion refers to the fact that you access your SharePoint instance over the Internet while you are online. Microsoft installs SharePoint on servers running in their data centers, and you connect to it and use it over the Internet.

SharePoint Site: A SharePoint Site is nothing more than a website. At its root, SharePoint is a website management system that provides a rich assortment of functionality that can be easily integrated into the SharePoint websites.

SharePoint Site Collection: A SharePoint Site Collection is a top-level site that contains other subsites. The difference between a Site Collection and a Site is that a Site Collection contains separate security and is isolated from other Site Collections. A Site, on the other hand, is contained by a top-level Site Collection and shares security and other aspects with other Sites within the same Site Collection.

SharePoint Workflow: A SharePoint workflow is a set of tasks and actions that can be associated with a list, library, or site. For example, you might have a workflow to request feedback on new documents. When a new document is submitted to a library the workflow might send an email to a list of people for feedback. When each person has finished his task of reviewing the document, the workflow might send an email back to the original author. SharePoint workflows are developed in a tool called SharePoint Designer.

SharePoint Workspace: SharePoint is great, but what happens when you aren't connected to the Internet and need to access and work with your website? SharePoint Workspace allows you to take SharePoint sites offline.

Silverlight: Silverlight is a technology designed to provide a rich user experience from within the web browser. The Web, in general, was not designed to provide the same rich user experience that an application running on your local computer provides. With a web application, the server is serving up pages that are viewed by the client computer by using a web browser. Each time the user interacts with the application, the web browser needs to send a message back to the server. This causes the web page to refresh and flicker. Silverlight runs on the web browser of the client computer and allows a rich interaction with the web application without the continual post-back of information to the server.

Skype: Skype is a consumer-based communications tool used by people all over the world.

Skype for Business: Skype for Business is a communications system for instant communication and ad-hoc meetings. Skype for Business used to be Microsoft Lync and is now being replaced with Microsoft Teams.

Visio Services: Visio Services provides SharePoint with the ability to render Visio diagrams through the web browser. Visio Services diagrams can be embedded right inside a SharePoint page. Visio Services is also used to provide a diagram of SharePoint workflow in real time.

Visual Studio: Visual Studio is a software application that is designed for development of Microsoft technologies. Visual Studio is called an Integrated Development Environment (IDE) because many development features are integrated into the application, such as the ability to run and test code, color-coded keywords, and IntelliSense. IntelliSense allows developers the ability to type the beginning of a keyword and have the editor show a list of available words. The list of words narrows down as the developer continues to type additional letters of the word. This aids the developer in finding the correct keyword without having to type the entire word.

Web App: A web app is a software application that is accessed over the Web, using a web browser. For example, if you have used Facebook or LinkedIn, then you have used a web app. The Office 365 product includes a number of different web apps. In fact, even the administrative interface you use to configure Office 365 is a web app because you access it by using your web browser. In addition, web apps are available for Outlook, Word, Excel, PowerPoint, and OneNote.

Web Part: A web part is a component of a web page that can be added, removed, or edited right from the browser. A web part is contained in a web part zone. A web part can be dragged and dropped between web part zones, using only the browser.

Wiki: A Wiki is a specialized website that allows community members the ability to update the content of the website on the fly. A Wiki is not specific to SharePoint; however, SharePoint provides Wiki functionality as a feature.

Index

About the Authors

Rosemarie Withee is President of Portal Integrators LLC (www.portalinte grators.com), Scrum-based software and services firm, and Founder of Scrum Now (www.scrumnow.org), the first Philippine-based Scrum organization with locations in Seattle, Washington and Laguna, Philippines. She is the lead author of *Office 365 For Dummies, 2nd Edition* (Wiley, 2016), *SharePoint 2016 For Dummies* (Wiley, 2016), *SharePoint 2019 For Dummies* (Wiley, 2019), and *Office 365 Apps For Dummies* (Wiley, 2019).

Rosemarie earned a Master of Science degree in Economics at San Francisco State University. In addition, Rosemarie also studied Marketing at UC Berkeley Extension and holds a Bachelor of Arts degree in Economics and a Bachelor of Science degree in Marketing from De La Salle University, Philippines.

Ken Withee works for Microsoft in the Office organization. He lives with his wife, Rosemarie, in Seattle, Washington. He is the author and coauthor of a number of books on Microsoft technologies and likes to spend his free time studying programming and electronics, and is studying to get his amateur radio license.

Ken is currently earning his Master of Science degree in Computer Science at the University of Washington. He also earned a Master of Science degree in Computer Science at San Francisco State University back before Google was a thing. He has more than 15 years of professional computer and management experience working with a vast range of technologies.

Jennifer Reed is a technology solutions professional who founded Cloud611 (www.cloud611.com), a Seattle area-based consulting and strategy implementation firm focused on helping small and medium-sized businesses, nonprofit organizations, and local governments achieve their goals using Office 365. The firm's core service offerings focus on increasing productivity, enhancing collaboration, simplifying communication, and enabling data-driven decisions using Microsoft cloud technologies.

Jenn holds a Bachelor of Arts degree in Economics and has for many years provided consulting services to a wide range of clients including a Fortune 500 company. She is a frequent speaker at business forums about Office 365 productivity and provides training facilitating user adoption of Office 365. She is a Microsoft Certified Professional (MCP) in Office 365 Administration, a certified project management professional (PMP), and a certified Scrum Master.

Jenn lives with her husband, Rick, a former All-Coast defensive back at Washington State University, writer, and retired Hawaii state senator. Jenn and Rick live where he grew up — in the lush farming valley of Snohomish through which run not just one but two rivers 45 miles northeast of Seattle. When not working on a cloud technology–related book, Jenn spends her spare time tending her organic garden, skiing, running, and hanging out with the Reed's son, Siddha, who has inherited his mom's interest in cloud technologies and his dad's writing skills.

Dedication

We would like to dedicate this book to our parents. — Rosemarie Withee and Ken Withee

My work on this book would not have been possible without the love and support of my husband and best friend, Rick, and our wonderful son, Siddha. I dedicate this book to both of you for understanding my late nights and hectic weekends. Thank you, Rick for stepping up and learning to cook and bake when I became too busy — especially for the delicious bread made with zucchini from our garden. Thank you, Siddha, for building raised flower beds for me even though you and Dad rolled your eyes when I assured you that I could write two books, work full time, and maintain a large garden simultaneously. Your unconditional love inspires me. — Jennifer Reed

Authors' Acknowledgments

Rosemarie Withee and Ken Withee: We would like to acknowledge our families in both the United States and Philippines. An extraordinary amount of special thanks to Katie Mohr, Katharine Dvorak, Guy Hart-Davis, and the rest of the *For Dummies* team for providing more support than we ever thought possible. It is truly amazing how much work goes into a single book. The work that goes into making a book correct, organized, and valuable is truly astonishing and it is the reason we will also buy a real book to learn a subject over searching for blogs and short Internet resources.

We would also like to thank Rosemarie's business partner Gen, who is the yin to the yang. Rosemarie and Gen are a formidable team and you can learn more about them at www.portalintegrators.com.

Genelyn "Gen" Ancheta holds a Bachelor of Science degree in Computer Engineering from Colegio de San Juan de Letran. She is a tireless seeker of knowledge, a thinker, and incidentally, also a web developer with Portal Integrators. Gen has more than ten years of web, mobile, and database development experience. She is a Microsoft Certified Solutions Developer (MCSD) specializing in SharePoint applications. She loves listening to music, and when she is not busy debugging codes, she indulges in watching movies and TV series.

Jennifer Reed: I owe my deepest gratitude to my customers and clients for giving me the opportunity to help them with their cloud journey as it has also provided me with valuable insights into the nuances of real-life application of Office 365 and other cloud technologies.

I am indebted to my employer, coworkers, and friends for the opportunities to learn and enrich my life, and I am grateful that I can share those positive, relevant experiences in this book. I want to call out a colleague, Aaron Holt, for recommending a sous vide tool which, unbeknownst to him, afforded me some semblance of normalcy by enabling me to cook healthy and delicious dinners with little effort in-between writing, gardening, and a full-time job.

It's been an honor and a pleasure to have the support and guidance of Katie Mohr, Katharine Dvorak, Guy Hart-Davis, and the rest of the *For Dummies* team. They are truly a dream team to work with.

Publisher's Acknowledgments

Associate Publisher: Katie Mohr
Project Editor: Katharine Dvorak
Technical Editor: Guy Hart-Davis

Editorial Assistant: Matthew Lowe
Production Editor: Siddique Shaik
Cover Image: © John Lund / Getty Images